HONOR DISHONORED

DON GARRETT, LTCOL, (RET) USMC

Richard & Barbara,

Enjoy!

◆ FriesenPress

Suite 300 - 990 Fort St
Victoria, BC, V8V 3K2
Canada www.friesenpress.com

Copyright © 2019 by Don Garrett, LtCol, (ret) USMC
First Edition — 2019

All rights reserved.

Members of 1st Platoon, Hotel Company, 2ndBn, 7th Marines.

No part of this publication may be reproduced in any form, or by any means, electronic or mechanical, including photocopying, recording, or any information browsing, storage, or retrieval system, without permission in writing from FriesenPress.

I want to especially want to thank my wife, Linda, for her undying support. And I want to acknowledge Mr. Larry and Mrs. Linda Wright for their enduring help.

ISBN
978-1-5255-3212-2 (Hardcover)
978-1-5255-3213-9 (Paperback)
978-1-5255-3214-6 (eBook)

1. *Biography & Autobiography, Historical*

Distributed to the trade by The Ingram Book Company

INTRODUCTION

"We few, we happy few, we band of brothers, for he today that sheds his blood with me, shall be my brother."

William Shakespeare

Semper Fidelis is Latin for Always Faithful—faithful to God, Country, and Corps. This is a unique and true-life story of a group of proud and determined young Marines and Navy Corpsman who served in Vietnam. They *belonged* to the same Marine platoon, 1st Platoon, Hotel Company, 2nd Battalion, 7th Marines, United States Marine Corps, from October of 1969 to November 1970 who were and remained "Faithful to God, Country and Corps"... ALWAYS! However, their country's faithfulness was, at the very best, cool and uncaring towards their sacrifices for their country.

I suspect over the period of time of mankind and a number of nations that have existed on this earth, that this story has been in fact been acted out before; however, I know of no other recorded event which included so many original members who remained so close and determined, and overcame tremendous obstacles—obstacles not of their making, but of those who they so valiantly fought to protect.

It took over forty years to write this book about these men's lives. The accounts are true, with the good, bad, and ugly. There have been reunions, fishing trips, countless phone calls, and emails with one goal: making this story as accurate as possible. This story was written to provide a snapshot of how it was at this time in history of the Vietnam War. This is a story of these men's personal combat experiences, day-to-day survival, hardships, endurance, support and/or lack of support, under extremely harsh conditions.

Their war experiences have haunted them, afflicted them, and in many cases stole sleep, or, when they could sleep, woke them with cold sweats and pounding hearts. Some gave their lives, others their mental and/or physical health; all were to some degree scarred, some scars not as visible as others. As painful as it was, those who survived will always remember the horror and suffering, but would rather focus on their comrades, their brotherhood.

These young men were from good, loving, middle-and lower-class families. They were high school graduates, and several had attended college and a few were college graduates. They were not street kids, uneducated or thugs. They were Christian patriots.

Most of these men's fathers had served in World War II. They felt an oblation to serve their country as their fathers had done. Like their fathers before them, they put country and duty before themselves. However, more importantly, this is a story of how these young men lived and survived, and how from this chaos grew a lasting brotherhood.

To begin with, these men were historically unique. Prior to Vietnam, American military units trained together then went to war as a unit. But these men, for the most part, had never met the people in the unit before they joined in Vietnam.

In a thirteen-month tour, on an average, they were in combat 240 days, while WWII vets served forty days of combat, on a three- to four-year tour. The average WWII vet was twenty-six years of age. The Marine Vietnam infantryman vet averaged only nineteen years of age. The WWII vet gained an average of ten pounds; the Vietnam Marine vet lost an average of forty pounds.

The single most profound difference from all other vets returning from war is that almost all returning Vietnam vets returned alone. There were no ticker tape parades or local school gyms crowded with cheering crowds, no dignitaries delivering speeches of gratitude or groups of well-wishers, and certainly no organized groups or politicians offering "thanks" or job opportunities.

These vet's units remained in Vietnam and individuals returned alone to face anti-government groups that cursed, spit upon, and in general took their wrath and hatred of the government out on the returning individual patriots. The individual Vietnam vet took the brunt of the anti-government activist while America's silent majority remained, well, very silent.

As history will show, these *un*-honored patriots gave their all in service to God, country, family, and community, and never organized rallies to demand anything from the government or its citizens—to the extent that they funded and built their own Vietnam monument. In most cases, these vets secretly shed their military clothing and quietly carried their burden of service to their country in silence.

One of the greatest stigmas carried by the Vietnam veteran is the perception they lost the war. The most rudimentary investigation will show all American combat forces were out of Vietnam in 1972. Vietnam fell to the communist in 1975.

Many Vietnam vets I have talked to have this nagging question to this day: Why, when we young men and women, who gave our hearts, souls, and many even lives, returned home, why did our fellow countrymen spit on us, curse us, and continue to treat us worse than criminals, why?

I am extremely proud to have served as platoon commander of these truly outstanding young men, and therefore I am honored to write their story. This story is of the actual Marines and Corpsman who served their nation with honor when their nation sadly reciprocated with dishonor.

CHAPTER 1
THE JOURNEY

Looking out of the airplane's window at the Da Nang airport below, the 22 year old farm boy from Oklahoma felt a flurry of emotions. He pondered, at least a million times, over all the events that had placed him on this plane as it made the final approach. He noticed that many of the other military passengers must have been having similar thoughts as they fidgeted in their seats. Or perhaps they were thinking about the two dog tags that were issued—one tag worn around the neck, the other in a bootlace. This allowed for a far greater chance of being identified if blown to pieces.

Second Lieutenant Donald R. Garrett of the United States Marine Corps was jerked from his thoughts by the sudden full throttle of the jet engines, forcing the plane to rapidly climb and quickly bank out to sea. Men immediately strained to see out of the windows, hoping to understand the reason for the pilot's actions. Don noticed the flight attendant's healthy skin tone had lost most of its rosy color and her hands shook as she handed a microphone to a Marine colonel who had jumped from his seat to speak with the pilot.

The colonel addressed the military passengers and told them the North Vietnamese were periodically rocketing the air strip and the plane would now circle out to sea. He also informed the passengers that the pilot had stated the attacks did not usually last long.

Don smiled nervously and thought, "The luck of the Irish. After months of excruciating painful training, only to have my plane shot down at the airport… DAMN!" He and his fellow passengers were about to enter another world, the one he had been training for since joining the

Marines. When he graduated from college he knew he would probably be drafted into the army, as were most of his peers. He decided he would rather go with the best and joined the Marines.

Don was not from a military family. As his father was on his way to the Navy Induction Center during World War II, he was removed from the bus and told he was more valuable to the war effort by staying home and working his job at the oil refinery than fighting in the Pacific.

Don knew when he got off this plane that he would be involved in the fighting. He had worked hard through pain, sweat, tears, and emotional stress to be prepared and he was ready mentally and physically for this combat challenge.

Finally, the plane made a long and very low approach to the air strip, as the pilot was hoping those shooting the rockets would not see the plane land. Once the plane landed and stopped, the ground crew quickly set up the mobile steel staircases at the front and rear side of the plane. Each row, starting with the row closest to the hatchways, exited in an orderly and timely manner. Once off the plane, guides directed everyone to the reinforced bunkers which paralleled the air strip.

The overpowering heat and humidity took the breath from everyone exiting the plane as they disembarked. Inside the bunkers the men sweated and watched the ground crews remove the staircases from the fueling plane.

After a short time, an airplane crew member waved off the refueling crew. Before they could pull their equipment away from the plane, the plane quickly lunged toward the end of the runway.

As the plane reached the end of the runway, the pilot did a half circle, aligned the plane on the runway, stepped on the brakes, revved the engines, released the brakes, shot down the runway, and leaped into the sky.

The plane, called the *Freedom Bird* by the troops, because it took you back home or freedom, left the airport without taking the military personnel who had completed their tours back to the real world. The crew, apparently having a great reverence for life, left the dangers of war to those better suited to deal with such matters.

The rest of the day was spent being shuttled from higher to lower commands, each requiring a recheck of the emergency notification data, and reading and signing of the "Rules of Engagement," indicating you understood the rules and would live or die, by them. Naturally, more endorsements of orders were asked for and handed over.

Military personnel entering Vietnam were sent to Force Logistic Command to swap their US currency for MPC (Military Payment Certifications). MPC was known by the troops as "monopoly" or "funny money," as possession of US dollars was illegal and could not be spent on the local Vietnamese economy. MPC's could only be used at military bases or on military contract services, such as barbers and launders.

The next morning a convoy of seven five-ton cargo trucks pulled in front of the Da Nang reception center. Each truck had a mounted 50 caliber machine gun and gunner located to the front of the truck bed. The entire floor of the truck bed and both sides of the bed were stacked with sand bags, reaching about forty inches high. These sand bags were to stop any shrapnel or bullets.

Don crawled onto a truck, armed with only his record book and two copies of his orders, as more officers boarded the truck. Several staff non-commissioned officers and enlisted troops were already wedged on board to be transported to their respective battalions to the front lines.

The convoy traveled south leaving Da Nang. The weather in mid-October was misty, about eighty degrees and extremely humid. It was the start of the monsoon season and the roads were muddy. It took about an hour for the first groups of military personnel to reach their new commands.

Late that afternoon the convoy pulled to the front guarded gate of Landing Zone Baldy. LZ Baldy was a hill which covered about forty acres of red mud and rocks, some about the size of a small house, and had a foul smell! The only other objects on the hill were buildings built by Seabees and Marines, which consisted of a camp exchange, mess halls, chapel, clubs (officers, staff NCOs, and enlisted), and hardbacks and tents for sleeping quarters.

Naturally, since this was a landing zone, a large landing pad was built below the hill on the one piece of flat ground in the enclosed perimeter. There were no trees or grass, and only a few scattered weeds. The hill was essentially stripped of vegetation.

The camp was enclosed by a mixture of concertina, barb and tangle foot wire, which extended at least fifty feet from the outer edge of the perimeter.

A large bright red sign with white letters and a painted 7th Marines logo greeted those entering the camp. The sign read "Prepare to March."

As the truck pulled through the gate, a Marine sergeant with an M16 laying across his lap turned to Don and said, "Welcome to the last Marine outpost sir."

Don said, "Thanks. Sergeant, I see you have a weapon, are you part of convoy security?"

"No sir, I was recently transferred to the 7th Marines from the 3rd Marines. I am Sergeant Joe Loerzel." They shook hands and completed the introductions.

Don found it odd the sergeant would be transferred from one rifle battalion to another, so being curious, he asked Sergeant Loerzel why he was transferred.

Sergeant Loerzel explained to him his former command was being sent back to the states; however, all personnel who had more than four months remaining on their tour were transferred to other units.

Additionally, the units continuing to be stationed in Vietnam would transfer those who had a month or so before they rotated to the 3rd Marines, so they would be sent to the states. Thus, it appeared an entire battalion was sent home; however, only the colors of the battalion and few "short timers" actually rotated back to the states.

Sergeant Loerzel continued to explain how he was currently placed in charge of different working parties at the regimental level, and would soon be sent to one of the rifle battalions.

Don looked across the camp and asked Sergeant Loerzel what caused the haze and odd smell. Sergeant Loerzel smiled and said, "Well the smell and haze is from the shitters... I mean latrines being burned, sir."

Don smiled and said, "In other words, it's from crap being burned?"

"Yes, sir, that's it," the sergeant grinned.

Don said, "Thanks for the information, sergeant; perhaps we will be assigned to the same battalion."

"That would be great, sir," replied Sergeant Loerzel.

Before they parted ways, Don noticed a rather large and long building on the spine of a hill in the center of the camp and asked Sergeant Loerzel about the building.

The sergeant pointed toward the building and said, "It's the crow's nest of the camp. The colonel's home, office, and officers' mess hall. It's also the official meeting place of Colonel Gildo S. Codispoti, the Golden Greek, and regimental commander of the 7th Marines."

The sergeant came to attention, saluted the lieutenant, did an about face, and walked away, leaving the lieutenant with many more questions.

The administrative processing went slowly. However, after what seemed hours, Don was finally assigned to 2nd Bn., 7th Marines. To his delight he met three new lieutenants assigned to the battalion, which were Lieutenants Thomas Baumgartner, Richard Jeppsen, and Alfonso Gerhardt. The four lieutenants immediately formed a "lieutenants protective society" and explored the camp.

They were invited, which was a mandatory showing, to dinner with Colonel Codispoti. They returned to their temporary tent quarters and began their preparations of shined boots and brass, and fresh jungle uniforms for the evening meal with the regimental commander.

Their new sharp, intense camouflage colors, polished jungle boots, and shiny brass made them really stand out, not only in sight, but also with the aroma of being "newbies."

As they were not used to the extreme heat and humidity, the lieutenants were sweating profusely. Therefore, they decided to arrive fifteen minutes early hoping it would allow enough time for their wet shirts to dry before their mandatory dinner.

About ten minutes after their arrival, Lieutenant Colonel McClintock, the regimental executive officer, suddenly appeared and gave the lieutenants a good look over, smiled, and said, "Good job men, we will enter the facility at 1800 hours. As you will be the last in and occupy the remaining seats at this end of the table, do not sit down. You are to remain standing in front of your chairs. When the colonel enters he will tell you to sit, you may then sit. Any questions? Good, stand by."

As other officers began arriving, the more senior officers were moving to the front of the line and lower ranked officers to the rear of the line leaving second lieutenants dead last, as usual.

Lieutenant Colonel McClintock looked at his watch, cleared his throat and in a commanding voice said, "Gentleman." He swung the two doors to the dining facility open and proceeded to the left of the long table in the middle of the room. The more senior officers followed in descending rank, peeling off to the left and right of the table according to their prearranged assigned seats.

Lieutenants Phil Santy and Tom Baumgartner quickly entered in front of Don. Phil grabbed the remaining chair on the left of the table while Tom snatched the remaining chair on the right of the table, leaving Don with the chair at the end of a very long table. Phil and Tom gave Don a "better you than me" smile. Don's only thought… "CRAP!"

As Don stared down the long table, maybe twenty-five feet long or longer, he saw the tables were covered in white linen, and each setting contained plates of china ware, crystal glasses, silver salt and pepper shakers, and silver napkin holders and linen napkins, all embossed with the 2nd Bn., 7th Marines.

Colonel Codispoti's seat was not at the long table, but rather at a smaller table against to the long table, forming a T. This table was about one inch higher than the long table, possibly to symbolize authority.

The room was about forty feet long and twenty feet wide. The walls were covered with wood about four feet up and then screen wire covered the remaining height to the top of the wall. The ceiling contained several ceiling fans, which ran on a low speed and hummed, circulating the hot humid air making it somewhat comfortable in the room.

Two stewards were behind Colonel Codispoti's place at the table, standing against the wall, maybe ten feet away. The stewards were dressed in camouflaged pants and green t-shirts with highly shined brass. There were eight more such stewards, four on each wall, waiting to serve the other officers their evening meal.

After several minutes, which seemed like forever to the lieutenants, Colonel Codispoti finally entered the room. The officers were called to attention by the executive officer. Colonel Codispoti walked slowly to his place at the head of the table.

The colonel was over six feet tall and his chest was wide and thick. He was a man of strength with no weakness. The colonel's eyes were dark and piercing. His eyebrows were extremely prominent as they were dark and

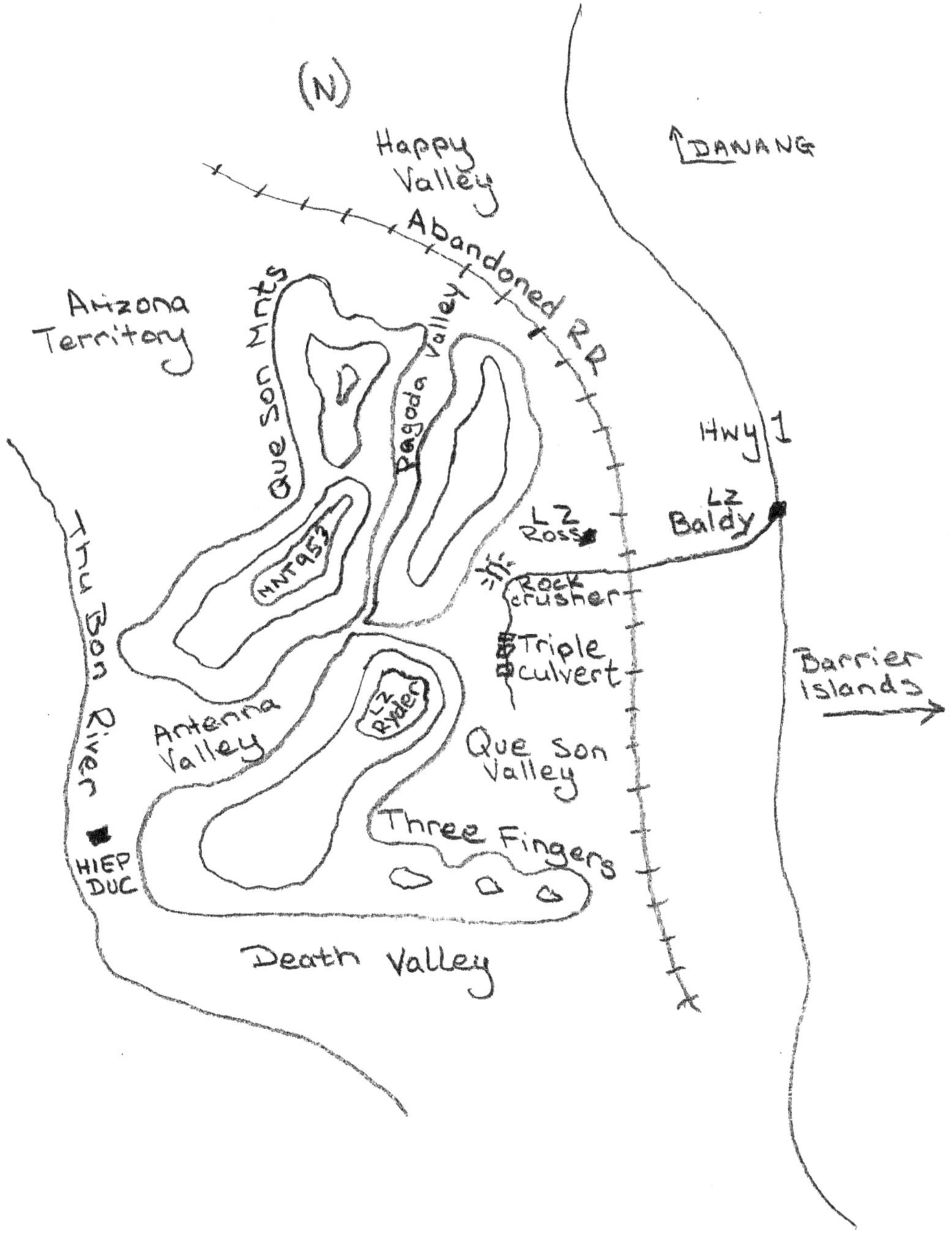

(N)
DANANG
Happy Valley
Abandoned RR
Arizona Territory
Que Son Mnts
Pagoda Valley
Hwy 1
LZ Baldy
LZ Ross
MNT953
Rock crusher
Triple culvert
Thu Bon River
Barrier Islands
Antenna Valley
LZ Ryder
Que Son Valley
Three Fingers
HIEP DUC
Death Valley

resembled a black hedge. Looking at the stewardess and the seating of his officers and the new officers, especially the new lieutenants, he then smiled.

Don and the colonel's eyes fixed on each other. Don felt the colonel's eyes were probing his soul and he wondered if he was finding his most secret thoughts.

"The Golden Greek" began to speak.

"Welcome young lieutenants to Quang Nam Providence, Republic of Viet Nam. Our mission is to 'close with and destroy the enemy,' while supporting the training of the Viet Nam military." The Colonel went on to explain that he and his staff were there for one purpose. To support the Marines in the bush!"

The colonel pointed to an ice cream machine standing in the far corner of the dining facility and said, "Any Marine can have ice cream, at any time, if his commanding officer requests it."

Lieutenant Phil Santy leaned toward Don and said, "Yea, right!"

Lieutenant Phil Santy had been an enlisted Marine before, going through the officers' training course in Quantico, Virginia, and had heard the same stories before and he had doubts.

After several minutes of explaining how effective the regiment was in supporting the battalions, the colonel asked the chaplain to say grace.

The meal consisted of roast beef, asparagus, baked potato, and ice cream with peach cobbler. It was a meal truly worthy of any infantry man in combat… or soon to be.

CHAPTER 2
HOTEL COMPANY, 2ND, BATTALION, 7TH MARINES

The next day, the lieutenants fell out and boarded another fleet of sandbag-laden trucks to complete their final mission since arriving "in country": to join their new combat units and hopefully take command of combat Marine platoons.

The drive to LZ Ross from LZ Baldy took about thirty minutes down a slippery and wet, red clay road.

LZ Ross was built by the US Army and manned by them for about three years. The high silhouette army bunkers were not what the Marines wanted to be in to fight the enemy. A large construction project was under way by the Marines, a "Destruction Project," to tear down the high silhouette army bunkers, deemed "unsafe and unsanitary," and replace them with dug out individual fighting positions.

The torrential monsoon rains did not help their efforts at all. LZ Ross was much like LZ Baldy but on a much smaller scale, and the camp was mostly flat and very muddy. It, too, was barren of almost all vegetation.

What the army had not told anyone in the turn over meetings was they had not ran a single foot patrol out of the camp into the surrounding valleys of Que Son, Antenna, Pagoda, and Happy Valley since the camp was built.

The NVA (North Vietnam Army) and VC (Viet Cong) had the run of the valleys for the last three years or so without any interference from the

American or South Vietnam Forces. This information chilled the blood of a Marine infantryman.

The trucks slid and skidded their way to the front of the 2nd Bn., 7th Marines S-1 shop. The lieutenants were soaked to the bone and once more waded through the mud into the S-1 Office (Administrative Office).

Lieutenant J. L. Matlack, the S-1(Officer), said nothing to the new lieutenants, rolled his eyes upward, turned to a PFC (Private First Class), and told him to get a table ready.

The PFC went to a table next to the wall and removed stacks of paper and maps from the table. He took each lieutenants' service record book and orders, placed them on the table, and turned on a fan to dry everything, as all documents were soaked.

Lieutenant Matlack finally greeted the new lieutenants and showed them to a room where there were waiting chairs, which they all flopped into, weary from the long, bouncy, and wet ride down to LZ Ross. He informed the new men the battalion desperately needed them, as the battalion had recently lost a lot of officers and enlisted men.

Don asked, "What do you mean by 'lost'?"

"Well, he said, "We have lost them to disease, wounds, and some KIA (Killed In Action.) The battalion was involved in a large operation a few weeks ago and took heavy causalities. You are the first replacements we have received."

The room instantly became quiet. The only sound was from someone typing in the next room. Lieutenant Matlack broke the silence by telling the lieutenants he had sent for runners who would direct them to check out sleeping gear, and show them the location of their temporary quarters and the officers' mess hall, which also served as the O Club (Officers' Club.)

He went on to explain he would make assignments that afternoon. However, the assignments would not be final until Lieutenant Colonel Hopkins, the battalion commander, approved the assignments, and the commanding officer was currently in the field. Weather permitting, they would fly out tomorrow, be interviewed by the colonel, and obtain approval of the assignments.

Lieutenant Santy asked Lieutenant Matlack which company was hurt the worst. "Hotel Company!" he replied.

The next day the flight was delayed a few more hours due to weather. This, to the lieutenants' delight, gave them time to draw their 782 gear (gear required for each man to live, fight, and survive in the bush) from battalion supply. Now they would feel more combat ready with all the necessary fighting gear when they met the battalion commander later in the day.

Their last stop in the checking-in process was the battalion armory. This is where they drew their 45 caliber Colt pistols, bullets, magazines clips (the clips which hold the bullets), and holsters... they then would be combat ready.

Don, however, was the last officer in line to get a 45 caliber pistol. When he stepped to the half door of the armory he found the armory was out of pistols.

He could not believe it; a Marine infantry battalion in a combat zone actually ran out of pistols. He stalked out of the armory and sat down on the side of the berm which separated the armory from the perimeter fence.

As he sat on the berm; he fumed and kicked the dirt with the heel of his boot. Could this hinder his chances of getting a Marine rifle platoon? He did not want to be stuck in the rear handing out volleyballs and other Special Services equipment in the battalion shop which provided sports gear and where sports tournaments were set up. He was pissed—he had not come this far and trained so hard to be left in the rear. Damn it, no way!

Suddenly, his boot heel struck a piece of metal. In an almost disinterested manner, he removed his newly acquired K-bar and slowly, while still burning inside, started digging at the metal. After a few minutes he abruptly realized the metal was in fact the barrel of a pistol. The tempo of interest changed dramatically as he briskly dug out the weapon and realized it was a US government Colt 45 caliber pistol.

He made his way back into the armory where he found Corporal Mount, the battalion armor, and notified him he had found the pistol.

After scraping the dirt off, they were able to find a serial number and discovered it belonged to the US Army. The pistol was probably lost during the turnover of the camp to the Marines.

Don said, "Give me some cleaning gear, Corporal Mount, and I will clean this baby up."

Corporal Mount grinned and said, "Shit, lieutenant, you can't strip that pistol down enough to ever fire."

Don smiled back at him and said, "Would you get me some cleaning gear? Tell you what, if I can strip it, clean it, and put it back together then it's mine to carry, agreed?"

Corporal Mount shook his head in disbelief and said, "Look lieutenant, I can't tear it down and put it back together. I'm not trained for that."

"I never said you had to do it. I'll tear it down, clean it, and put it back together." Don thought for a moment then said, "Tell you what, you get your pistol and I'll teach you how to tear it down and put it back together. It won't take long. Come on, we are wasting time."

Corporal Mount looked at him, and then at the pistol, grinned and said, "Well… they promised me the school several times, but when it came time for it they said they couldn't spare me for the school. Are you sure about this, lieutenant?"

"Yep, get your pistol, Corporal."

Corporal Mount handed his pistol to the lieutenant and watched in awe and said, "Jesus lieutenant, I have never seen a 45 pistol tore down that smooth and fast before."

It took two and half hours to soak the pistol, clean all parts, and replace several springs and the firing pin, which were too rusted to save. While the pistol parts soaked in the cleaning fluids, the lieutenant instructed Corporal Mount on the procedure to tear down and reassemble his own pistol. After several times the corporal had it down perfectly. Finally, the newly found pistol was reassembled, taken to the range at the camp trash dump and fired.

The pistol's coloring was gray, not black, as the acids in the soil had destroyed the bluestocking. The corporal and lieutenant were both happy with the results. The lieutenant got a pistol and the corporal learned to completely tear down and reassemble the Colt 45. The Marine Corps teaches to improvise, adapt and overcome and they did.

Later in the day the four new lieutenants went to Lieutenant Matlack's office to learn where they had been assigned.

He informed them they were all being recommended to be assigned to Hotel Company. They were ecstatic!

The next morning the CH-46 Chinook helicopter slowly landed on the wet asphalt helo pad. Morning rains flew like sheets of water from the helo's blades as it landed. Lieutenant Matlack waited until the water subsided. He motioned to the new lieutenants to follow him on to the helicopter. They all boarded, following single file onto the "bird" and were directed to the front. They sat on nylon strap seats, which lined both sides of the bird.

The crew chief studied the new lieutenants through his sunglasses, smiled and chuckled and then began talking on his headset to the pilot and co-pilot. Both stuck their heads out of the cabin of the helicopter to stare at the passengers. A casual glance would have told the most novice Vietnam service personnel that these lieutenants were newbies.

The lieutenants were dressed in brand new camouflaged utilities, unsoiled and unscuffed boots, and had new 782 gear (Gear is called 782 because it's checked out on form 782) properly attached to the web belt. They were clean, shaved, and dressed as if they were headed for a Marine personnel inspection.

The lieutenants did not seem to mind the attention. Their immediate objective, after over a year of daily long grueling hours of physical and academic training, was to present themselves to their new battalion commander so that they might be assigned as Marine combat rifle platoon commanders.

About thirty minutes after takeoff the crew chief stood up and pulled the bolt back on his side-door-mounted machine gun as he began searching for targets. The helo made descending circles, landing where a white M18 smoke-grenade was thrown to mark the LZ.

The helicopter's rotary wash kicked up unmanned and untethered gear and trash, sending it flying through the air. The passengers immediately got off the helo and headed for a small CP (Command Post) located a short distance up the trail.

The helo quickly lifted, the crew preferring to wait in the safety of the sky rather than taking a chance at being a sitting target from enemy ground fire.

The group of officers walked up the trail where Marines guarded the trail and perimeter of the CP and shouted out cat calls: "Newbies, new meat, welcome to Hell, sirs."

Lieutenant Matlack lined the new lieutenants up in a single line shoulder to shoulder. They were told to stand at ease and he proceeded to the battalion commander, who was lying on a weight bench lifting weights. The lieutenants looked at each other but said nothing.

Colonel Hopkins was a tall, heavy, muscled man who was bare chested and wore combat boots, jungle trousers, and no cover (Marine hat). After about five minutes of lifting weights he stopped and sat up. The corporal spotting for the commander handed him a towel.

The colonel stood up, dried the sweat from his neck and chest, stretched, and seemed to ignore the new lieutenants. He then looked at Lieutenant Matlack.

Matlack took the armful of officers' jackets to the battalion commander, who slowly scanned through each of the jackets. Once he was through looking at the jackets, the commander walked over to the lieutenants, who immediately came to attention. He stared at the new lieutenants a few minutes, then told them to stand at ease.

He walked up and down the row of young men and said, "Welcome to the 2nd Bn., 7th Marines. I am Lieutenant Colonel Hopkins, the commanding officer. I understand you have met and dined with our regimental commander, Colonel Codispoti. My remarks will be short. You have had the best training in the world. You have mastered it or you would not be here. However, you must hone those skills quickly, as mistakes cost lives, yours and your men, and we can't afford mistakes."

"The policy of the Marine Corps is for you serve six months in the bush as a combat platoon leader, and then be pulled into the rear filling a staff position. Any questions?"

The lieutenants had none.

The CO turned to Lieutenant Baumgartner and said, "Baumgartner, are you a football player?"

"No sir, wrestler from Iowa State, sir."

The CO smiled and turned to Lieutenant Jeppsen and asked where he was from. Lieutenant Jeppsen told him he was from Utah and Brigham Young University.

The colonel nodded his head and then asked Lieutenant Garrett the same question.

Don replied, "Oklahoma sir, Northwestern State College, sir."

The CO turned and started walking away then said, "Are you an OU (Oklahoma University) fan?"

"Yes sir, unless they are playing Oklahoma State, sir."

The colonel stopped, turned to look at him, said nothing, looked down, then turned to Lieutenant Santy.

Lieutenant Baumgartner gently shouldered Don and whispered "Nice going!"

As the colonel looked at Lieutenant Santy, he immediately replied, "Marine Corps School of Hard Knocks, sir."

Lieutenant Gerhardt was prepared to speak, but the CO turned his back on the group and began wiping the sweat from his head and bare chest. The CO placed the towel around his neck and held both ends of the towel next to his chest and said, "Hotel Company has had some bad luck with their officers lately due to emergency leaves, rotation dates, and combat causalities. Therefore, I am going to assign you all to Hotel Company. Your company commander will further assign you to billets within the company. Good luck, gentlemen." The colonel walked back to the weight bench and started lifting weights again.

Once back at LZ Ross, the lieutenants finished their processing at the battalion level, thanked Lieutenant Matlack for his recommendation, and headed for Hotel Company.

The road to "H" Company was muddy and very sloppy, due to the rain and countless number of Marines who had walked through the mud, stirring it up throughout the day. The lieutenants did not mind the conditions, and the cat calls had stopped because the personnel in the rear were dressed in "respectable rear echelon uniforms."

As they discussed the meeting with the battalion commander, each lieutenant was extremely happy to be assigned to the same Marine combat rifle company, but each had various opinions as to the "leadership style" of the battalion commander. All were excited, thankful, and in full agreement about finally arriving at their permanent duty station and, hopefully, being assigned as a combat Marine platoon leader in the "Nam."

When they arrived at Hotel Company, the lieutenants noticed a large sign standing in front of the company headquarters office, a four-by-eight painted red with white stencil lettering. The sign identified Captain K. E. Kramp as the commanding officer and 1st Lieutenant C. A. Vallence as the XO (executive officer.) Lieutenant Jeppsen led the officers into the company office.

A corporal was sitting behind a field desk on a fold-up stool. He looked up and then went back to his typing, then jumping to attention, knocked over the stool, and said, "Yes sirs', may I help you?"

The lieutenants in unison mumbled, "We're checking in."

The corporal stared at each officer, and asked, "Sirs', are you supposed to be checking into Hotel Company, 2nd Bn., 7th Marines?"

The lieutenants all nodded. The corporal quickly turned his head over his shoulder and slowly stammered, "Lieutenant. Vallence… sir, could you come out here, sir?"

Lieutenant Vallence came out of his office. Focused on a piece of paper in his hand and without looking up, he asked, "What's up?"

"Sir, these officers claim they are to check into the company."

Lieutenant Vallence immediately glanced up and began to check out each officer, especially their lapel rank insignia, then turned to the corporal and asked, "Are you sure?"

Then, without waiting for an answer, he reached out to the lieutenants and asked each one of them to give him a copy of their orders. He glanced at each set of orders, and then handed them to the corporal as he finished reading them.

Lieutenant Vallence walked over to a desk, picked up a landline phone hand set, placed it to his ear and cranked the phone. "This is Lieutenant Vallence, Hotel Company. I want the battalion S-1, Lieutenant Matlack. Thank you." After a few seconds he quickly said, "Jack, what… yes, all five of them… really, has the battalion commander approved it? He has. I owe you a beer… okay a six pack, thanks!"

Lieutenant Vallence hung up the phone, reached over and picked up a writing tablet, and then asked the new lieutenants to turn their record books and orders into the administrative chief. He then asked each of the lieutenants, as he handed the tablet to Don, to write their name, serial number, and date of rank, and to leave an inch to two between each name so he could write down some notes.

When the names were written on the tablet, Lieutenant Vallence looked it over and asked them to follow him. He told them they were going to the Officers Club, where he would have room to brief them on the current situations.

Once again, the lieutenants trudged through the mud toward the O Club, knowing they were so close to the final hurdle of where they would be assigned.

When they reached the O Club, Lieutenant Vallence cleaned his muddy boots on a steel grate outside the front door to the club and indicated for the others to do the same. He waited patiently while they finished cleaning their boots, gave a quick glance at their boots, opened the door, and entered.

A sergeant who was stocking a beer cooler behind the bar looked up and told the officers the club wasn't open yet. Lieutenant Vallence waved him off and told him they weren't there to drink, but rather to have a meeting.

The sergeant looked the group over, as to see if he could possibly find a flaw in the statement, then waved toward the tables, indicating for them to sit.

Lieutenant Vallence selected a large round table in the middle of the room, which offered more seating than required. When everyone was seated and comfortable he asked if anyone knew the battalion motto.

Don raised his hand, like he was back in a college classroom.

Lieutenant Vallence smiled, looked at Don, and said, "Yes, Lieutenant…" He glanced at the paper with the lieutenants' names in hopes of identifying the lieutenant who held up his hand.

Don quickly replied, "Lieutenant Garrett, sir."

"Yes, Lieutenant Garrett, you know the battalion motto?"

"Yes sir, I read it on a sign at the front gate of the camp. 'Ready for Anything and Counting on Nothing.'"

Lieutenant Vallence slapped the table, and in a loud voice said, "That is absolutely correct! Gentlemen, remember, and live by this motto, because it is the closest thing to the truth you will ever find in this living hell."

Lieutenant Vallence continued to explain the mission of the battalion was to deny rice and reinforcements to the enemy. The NVA (North Vietnamese Army) and VC (Viet Cong or National Liberation Front) units were scattered throughout the Que Son Mountains. Their personnel strength was around 2,500 and comprised of infantry, sappers, rocket, transportation, and intelligent military units.

These enemy units were battle-hardened, well-disciplined, and always ready to fight. To stop the flow of rice and man power, the Marines sent out squad-size patrols during the day, hunting for the enemy, especially those trying to carry rice or leading reinforcements into the mountains.

Additionally, ambush squads were sent out at night along the trails going into the mountains, preventing the enemy from robbing the local villagers of their hard-earned rice.

He went on to explain in the 7th Marines TAOR (Tactical Area of Responsibility) was averaging about 300 enemy killed monthly and between thirty and forty tons of rice per month captured from the enemy, which was then redistributed to the local, friendly, villagers.

The lieutenants listened and eagerly adsorbed the information, with few questions at the end of Lieutenant Vallence's brief. The XO was now ready to assign billets.

He studied the roster methodically, for what seemed forever to the lieutenants. Finally, the XO said, "You are probably wondering why I, as the XO, am making these assignments instead of the CO. Well, I don't know if the CO will be back today, tomorrow, or any day. I really don't even know if Captain Kramp is still the commanding officer. A brand new captain is supposed to take over in the next few days, whatever the hell that means. So, to move things along and get you platoon leaders out with the troops, I am going to make the assignments."

"Lieutenant Jeppsen, you are the most senior of this group and therefore you will be filling my position as the XO of the company. We have a few days before I rotate, so we can spend some time together to discuss the position."

"As for you remaining officers, Lieutenant Santy, I see you have some enlisted time in a weapons platoon. Therefore, I am going to assign you as the company weapons platoon commander."

Phil smiled, rubbed his hands together, and thanked the XO.

"We have three lieutenants and three rifle platoon positions, so I guess the only questions remaining, who gets what platoon?" Lieutenant

Vallence paused a couple moments then said, "Lieutenant Garrett, you answered the motto question correctly so I will give you first choice, which platoon do you want?"

Don thought for a moment. "Well the chain of command is CO, XO, weapons, then the rifle platoon commanders, and they are numbered one through three. Might as well start as number one. Sir, I would like 1st platoon."

"It's yours. Gerhardt, 2nd platoon, and Baumgartner you have 3rd platoon. Any questions? Good, let's have a beer. Sergeant, the bar is now open."

CHAPTER 3
THE TRUTH

Lieutenant Vallence promised the lieutenants he would give each of them a thorough briefing on their respective platoons. A lot of information had been passed around last night at the O Club. However, there were many interruptions by officers from the battalion, who wished Lieutenant Vallence a congratulatory "going home" and safe trip. Naturally, the other lieutenants had as many questions as Don about their platoons. As the night wore on, perhaps too many beers were consumed to draw a real accurate mental picture of the platoons.

Anyway, it was a new day, and Don sloshed through the sticky red mud, the increasing heat, and humidity, cheerfully making his way to the company office to meet with the XO at his appointed briefing time.

Arriving at the company office, Don entered. The administrative chief was once again behind his field desk. He quickly looked up and began to rise. Don told him to, "Carry on."

The admin chief slid back into his chair, continued typing, and shouted over his shoulder, "Lieutenant Garrett is here for his appointment, sir."

A shuffling of wooden chair legs against the wood floor could be heard in a back room. Lieutenant Vallence appeared in the doorway of the nearest office, walked out, and extended his hand. The two shook hands. The XO asked, "Did you get a good night's sleep?"

Don told him he did.

"Good, because in the future a good night's sleep will be allusive as snow in Vietnam. So, tell me, do you have a lot of questions?"

Don did have several questions, especially about how effective the support in the field was, and what the company and platoon's current history in combat was, to name a few of the "big" questions.

The XO suggested they go have lunch and there he could answer any questions Don might have. Both agreed and headed off to the O Club.

The XO told Don to grab a table and he would order some burgers and fries, the only items on the menu being served this late in the day.

Don surveyed the room and saw a table in the corner next to a large screened window. The window offered a slight breeze to pass through the room and provided a comfortable place to sit. He pulled up a chair, sat down, and looked out the window toward a mountain range, more than likely the Que Son Mountains he had heard so much about. Slightly to the right of the center of the mountains was a peak, which rose up beyond the clouds.

The XO plopped into a chair at the table and said, "Don, thanks for coming over here and having lunch with me. I didn't get around to having breakfast this morning, due to my later-than-usual turn in time because of a bunch of newbie lieutenants. And apparently I did not allow enough time for each of you because of the many, many questions."

Don smiled and continued staring at the mountains and finally asked, nodding toward the mountains, "Are those the Que Son Mountains?"

"Yes," the XO offered, "and the peak over there is the notorious Hill 953, as shown on the maps."

Don, mimicking the XO said, "Notorious Hill 953."

The cook told them the order was ready for pick up.

Lieutenant Valence said, "Yes, notorious, let's get our lunch, then I will tell you about the mountain top."

The officers went to the bar, gathered up their meals, and returned to the table. They both sat down and began eating. After several minutes of silent eating, the XO asked Don what he wanted to know.

He thought a moment and said, "I don't understand, when we had dinner with Colonel Codispoti he said he and his staff were here for one reason, and only one reason, to support the troops in the bush. Yet, when we went out to Lieutenant Colonel Hopkins's field CP, the Marines providing security there... well, looked like a 'rag tag' unit. Why, if the support is so good? And what the hell was with the battalion commander's 'body building' show? And last, what can you tell me about the platoon I am going to be leading?"

The XO stopped in mid-air as he started to take another bite of his burger, paused a moment, placed the remainder of the burger on his plate, pushed his chair back from the table, and stared at Don. Then the XO said, "Do you always go straight for the jugular?"

He shrugged and said, "Well you asked what I wanted to know."

"Yes, I did," replied the XO. "Where should I start?" Apparently it was a rhetorical question, because he continued to speak. "Well let's start with the first question, as to how well the support works. At times it works well, others not so good. Do you want the 'official' answer or the raw, naked, and realistic truth?"

Don, going through mental gymnastics, thought for a moment and sarcastically said, "Well, I like nakedness; you know, with the right person the truth is good and I can accept realism... I think. So, yes I want the real truth!"

The XO interlocked his fingers, placed his hands behind his head, and slowly slid slightly down in his chair. He stretched his legs out, closed eyes, and was quiet for a few minutes.

"Support is a big area to have questions about," the XO said as he opened his eyes. "Let's divide it into two areas, Ordnance and Supply. Ordnance, air, naval gunfire, artillery, tanks... the supporting arms folks have been unbelievably good, no, outstanding!"

"On the other hand, supply, as a system, which you were alluding to, has had its good days and very bad days. Why? Because of several factors: availability of supplies, transportation, weather, I mean you can go through a laundry list of reasons of 'whys.' However, the real and most damning factor as to why the supply system fails the Marine on the front lines is because of the Trickle Down System of human nature."

"Let's say, for discussion purposes, there are 100,000 Marines in Nam. Ninety thousand are 'pogues,' support personnel. That means only 10,000 are combat personnel and they are further broken down into the air, artillery, tanks, reconnaissance, and finally the 'grunt,' the rifleman on the front lines, the last in line for supplies, think about it. These, pogues are the same people in OCS (Officer Candidate School) and TBS (The Basic School) who voiced slogans like, 'In the rear with the beer,' 'Party with arty,' 'Why die, go supply.'"

"Is a Marine at the wing, working with the air support going to take a five-hundred- or two-hundred-pound bomb to his quarters, or a navy guy going to take sixteen-inch shells back to his quarters, or an arty man going to swipe a 105 round for his personal use? Hell no! Ordnance is something that does not 'trickle down.'"

"On the other hand, supplies, food, clothing, booze, all kinds of comfort items are continually being siphoned out of the system by the 90,000 pogues, to support what they need… there is a *big* difference between *need* and *want*. The further you get away from the 'high command' the less you get. Now, who is the furthest away? The 'grunt,' the fighter, the warrior; he is the last man in the supply system."

"The grunts at Lieutenant Colonel Hopkins CP, the 'rag tag' Marines you saw, are a good example of those grunts, last on the list to receive supplies; that is why they look like they do. Look at you, you are a good example. You have a new clean set of jungle utilities, new boots, and 782 gear. You are dressed much like all the Marines in the rear, regardless of rank. You have never even been in the real bush in Nam."

"Look at the 'rag tag' Marines coming out of the bush… big difference. Mark my words, in a month or less, you will be just as rag tag, hungry, tired, and sleepless, and you'll stink as much as your troops do. You and your troops are grunts, warriors, fighters, who carry their supplies, body armor, fighting equipment, weighting over a hundred pounds on your back, all the time."

"You will encounter the heat, rain, leeches, tons of insects, malaria, jungle rot, booby traps, antipersonnel mines. You will sleep on the ground, eat cold food out of a can, not bathe for weeks, sweat and stink and, oh yes, and *fight the enemy*! Does that answer your question on support?

"And by the way, rumor has it that the battalion commander is on the way out."

Don sat quietly for a minute then said, "Well, they taught us about the supply system in OCS and TBS, maybe not as graphic and I don't remember anything about the Trickle Down System, but it sounds like your assessment of the system is probably right on target."

"Mark my words, you will find out I am squarely on target," replied the XO.

"Okay, what about the Marines in my platoon, what can you tell me about them?" Don asked.

The XO sat up straight in his chair and turned and looked toward Hill 953. In a low audible voice he said, "In my mind, you have the best platoon in Nam." He continued to stare at the mountain. He finally said, "You have three of the best squad leaders in the Nam. They all are seasoned vets who can handle almost any situation. They can teach you a lot, listen to them."

"What about my platoon sergeant and right guide. You know, the guys second and third in command of the platoon," Don inquired.

In a very matter of fact manner, Lieutenant Vallence said, "You don't have a platoon sergeant or guide."

"WHAT! You said I have the best platoon and I don't have a platoon sergeant or right guide?! What the hell do the other two platoons have? Do they have any personnel?"

The XO took his hands off the back of his head, crossed his arms and laid them on his chest, and slowly said, "Well, the other two platoons have a platoon sergeant and a right guide, but like your platoon, they also are short on riflemen."

"Shit, this gets better and better; not only am I short two of the three personnel that make up my command group, but now I am short riflemen. So, what have I got? The three musketeers, and I make four?"

The XO began to laugh. He laughed so long he could hardly talk, but did manage to choke out, "I'll get us some beers. God, this is funny!"

Don did not share the XO's humor and thought, "What the hell."

The XO returned with two beers, and set one in front of Don as he chuckled under his breath.

Don was now stretched out in his chair with legs extended and arms crossed, and a frown on his face.

The XO sat down and said, "Listen, I know you aren't finding the humor in this but let me explain. I will tell you about a recent event that happened and I think it will explain why I think you have the best platoon."

The XO hesitated a moment then said, "This story could be about any one of the three squad leaders or any Marine in the platoon. They all are so much alike in action, decision-making processing, discipline, you name it. And, by the way, before I tell you this story I want you to know the entire company office, along with the battalion S-1, are working on getting you a platoon sergeant and right guide."

Don muttered, "Thanks."

The XO took long swigs of his beer, then reminded Don this event could have been about any one of the three squad leaders in the platoon but it was about Corporal Gary Howard, nicknamed Jersey. The XO's narrative began somewhat slow and meticulous.

"A few weeks ago, the battalion was conducting a battalion size operation on Hill 953. Hotel Company, along with another company within the battalion, was to be inserted on the mountain top by helicopter, while the other companies in the battalion were to start up the mountain. The idea: catch the NVA in between the two Marine forces."

"Weather was a factor; the monsoon rains were not heavy at the start of the operation. However, right after the first bird landed at LZ Flamingo, grid 970393, the mountain became socked in and the enemy opened fire on the Marines and helicopters. Before the birds lifted off the mountain, Jersey and fourteen men of his squad and seven men of 3rd squad jumped off the birds."

"The Marines landing on the mountain immediately took enemy fire. Jersey quickly organized the men into a defense position, resulting in them killing twelve NVA. The squad leader of 3rd squad informed Jersey he was the senior Marine on the mountain and therefore in charge. Jersey then radioed the company and informed them he had contact, killed the enemy, had no causalities, and secured the landing zone."

"The company commander was extremely happy. However, a new plan was given to Jersey. The new plan... no more Marines were going to land; the mission had been aborted. Jersey was to bring his Marines down the mountain."

"Intelligence estimated there were twenty-five hundred NVA in the area of Hill 953. That was, potentially, a lot of NVA for twenty-one

Marines to fight through. Being a Marine, Jersey rallied his men, locked and loaded, and swore they would not become prisoners."

Lieutenant Vallence picked up his beer and slowly sipped on it. He waited a few moments then, leaning into the table, began again in a low serious voice. He said, "PFC Donahue was selected as the point man. He had been with the squad about three months and was eager, as were the others, to move down the mountain. The squad moved about a hundred meters down the trail when three NVA snipers, in spider holes, popped up and shot Donahue. Jersey and the rest of the Marines killed the three gooks."

"Once again Jersey contacted headquarters and informed them of Donahue's death. Battalion told Jersey to bury the body and mark the grave so that they could come back later and retrieve the body."

"Jersey wasn't having any part of this; he told his men to cut a couple of limbs off a tree and make a stretcher out of the limbs and ponchos. They were going to take Donahue's body down the mountain… *nobody* was going to be left behind!"

"Jersey's men fully supported his decision and agreed they would all help carry the body down the mountain. At times they could smell the gooks, hear them, and the hair on the Marines arms would literary stand up as an affirmation of the enemy's presence. Oddly though, the gooks never attacked the Marines again."

The XO turned and looked out the screen widows toward Hill 953 and said, "The trip down was on an extremely long finger, only wide enough for the unit to travel in single file, but it provided adequate cover most of the time. In many places the trail was so narrow, and the sides so steep and slippery due to the continuous rain, that if they had dropped Donahue's body, it would have been impossible to retrieve."

"Jersey and his men trekked down the mountain for five fatiguing days and sleepless nights, filled with anticipation, anxiety, total appall, and an unequaled but rather astonishing brotherhood determination."

The silence in the room was deafening once the XO stopped talking. Don looked out through the screen window at Hill 953. He stared at the mountain for a few moments, cleared a lump in his throat, and said, "I see what you mean, thanks. I hope I can live up to the men's standards."

Doubt began to creep into Don's brain. He could sense it. He was starting to feel physically unbalanced and nauseous. *No*, he had no place for doubt in his life or command. He had been a good leader in high school. He held several successful leadership positions in college. The Marine Corps had trained him in all the principals of leadership and he fully understood each and had put them into practice many times. *Yes*, he could and would be an excellent platoon leader; after all, he had trained hard to acquire the skills, the ability, and a deep desire to succeed as a Marine Officer.

He had learned early on in OCS that one had to buy into the Marine Corps program totally, not fifty, eighty, nor ninety, but one hundred percent, if you were to be successful as a Marine Officer. He had done that; he was ready to command a Marine rifle platoon. No, not any platoon, but 2nd Bn., 7th Marines, Hotel Company, 1st Platoon!

The XO stood up and informed Don he had to get back to the office.

Don graciously thanked the XO for the story and insight on the platoon but immediately wanted to join the platoon. The XO told him it would be another day or so before he could join the platoon; besides, the platoon was out in Happy Valley and due to move to the Rock Crusher in two days, and he could join them there.

As the two headed back to the company area Don continued pressuring the XO to get him out to the platoon today or at latest tomorrow.

Wanting to get the lieutenant off his back, the XO agreed to see what he could do. He told him to come by the company office later that night and check on what he had been able to arrange, if anything.

Don went back to the tent that served as the transit officer's quarters. None of the other officers were there, probably at the O club. That was fine with him. He wanted, and preferred, to be alone. He did not want to be bothered so he could do some uninterrupted thinking.

After an hour he decided to write letters to his fiancée and his parents. Once he had finished the letters he decided the best place to get them mailed was at the company office. Since he had agreed to stop by there later to find out if any arrangements had been made to get him into the bush, he could accomplish two things with one trip through the sticky mud.

Upon entering the company office the admin chief started to rise, and Don told him, "As you were."

The chief relaxed back into the chair and over his shoulder told the XO Lieutenant Garrett was in the office.

The XO yelled, "Pain-in-the-ass lieutenant, get in here!"

Don sheepishly walked into the XO's office and said, "Yes sir."

"Do you have any money to buy beer? I sure hope so because you owe me more than a single beer. Be at the LZ 0900 hours tomorrow to catch the bird resupplying the platoon in the bush. Don't be late!" the XO said smiling.

Don was fervent with joy as the two walked to the O club through the hot, sticky, humid air and the slushy, gluey, red mud. Finally, his chance to join his men!

CHAPTER 4
THE PLATOON

Don walked down to the landing zone, arriving early; he did not want to miss the flight out to the platoon. The temperature was rising along with the humidity, making for a stifling hot day. His back was already completely soaked in sweat. He took off his pack and laid it down on the ground.

Several Marines were busy stacking supplies into a large cargo net. Four other Marines were dragging the corners of another loaded cargo net toward the center where a fifth Marine stood holding a large hook. He held up the hook and each Marine placed his corner of the net into the hook. The Marines were all dressed alike: jungle boots, camouflaged trousers, green t-shirts, camouflaged hats, and no rank insignia. He assumed the Marine holding the hook was in charge and asked him if these supplies were going out to Hotel Company.

The Marine turned to him looked him up and down for a few seconds then said, "Yes sir, do you want a lift to Hotel Company?"

Don told him he wanted a ride specifically to Hotel's 1st platoon.

The tall Marine looked over to his right and pointed to a smaller cargo net of supplies and said, "Lieutenant, that net is going to Hotel 1st Platoon. The bird should be here," he quickly glanced at his watch, "in about ten minutes. I will have the bird pick you up then the net. The bird will land down at that end of the pad. When it lands the crew chief will exit and motion for you to board the bird. After you are aboard they will lift off and pick up that cargo net. When you get out to the platoon they will drop off the net then land and let you off. Any questions sir?"

Don had no questions but could feel his excitement rising.

Far up the valley came a faint "thump, thump, thump" of the helo's rotary blades slapping the moist, hot air. The bird came down the valley to the landing zone. The tall Marine had gone back to the working party and was supervising the readying of the cargo net for the bird. He then walked toward Don and said, "Lieutenant, are you going out there to take over the command of 1st platoon?"

Don told him, "Yes."

"By the way lieutenant my name is Sergeant Sullivan, I am with FSSG," the sergeant informed him.

"I am Lieutenant Garrett, 1st Platoon Commander of Hotel Company."

Sergeant Sullivan again looked over the new lieutenant and said, "Hotel Company has really seen a lot of action the last few months and their officers and senior enlisted have been decimated."

Don quickly looked at the sergeant. DECIMATED was a harsh word and the sound of it sent chills down his spine.

"Lieutenant, I have a hometown buddy who was with Hotel and was recently medically evacuated to the states. Sir, I wish you, and your men, the best of luck!"

"Thank you, Sergeant Sullivan. And by the way, sergeant, keep those supplies flowing to the bush as long as you can."

"Yes sir... here comes your bird," he replied as he moved to the other end of the landing zone to direct the bird into the LZ.

Don watched the bird as it began to land. It had a large purple fox painted on it's side. He knew, from basic school, it was the sign of the Purple Fox Squadron.

As directed by Sergeant Sullivan, the bird landed. Don boarded, and the men then hooked up to the cargo net of supplies. Don sat on a seat next to the "hell hole," a square trap door in the floor of the helicopter; from here he could see the cargo net slowly swinging gently against the wind caused by the speed of the helicopter. He also noticed the ground below the cargo net was once a rice paddy which had produced an abundance of rice. The rice basket of the Far East now lay dormant, unattended, and unproductive.

He thought of his home back in Oklahoma. From his father's place he could look west and see the flat, highly productive ground that produced wheat for America and much of the world. This ground ran for hundreds of miles across Oklahoma. To the east one could see into the Osage Hills of Oklahoma and the Flint Hills of Kansas, both the best grasslands in the world and his favorite place.

Suddenly, the melancholy was broken by the slight squeeze of the crew chief's hand on his shoulder. The crew chief leaned over and pointed to his ear. The lieutenant knew the chief wanted him to remove the ear plug in his ear so he could talk to him. He removed the ear plug and the chief informed him they would be landing pretty quick and he wanted Don to get off the bird quickly and have the grunts get the supplies out of the cargo net, and that the bird would be back after delivering the other supplies to pick up the cargo net. Not wanting to yell over the roar of the helicopter engines, Don merely gave the crew chief a thumbs-up, indicating he understood.

A green smoke was popped on the ground, and the bird banked and flew toward the green smoke, hovered over it, and dropped the cargo net. It then flew backwards a few yards and landed. Don immediately got off the bird. He ran a short distance away from the bird when the pilot opened its engines to full thrust, which caused Don to stop and drop to one knee before he lost his balance and fell over from the force of the rotary wash.

He looked back at the helo leaving the area "like a bat out of hell" and thought, "That pilot must be really nervous." He looked up the small hill in front of him as he brushed himself off, and then saw two Marines heading towards him from the hill. One was short, maybe five six, the other maybe six feet tall.

The short Marine was in front and shook Don's hand and said, "Damn sir, I am so happy to see you. I am Corporal Lipsky. And this is Corporal Howard." He released his grip then pointed to the Marine right behind him.

Don shook hands with Corporal Howard and then, as he pulled his hand back from Corporal Howard, Corporal Lipsky once again grabbed his hand and said, "God, it's good to see you, lieutenant."

Don smiled and said, "I can't ever remember anyone being so happy to see me like you are, how come?"

Corporal Lipsky smiled and said, "Because I am no longer the platoon commander, you are. You now have the responsibilities' and I am free of them. God, it feels great!"

Don smiled even harder and assured Corporal Lipsky that as happy as he was to shed the responsibilities, he was equally happy to accept them. He then told them the bird was going back to LZ Ross to pick up another resupply and deliver it to Hotel Company Headquarters, then to return to this site to pick up the cargo net; therefore, the supplies needed to be removed from the net and folded so it could be placed on the returning bird.

Corporal Lipsky said, "Okay." Then he turned to Corporal Howard and said, "Take care of it, Jersey."

Jersey—the name sent shock waves through the lieutenant's brain. He looked at Corporal Howard. Jersey quickly moved down the hill to take charge of the working party on the landing zone.

He turned to Corporal Lipsky and slowly said, "Is that the same Jersey that led twenty-some Marines off Hill 953 a few days ago?"

Corporal Lipsky said, "Yes sir, is something wrong?"

"No. He looks so young. He looks to be maybe eighteen or nineteen. I had envisioned someone much older... much older."

Corporal Lipsky said, "He is eighteen or nineteen. If you don't mind me asking lieutenant, how old are you?"

"Twenty-two," Don replied.

"Well, sir you have about forty Marines under your command and only one of them is older than you and that is Lance Corporal Moc Sabanos. The rest, seventeen to nineteen. This is a *young man's war,* anyway out here in the bush, it damn sure is!"

Corporal Lipsky led the way up the hill to the platoon command post. The CP consisted of four sticks driven into the ground, about three feet high and four feet apart, forming a square covered by a camouflaged poncho liner.

Partially covered under the poncho was what appeared to be a very slim, muscled Marine and two radios he apparently was monitoring. As he approached the CP, the Marine, as agile and gracefully as a cat, exited the make shift CP and stood at attention with a mile wide smile said, "Lance Corporal Mosher 1st platoon radio operator sir."

Don stared at the Marine; he had wide shoulders, a slim waist, and a somewhat sad face. Finally, he stammered out, "Carry on Lance Corporal Mosher."

Mosher immediately slid back under the poncho and resumed his previous position. Corporal Lipsky asked if the lieutenant would like to take his pack off and get more comfortable. He did, in fact, take off the pack and laid it under the poncho; after all, it was now his command post.

Don looked down the hill, evaluating the tactical position. He then turned to his left checking out the fighting positions on the line and then those on his right. After a few moments he slowly started walking up the hill so he could see the entire perimeter. Corporal Lipsky followed in silence. Don thought the hill was a defendable piece of terrain. The fighting positions were solid. The machine gun position was good and the pit for a single mortar was adequate.

The hill had a few large boulders and several small, bushy trees providing some cover for him to move about during a fire fight and control the platoon. He walked over to one of the bushy trees and sat down in the shade. It was about ten o'clock in the morning, ninety percent humidity and some ninety degrees, and the sweat was starting to bead up on his arms and forehead.

He motioned for Corporal Lipsky to sit down. Corporal Lipsky found a relative comfortable place to sit.

"Tell me, did you select this position or were you told to move on this hill?" Don asked.

"I was told to move in this general area and find a position to cover the main trail in the area leading into the Que Son Mountains. So the squad leaders and I thought this was a good place," Corporal Lipsky replied.

"And they dug individual fighting holes? Machine gun and mortar position all decided by you and the squad leaders?" Don inquired.

Corporal Lipsky twisted his face, looked up into the sky, and said, "Well I guess so, but maybe more Jersey and I made the final decisions."

Don slowly placed his left hand on his chin and began to rub his hand around and around. He could feel the stubble of his beard. He had not shaved this morning; he had wanted to appear older and his black stubble always made him appear older than his real age, but then, he had already let that "cat out of the bag" by telling Corporal Lipsky he was twenty-two.

He turned to Corporal Lipsky and merely looked at him for a few seconds then said, "Your selection, by committee or whatever leadership style you consider it, of this site—fighting holes and crew-served weapons positions—is really excellent in my opinion. Now with that said, we both know my vast combat experience is really rather limited. So don't let this complement go to your head."

Both were silent for a moment then began to chuckle then broke into laughter. A long pause of silence followed the laughter until the Don broke it by asking Corporal Lipsky, "What is your first name?"

"Stuart, sir, but they call me Lippy," he replied.

"Well Corporal Stuart 'Lippy' Lipsky of the United States Marine Corps, we need to have a down-to-earth meeting of the minds." Don's demeanor changed from joyous to serious as he went on to say, "I really don't know how to say this other than I need to know how you really feel about me, kind of falling from the sky into the platoon position, and taking over as the commander? Because if it bothers you, I will do all I can to get you a transfer to another unit."

Lippy leaped up from his sitting position and faced the Lieutenant and in a very emotional voice practically yelled, "LIEUTENANT, I don't want a transfer. I want to stay with the platoon. I never wanted to be the platoon commander. I told you earlier I am thrilled you are here: I am not a person who likes to be in control. You noticed I command by 'committee,' I think you called it. I will do all I can to help you in any way. *Please*, don't transfer me. These are my Marine brothers. War has forged us together. I have less than a month to go before I go back to the world. Before I go back, I want to know that my Marines have a good leader and will take care of them. I can help you be that leader. Give me a chance!"

Don could easily see the emotion swelling in Corporal Lippy's face and knew he was being genuinely honest. Don stood up, smiled, and reached out to offer his hand, and the two vigorously shook hands.

"I was hoping you would say that! So, you don't mind being the platoon sergeant instead of the platoon commander?"

"Shit, sir I would love to be the platoon sergeant, right guide, anything I can do to stay and help."

They stopped shaking hands and he slapped Lippy on the back as they walked back to the platoon command post. As they neared the platoon CP, Lance Corporal Mosher quickly came out from under the poncho and informed Lippy the CO wanted his night acts (Patrols and ambushes conducted at night) sent in before 1400 hours.

Lippy gave Mosher a stern look and then jerked his head toward Don. Mosher looked at Lippy funny like and then turned bright red in the face and, looking at the new lieutenant, said in a very low and stammered voice, "Sorry sir, the CO wants night acts routes sent to him before 1400 hours."

Don smiled and said, "Thank you Lance Corporal Mosher."

He turned to Lippy and said, "Well Platoon Sergeant Lipsky, I guess you and I need to set down and have additional discussions and briefings on things such as our mission, required patrols, day and night acts, pre-planned fires, personnel strengths, what has been done in the last few days and nights, who is who, and oh yes, I need to work up a night ambush for tonight."

Lippy broke out in a big smile and offered a place under some brush type trees about twenty feet from the CP. Both young Marines sat down under the trees and began their discussions and briefings. One Marine had countless hours, days, and months of battle experience, the other had a tremendous amount of the best battle classroom lecture and field training in the world.

The meeting went on for what seemed an hour when Don abruptly held up his hand, much like a traffic cop and said, "Let's stop for a while. This is starting to feel like I'm drinking from a fire hydrant."

He stood up stretched and then heard the sound of a helicopter in the far distance. He turned to Lippy, and said, "It must be the helo returning for the cargo net."

Lippy immediately rose and said, "I'll go down and see that the net gets loaded."

Don thanked him, reached down picked up a handful of small rocks, and began tossing them aimlessly at large boulders and small bushes, trying to decipher all that he had heard.

CHAPTER 5
THE NEW PLATOON COMMAND GROUP

Don finally sat down and picked up his small field map case, plotted his platoon position, and worked up a night ambush. The resupply bird had picked up the cargo net and left before he had really been aware of the situation around him. His thoughts were broken by Lippy's return and low cursing after he slipped coming back up the hill.

Lippy looked at the lieutenant and said, "You have to watch those contour lines, they can trip you up."

The lieutenant immediately grinned; the contour lines were the lines on the maps showing the distance between evaluations usually every twenty meters in height. Humor was good and no doubt a rare commodity in war; he thought, "Cherish it!"

He learned Lippy was from a military family and he considered himself an air force brat; his father was on active duty with the US Air Force. He was the oldest sibling, with two younger sisters. And he was proud of the fact that he was the shortest male in his high school of seven hundred students. He stood five foot six, with brown hair and blue eyes, really shinning blue eyes. He was no delicate porcelain tea cup, though, but rather a tough, durable, Marine Corps metal canteen cup, which held a tall drink of courage, determination, and conviction.

He handed Lippy a piece of paper he had written the ambush site and supporting fires positions on, and asked him to look at them and tell him what he thought.

Lippy took the paper, immediately reached in his cargo pocket on the side of his utilities, and pulled out a very worn map. He slowly sat down and very carefully plotted the positions on the map and said, "I was thinking of putting an ambush here too. I wasn't sure where to put the supporting fires though. Do you want me to give them to Lance Corporal Mosher to send into the company?"

"No. I think I will give them to him."

"Right," Lippy said with a slight smile.

"I do want to talk to the squad leaders all together. You said Corporal Olsen was on patrol, when will he be back off patrol?"

As Lippy checked his map, he slowly muttered, "That depends…"

Don looked at Lippy in a questionable manner and said, "Depends on what?"

"Do you want them to hit each check point? If they don't go to check point six and seven but go from five to eight they could be back in maybe two hours," he replied.

"You have their check points plotted on your map? Let me see your map for a second."

Lippy quickly handed him the map.

Don swiftly studied the map and finally said, "Yes, let them skip six, seven, and eight. From their current position I want him to go to this grid," he scribbled it on the paper containing the night ambush, "then into the perimeter. Where are they now?"

Lippy yelled at Lance Corporal Mosher, "Mosher, where is Olsen? Heard from him lately?"

Mosher jumped out and up from the makeshift CP and yelled back, "They recently reached check point five, maybe ten minutes ago, and are going to set up a perimeter and take a break."

Don and Lippy slowly walked back to the CP, each knowing there was more that needed to be discussed. He gave radio operator Mosher the night ambush coordinates to be sent to company headquarters and notified Corporal Olsen of the new check points and mission. He then sat next to his pack under the poncho liner CP and reached over and opened the flap covering the large pocket on the pack. He looked at Lippy and said, "I noticed your map is not coated with lamination and very worn. By the way, what is your map covered with?"

Lippy grinned, more than usual, and said, "Scotch tape, sir."

Don merely shook his head in disbelief. "Okay, Lippy, how many maps, compasses, binoculars, and night starlight scopes does the platoon have?"

Lippy looked down at the ground and after a few moments looked up and said, "Well we have four maps, three compasses, no binoculars, and no starlight scopes. We share the compass; you know, the three squad leaders and me."

Don said, "Okay, I brought with me four laminated maps, three compasses, a set of binoculars, and one night starlight scope. So that gives us eight maps, six compasses, a set of binoculars, and a starlight scope. Each of the rifle squad leaders gets one of the new laminated maps as well as the weapons section. They also will get their own compasses. I'll carry the binoculars and night scope and will dole them out as needed. The rest of the maps will be given to the assistant rifle squad leaders. What do you think?"

"That's great!" Lippy said.

"Okay, I want a meeting at 1730 at that group of bushy trees we left a moment ago. I want you, the three rifle squad leaders, machine gun leader, and mortar leader at the meeting. Can you make that happen?"

"No problem sir!" Lippy responded with a noted amount of enthusiasm and walked off to notify people of the meeting.

Don turned to Lance Corporal Gary Mosher and asked him to tell him about himself. Mosher started to slide out from under the poncho but Don stopped him and said, "Mosher don't jump to attention every time I talk to you. This is a war zone and the enemy, no doubt, is watching us and we both will have a longer life expectancy if you don't jump up every time I talk to you. Do you agree or disagree?"

Gary Mosher paused a few moments and agreed, then slowly relaxed under the poncho.

Gary explained he was from Minnesota and was married, and soon would be a proud father. He was an infantry man, but was "drafted" as the radioman because the regular one was killed a few weeks ago. Don stared at Gary in disbelief and finally asked him if he really wanted to be the platoon radio operator and if he enjoyed it.

Gary explained that he did in fact really liked being the platoon radio operator and thought the Marines of 1st platoon were the best. The platoon members had named him "Poor Boy", probably because the "Poor Boy" was separated from his wife and new baby he had not seen yet.

Don rubbed his face with his hand in a slow circular movement and finally stopped, unbuttoned his flak jacket, reached into his camouflaged shirt pocket, and pulled out a small two-by-three-inch Field Marine Corps PRCN 25 Radio Operators Manual and handed it to him and said, "I have no idea how much you know about the radio, but look at this, it may help."

Poor Boy smiled, thanked him, and took the manual.

Don picked up his pack from under the poncho CP and informed Poor Boy that when the squad leaders arrived they should go to the group of trees where he and Lippy had been meeting.

Poor Boy started to rise. Don waved him down and Poor Boy smiled and said, "Yes sir."

Don made his way back to the group of trees and rocks, and selected a place where he could see the valley and which allowed room for the squad leaders to sit next to each other. He pulled out his map and began looking for the hills that were shown on his map.

He did not want the platoon to stay on the hill another night. He was told a million times in basic school if you stayed in a position over two days you were more than likely going to be hit the third night. Secondly, he knew in a day or so the platoon would be moving to the Rock Crusher.

The Crusher was about fifteen clicks, or about seven and a half miles to the north, north east. He wanted to move in that direction and cut down the distance they would have to walk in a single day. At the meeting point. He checked his watch; the squad leaders would be arriving any moment.

He heard a loud voice coming from the CP area and looking up he saw two people approaching him. One was Jersey. Jersey was the source of the noise. He was about six feet tall and had a very large and very black mustache—very illegal in a garrison situation. He was wearing a green t-shirt with a flak jacket over it and a bush cover. His camouflaged trouser pockets were jammed full of what appeared to be fully loaded magazines for the M16 he carried over his right shoulder. His left shoulder was loaded down with bandoleers of M16 ammo. His cartridge belt contained at least six canteens of water, a jungle first aid kit, and a K-bar.

Walking next to Jersey was a much shorter Marine, maybe five seven, with blond hair and a wiry appearance. His waist was so small his buckled cartridge belt, which had identical items as those Jersey carried, hung loosely about his waist and was held up by suspenders. He wore a camouflaged utility jacket which had the arms cut off at the elbows and then rolled up to the shoulders. He, too, shouldered an M16 rifle.

Don knew this Marine had to be Corporal Rathbone, the squad leader of 2nd squad, because the squad leader he had watched through his binoculars returning from the patrol was much taller. They greeted him and introductions were made. Don offered them seats in the shade of the trees.

No sooner had they taken seats when Corporal Lipsky showed up with two more Marines and a corpsman. One Marine was Corporal Olsen. He was six one or two, had a very heavy head of long blond hair, not hippy long but long for Marine Corps regulations. His face was long with deep, piercing eyes and he seemed friendly but surly, a no-nonsense person. His dress was much like the other squad leaders, except he appeared to be much tidier in his dress; he shouldered a M16 and cartridge belt, and his utility jacket sleeves were buttoned at the wrist. His trousers were also stuffed with loaded M16 magazines.

The second Marine stood about five eight with dark hair, slim, very soft spoken, clearly Hispanic, and he wore a genuine smile from ear to ear. "Corporal Ray Alcala, the team leader of the machine gun and the 60mm mortar teams, sir."

The third person, a Naval Corpsman, was, like everyone else, very slim, about five nine, and wore glasses and a big smile. He appeared to be older than his Marine counterparts and certainly as battle hardened. He was dressed much like the Marines except he had a 45 pistol instead of an M16 and a "Unit One" bag draped across his chest. Shaking hands, the Naval Corpsman said, "Doc Smith, lieutenant, senior corpsman in the platoon and part of your CP group."

Don asked everyone take a seat and silently looked over the group. "So, this is my platoon leaders, said Don. In basic school we were told our platoon of forty-six enlisted Marines would consist of one staff sergeant, five sergeants, nine corporals, and that the remaining thirty or so would be lance corporals, private first classes, and a few privates. I see five, no doubt, outstanding corporals. Is everyone in the platoon a corporal?"

The group looked at each other in silence then broke out in laughter. Lippy finally said, "No, the rest of the Marines in the platoon are lance corporals, except for a couple rare exceptions, sir."

Don chuckled with the group then, in a serious tone, said, "Well I am glad we got that cleared up. I would also like to make clear some fundamental facts now to be understood by each of you regarding my leadership and tactics." The group became not only very quiet but motionless as they stared at the lieutenant. He immediately sensed he had their undivided attention and seized upon the opportunity to explain in detail what he wanted them to know about his leadership and tactics.

"I will keep *you* informed and I expect you to keep *your men* informed. I sometimes may not like what I have to tell you and you may not want to hear what I have to say, but *we* will complete the mission. I will do my part. As they say, there is no 'I' in team. I believe one of the most basic elements of sound tactics is using *supporting arms*.

"I want all day patrols to have pre-planned artillery fires plotted and called in before the patrol leaves the perimeter. That also goes for night ambushes; any time a unit leaves the perimeter, pre-planned fires are required. The last thing I want made perfectly clear is when a Marine is on watch, 'hole watch' as you call it here in Vietnam, I want the Marine completely dressed, helmet, flak jacket, weapon, and ammo. It's not the time to write mom and dad letters, nor time to catch up reading or get a suntan. I want the Marine on watch focused, and ready for anything. Does anyone have any questions or not understand what I said?"

The group looked at each other and all seemed to be nodding their heads in agreement. Finally Lippy said, "We understand and most of the time have been doing the pre-planned fires. Our hole watch has been good but I'm sure we can make some improvements on it. We probably have not been using supporting arms as much as we should have."

"And speaking of supporting arms, I understand we have only one machine gun. Do we have another one on order?" Don asked, looking at Corporal Alcala.

Alcala squirmed in his seat for a few moments then said, "Yes, we have had a gun on order for about a year sir."

"A YEAR! Are you serious?" Don yelled, at what he had just heard.

Once again Lippy jumped in and explained he had been with the platoon a year and was told it had been on order for several months when he joined the platoon.

Don could not believe a Marine Corps combat unit in a war zone could not get an M60 machine gun in over a year. He got up from the place he was sitting and walked out into the sun. He took his cover off and rubbed his hand through his hair then slowly walked back to the small group of trees and leaned against a larger rock next to where he had been sitting before and said, "Okay, we will deal with this later, let's move onto another subject."

He crossed his arms over his chest and asked, "How many nights has the platoon been in this position?"

Once again Lippy volunteered the answer. "Tonight will be the third night lieutenant."

Don unfolded his arms and walked over to his pack, opened it, and pulled out the laminated maps and compasses. As he started passing out the maps he turned to Doc Smith and asked him to open the side pocket of his pack and get the grease pencils—black, red, blue, and green ones—and pass one of each color to the corporals. The lieutenant asked who did not have a compass.

Corporal Rathbone and Alcala held up their hands and he gave each one a compass.

"All right, we all now have laminated maps and a compass. I also brought a pair of binoculars and a starlight scope for night vision," he announced.

The corporals were all smiling and making comments about Christmas coming early. Don instructed the squad leaders to give their older maps to their assistant squad leaders and team leaders.

"Okay, the last thing I want to talk about is the subject of spending another night on this hill. I want to throw out to you a plan and I would like your honest opinion on it. What I don't want is a bunch of yes guys. If you don't or do like the plan let me know."

Don looked at the group. They appeared to understand and indicated they would be honest about their feelings on the plan.

"Now before I reveal my plan I want you to know what 'rumor control' has in stock for us. It says we are going to move to the Rock Crusher or the Triple Culvert maybe as early as tomorrow. Now that is about 15 clicks from where we are right now. My plan would cut about a third of the distance off and make it easier to reach the Rock Crusher or Culvert without killing us if we are told to move tomorrow."

He then gave the group grid coordinates on the new location where he wanted to move to. This also gave the platoon leader a chance to see how good, or bad, the squad leaders were at reading and locating positions on the map. They all quickly located the position. This made him happy, extremely happy.

"Great. Now here is what I want to do. The platoon leaves this position and patrols going toward the hill about a click and a half northeast of the hill I want to finally occupy. We need to get to the temporary hill at least a half hour before dark. We can observe our final position from the temporary hill with the binoculars in order to make sure the enemy doesn't move on to it."

"At dusk the platoon moves on to the hill and digs in. Jersey, since you have the night act tonight I want you to lead the platoon. After we get dug in you and your squad will slide down the southwest side of the hill and set an ambush on this side of the blue line and tree line about 350 meters from the base of the hill, where the rest of the platoon will be. We can support you with the platoon mortars and machine gun, and hopefully provide early detection with the starlight scope. And remember, no fires, smokes, or lights after dark. Well, what do you think?" There was a long pause, no one said anything. Don broke the silence with another question. "Anybody ever been on the hill before?"

As the silence continued, Don, noticed he was sweating. He hoped no one noticed. Was it from nerves or the sun? After all, today was the first time the sun had shone since he'd came to Vietnam; maybe it was the heat from the sun... or maybe not.

Lippy slowly rose and walked up to him as he stared at his map and finally said, "Well, we will have to leave real soon to make it before nightfall. It sure will keep the enemy guessing where we are and it gets us off this hill which I am really in favor of."

Jersey cleared his throat, grinned then said, "I like it, especially having the platoon guarding my back and the starlight support. My only concern is does it gives me enough time to set up my ambush? I think it will if we don't have any complications."

Corporal Rathbone immediately jumped in the discussions by stating he really liked the idea of cutting down the distance from the Rock Crusher and was pretty excited about possibly moving to the Rock Crusher for some long-needed rest.

They all agreed the plan had merit and should work. Don was almost ecstatic and said, "Great, gentlemen, let's move out in twenty minutes. Jersey, once your squad is ready, see me and we will make the final decision as to the route you will take."

Jersey left, kissing his new map, and uttered, "Yes sir."

CHAPTER 6
FIRST AMBUSH

The foot movement to the new platoon position was uneventful. It had not rained heavily in two days and the ground had dried out some, providing solid footing for the patrol. With no slipping and sliding, which was always a problem in mud, especially when they carried eighty to hundred pounds of additional weight on their back, the platoon arrived a good forty-five minutes before sunset.

After sunset, the platoon moved onto the main objective. Don assigned the two squads their perimeter responsibilities and the crew-served weapons positions. By 1830 hours all perimeter positions were dug and every Marine was in position.

Jersey reported to the lieutenant that he was ready to leave the lines and set up the ambush.

Don, Lippy, and Jersey all crawled under a poncho and with a red lens flashlight checked the position coordinates, pre-planned fires, call signs, and routes from withdrawing from the ambush site back to the platoon position if necessary.

Don handed Lippy the starlight scope and said, "You know what to do with it."

Jersey looked at the two with a puzzled look on his face and said, "What... what's up?"

Don looked at him and said, "The radio watch can watch the trail up from your ambush site, at least as long as the clouds don't thicken up and filter the light out. Therefore, the starlight scope can, hopefully, allow the radio operator to warn you if an enemy unit is headed your way."

"And one more thing," said Don with a short but very silent pause, "I'm going with you on the ambush."

Jersey quickly looked at Lippy and got the old shrug-of-the-shoulders, then back to the lieutenant and said, "So you are going to take control of the squad and ambush site?"

Don smiled at Jersey and put his hand on his shoulder and gently responded, "No. It's your squad. You run the squad, I control the platoon. I'm only going as an observer. Understand?"

Jersey looked at the lieutenant then Lippy. Both corporals, as if a non-verbal message had passed between the two, smiled. Jersey looked back at the lieutenant with an even a bigger smile and said, "Damn straight! Are you ready to go lieutenant?"

Jersey and Don crawled out from under the poncho and moved down to where Jersey's squad was waiting to go out on the ambush. Jersey immediately placed himself in front of the semi-circle of Marines waiting for further information, and in a low voice passed out the needed information.

His voice was so low Don could barely make out what was being said until Jersey said, "And the lieutenant will be going with us." All of sudden in the dim moonlight Don could make out the quick turn of heads toward him, combined with the sounds of mumbling voices.

He immediately assumed there might be some reservations about him accompanying the squad, but was somewhat relieved when Jersey said, "Knock it off! He is going to observe. I'm in charge and you damn will do what you are supposed to do. Got it?"

A low mumble of agreement could be heard, then silence. The group moved to the edge of the platoon perimeter. There Jersey lined the squad up in the order they were to exit the perimeter. As each Marine exited in the dark, Jersey tapped each one on the shoulder and in a low voice said their names, "Pizza, Little John, Speedy, Frenchy, and Cowboy." He then quickly stepped into the line and passed the perimeter, leaving Don and a couple squad members left behind.

Immediately, one of the remaining squad members took Jersey's place and began repeating single names as the individuals finally passed through the platoon perimeter.

Don stood staring at the squad member who had taken Jersey's place.

The squad member identified himself as Lance Corporal Ed Cherry and said, "Jersey… I mean Corporal Howard said you were to go before me. I'm to be the last person in the squad, sir."

Don looked at him and said, "Do you have a nickname?"

"Cherry, sir."

Don smiled and stepped past the perimeter thinking, "Does everyone in this platoon have a nickname?"

The squad moved as silently as a fog moving over the landscape into the ambush site. Jersey quickly set each member into his ambush position; Claymore mines were set out and a radio check was made to insure they had communications with the platoon.

Don positioned himself about ten feet behind Jersey. Jersey was located in the middle of the squad, which formed a line from his right to his left, making up the ambush site. Once Jersey was satisfied with the set-up of the squad, he slowly moved back to the lieutenant and quietly asked if he was okay in his position.

Don ensured him he was okay and told Jersey, "You have set up an ambush site that is text book Marine Corps doctrine."

Jersey smiled and said, "Lieutenant, I have been taught by the Bush Masters." He then moved back to his squad position where he could control the springing of the ambush.

Don slowly and very quietly rolled over on his side. The ground was not muddy, but damp and very cool, which made it even more uncomfortable to lie in one position for a long period of time. The mosquitoes were beginning to arrive in black clouds. Don immediately pulled his small plastic bottle of "bug juice" from under the rubber band around his helmet and quickly smeared the juice on all the places his skin was exposed. The back of his hands had already been bitten at least three times and was starting to swell. He slowly rubbed his hands and thought, "These damn mosquitoes can not only suck the blood from your body, but maybe from your soul too."

He then began to think of what had happened in the last twenty-four hours. He had gone from a comfortable warm, dry, and somewhat safe cot to the damp, hard, mosquito infested ground Additionally, he was now responsible for the lives of about forty young men. The new responsibilities were now starting to weigh on his mind.

The morning did not come any too soon. The ground, it seemed, had become damper, colder, and much harder than when they first set up the ambush. Don had fought sleep all night and tensed up with every rustle in the grass or brush, which seemed to happen every minute or so. He was exhausted—his first night on ambush—yet he was extremely pleased. Jersey did in fact know how to set up an excellent ambush. He did have mixed feeling about not having the ambush sprung and it appeared, since it was getting light, it would not happen this morning.

Don was watching Jersey when he slowly rolled over on his back, raised his head, and looked at the lieutenant. Both men stared at each other; the spell was only broken when the corporal broke out in a big smile. He then gave a thumbs-up to the lieutenant, rolled back over, and took the handset of the radio and very lowly talked into the mouth piece.

He stopped talking and waited several minutes then said, "Roger, copy that," then rose up, his weapon on the ready. The other squad members followed.

Jersey signaled the men on the ends to gather in the Claymore mines. The Marine on each end of the ambush site silently, and quickly, retrieved the mines and returned to their former positions.

Don felt a tap on his shoulder and he turned and saw Lance Corporal Cherry, who motioned for the lieutenant to follow him. The squad returned to the perimeter in the reverse order they had left.

Once through the perimeter, Don walked about ten feet and then stopped and turned to watch as each member of the squad returned. When they all had cleared the perimeter, Jersey walked up to the lieutenant and in a voice that could be heard throughout the platoon area, thanked the lieutenant for going on the ambush and observing how ambushes were done in the Nam.

The two talked for a few minutes before Jersey left to check on his men and to make sure they got some rest. All of a sudden, Don was uneasy. He turned to look around and immediately noticed that it seemed every member of the platoon was watching him.

He smiled and walked to the CP, aware of the eyes fixed on him and the critical evaluation of the new platoon leader. He walked up to the CP and with some effort slid under the camouflaged poncho; his muscles were sore and starting to stiffen from lying on the cold, wet, hard ground all night and the burning mosquito bites. Poor Boy immediately handed him a canteen cup of steaming hot coffee.

He looked at the coffee, then at another canteen cup of water being heated up by a heat tab. He asked what the other cup was for? Poor Boy informed him that it was for his own cup of coffee. He offered to trade his newly acquired cup of hot coffee for the cup of hot water. He did not like coffee.

Poor Boy thought this odd, because everyone loved his coffee. However, the two quickly came to an agreement they would trade each other's C-ration coffee for the other one's cocoa.

Corporal Lipsky walked up and sat down cross-legged right outside the camouflaged poncho CP and asked the lieutenant how things went last night.

He looked at Lippy, smiled and said, "Tense, uncomfortable, tiring and boring; yet very informative."

Lippy laughed and said, "That sounds about right. Did you get any sleep?"

"Not a wink."

"May I make a recommendation, lieutenant?"

"Sure, what is it?"

"Get some sleep. We will let you know if anything comes across the net. I have Jersey's report and Poor Boy will send it in to headquarters. You will need all the sleep you can get in the next twenty-four hours, especially if we are ordered to move out to the Rock Crusher or the Triple Culvert today."

Don unbuttoned his flak jacket, leaned back, threw his poncho liner over his body, and, through almost completely closed eyes, looked at a smiling Poor Boy and Lippy. Then, all went blank.

"Lieutenant… lieutenant!"

Don jerked up quickly, partially throwing off his poncho liner, startled. He immediately looked around. It wasn't Oklahoma or Quantico. It was

Vietnam, he now knew as his brain caught up with reality. He turned to Poor Boy and said, "What's up?"

"Sir, Hotel 6 wants to talk to you."

He rubbed his hands through his hair then asked, "Is the six on the net now?"

Poor Boy informed him the six was not yet on the net but would be coming on in a couple minutes.

Don thought of his new call sign, Hotel…Hotel Company, 1st platoon, he liked it. 2nd platoon's lieutenant's call sign, Hotel 2, 3rd platoon, Hotel 3, weapons, Hotel 4, executive officer, Hotel 5, and the commanding officer of the company, Hotel 6.

This allowed for anyone talking on the net to know who they were talking to and what command, without giving up the actual names of the officers. This practice denied the enemy from getting these officers names and using them in covert operations. He thought this practice was extremely simple, effective, and tactically sound.

"How long have I been asleep?"

"Oh, about two hours."

Then the net squawked and crackled, yet Don could hear the voice on the other end of the net clearly say, "This is Hotel 6, put on Hotel 1." Poor Boy immediately handed him the hand set.

He quickly stretched out his hand to receive it, and said, "Hotel 6, this is Hotel 1, over." As Don started talking, Poor Boy instantly pulled out a small notebook from his utility jacket pocket and with a pencil in hand listened intently and began taking notes.

As he talked, he looked at Poor Boy from time to time making sure the words were said slowly to insure Poor Boy could clearly get the information. As he finished up the conversation with the CO, Poor Boy leaned over and withdrew a Whiz Wheel from his pack and began deciphering what had been passed in code.

As he waited for Poor Boy to finish the deciphering he pulled out his map case and located the Rock Crusher's location and grid numbers on the map.

"The top numbers are the grids, the bottom ones, the time," Poor Boy said, as he handed the lieutenant the notebook.

Don quickly looked at the grid numbers, then the times, and mumbled, "We need to be there by 1630 hours. Do you know where Lippy is?" He looked up from his map.

Poor Boy raised his hand, pointed a finger about a foot to the right of him, and grinned. Don turned and there, sitting on the ground crossed armed and legged, was Lippy.

Don smiled and said, "What the… you… like a Genie in a bottle showing up when needed?"

"I try, lieutenant, I try," chuckled Lippy in response.

Don and Lippy quickly drew up a route, pre-planned supporting fires, check points, and an order of march, finalized it, and called up squad leaders and briefed them. Headquarters was notified and reports were forwarded.

Don informed the squad leaders, he and Lippy, would do a final inspection of the hill, ensuring that all fighting holes were covered up, and that trash had been buried and ordinances were not being left behind.

This was critical because the enemy would almost always check positions where friendly forces had occupied for anything they could find to use in making weapons of war, such as booby traps.

CHAPTER 7
MOVEMENT TO COMBAT

The platoon did an excellent job in burying the trash and taking with them what they had brought, leaving the hill pretty much as they had found it. Also, in the process of checking the hill, Don was able to introduce himself to the members of the platoon and briefly talk to each one of them.

He now understood better why Hotel Company was known as the "Horrible Hogs": the uniforms of the Marines were far from uniform. They were dressed in a mirage of different hats, helmets, bush hats, and baseball type camouflage covers, along with camouflage utility jackets, some without sleeves. Others had no utility jackets, only green t-shirts.

The one piece of clothing they each had was a flack jacket. Some contained, however, more colorful graffiti than others. Much to his delight, on the march he noticed how quiet the platoon moved and how, when stopped, the members would face outward in a tactical position. They did not drop equipment or start running around talking and clowning around... they were focused to fight.

As the platoon tactically moved toward their new position, Don missed very little as he silently walked along, watching and taking mental notes. One of the more glaring facts that began to jump out to him was how young or old the different Marines looked, yet according to their records they were all about the same age, eighteen to nineteen.

Those Marines, like himself, who had been recently assigned to the unit, wore newer clothes and had fuller faces, while those having been assigned for some time to the unit wore dirty, faded clothes and had more sunken faces and a greater assortment of nonstandard uniforms.

He began quickly picking out those who had been with the unit for less than four months, for four to eight months, and for more than eight or nine months. Those close to ending their tour, like Lippy, had clothes which were extremely faded, ragged, and very dirty. They had in some instances thrown some of the clothing away, which helped explained for the assorted clothing in the platoon… not totally though.

The platoon reached check point four and a perimeter was set up so the Marines could eat lunch and rest. Don selected a position with some cover and dropped his pack. He then went to check the perimeter to make sure the squads were linked together and they knew their area of responsibilities in case of an attack.

When he returned to the CP area, Poor Boy had already started heating his C-ration meal of beans and frankfurters. His field stove was a C-ration can with the top removed and slits cut into the side. The heat tab was placed into the can and then lit. The slits allowed for the heat tab to breathe while the can of food being heated was placed on top of the stove. In most cases, the food was heated to an acceptable temperature.

Don sat down and said, "So, Poor Boy, you said I slept for about two hours this morning, right?"

Poor Boy informed him that, yes, he had slept for about two hours and that he would always get about two hours of sleep during the day and about the same at night. "That's the norm, lieutenant."

Don heated a C-ration can of beef slices and potatoes in gravy, ate his lunch, and felt good. He once again began to look around and didn't look far when he noticed Poor Boy had a series of packs he carried on his backpack frame. The first one contained the radio, the second had his personal items and a third small pack at the bottom of the other two larger packs contained two extra batteries, an extra hand set, and a whip antenna, plus some cleaning gear for the radio.

Don sat up and carefully studied the packs and, to his amazement, figured the three packs had to weigh at least a hundred pounds. He turned to Poor Boy and said, "You are carrying a hell of a lot of gear. Do you always carry this much with you?"

Poor Boy looked at his packs, smiled and said, "Yes sir, you get used to it. I don't have to carry any machine gun ammo or extra mortar shells like the other guys do though."

Don got up and walked up and down the lines of the Marines. He noticed some were carrying cans of machine gun ammo and others a mortar shell on their packs. However, as he neared the CP he noticed one Marine with two mortar shells on his pack. He stopped, sat down next to the Marine and said, after looking at him in the face, "I can't remember your name, but you are from New Mexico."

The Marine started to stand, but the lieutenant motioned for him to stay where he was. He then said, "Lance Corporal Louis Lujan, sir."

"And what do they call you?"

Lujan looked at the lieutenant and with a rather puzzled expression on his face said, "Lujan, sir."

Don did a low chuckle and said, "Okay. Tell me, Lujan, why are you carrying two mortar shells and why does everybody else have one?"

Lujan looked at the lieutenant rather seriously and somewhat questionable again and said, "Well sir, it was an extra one and someone has to carry it."

Don took the mortar shell, returned to the CP, tied the shell to his pack, helped his radioman put on his pack, and informed the squad leaders to move out.

He didn't say much the rest of the way to the new position. He did do a lot of thinking and studying of "his Marines." He found the level of responsibility among these Marines almost unbelievable. Apparently, like all good Marines, whatever it took to get the job done, they did it. This didn't surprise him; what he had trouble grasping was the *age* of these young Marines. They respond as if they were old seasoned veterans.

His silence and thoughts were instantly broken by the crackling and squawking of the radio followed by a frantic voice yelling, "Hotel 1...Hotel 1!" Poor Boy, who was walking behind him, leaped forward immediately, handing him the handset.

"This is Hotel 1. Over." Don strained to understand the caller's words and while listing to the caller, he quickly pointed to Lippy, who was running up from the rear of the platoon. He raised his hand and made a circular movement, telling Lippy to stop the platoon and setup a quick defense position.

Poor Boy immediately grabbed his notebook from his pocket and knelt down on one leg, using his leg as a hard surface to take notes.

Poor Boy quickly scribbled down grids as the lieutenant repeated the information loud enough for him to hear. He then told the caller to "wait one," while he jerked his map case from his shoulder and plotted the grids on the map. He then informed the caller it would be about fifteen "mikes" (minutes) before he could reach them. The call ended with the Don yelling, "SQUAD LEADERS UP!"

In a matter of seconds, the squad leaders, and Lipsky, were kneeling in a half circle in front of the lieutenant. "Golf Company is in contact with an NVA unit. We are to linkup with them and assist them in the fight." Laying his map out on the ground, Don showed the squad leaders where Golf Company was located and the platoon's current position.

"We will travel along this route in an inverted 'V' with the point of the V being the front of the platoon. 3rd will be the point, 1st on the left, 2nd on the right, the CP will move in the middle of the V, right behind 3rd. We must move fast but stay tactical and be ready for anything that may pop up on the way. Any questions?"

Each of the squad leaders looked at their maps then the lieutenant and said, "No, sir."

"Okay, we move out in two minutes. Let's go help Golf!"

The squad leaders quickly scrambled off to their respective squads to brief their men and set up the tactical movement.

Don's adrenaline was pumping wildly through his body. No doubt, his blood pressure was sky high. He could feel it pumping through his head to the point that it hurt. The platoon's movement was at a very good pace, uniform, and surprisingly quiet.

He could sense he and the men had now worked off a lot of anxiety and tension; however, they knew they were very close to the fight as they could hear rifle fire and explosives not very far up in front of them. Suddenly, Jersey dropped to the ground and held his rifle over his head with both arms, indicating enemy was in front of him.

Immediately, the squads on each side of him swung out to form a platoon line.

Eight NVA came running straight into the line. The platoon opened fire, dropping six of the NVA instantly. The two on each side and, behind the main NVA group, somehow managed to escape into the bushy terrain.

A quick search of the dead NVA produced some documentations and an immediate area where one of the enemies escaped. A few drops of blood were found, probably a slight wound. However, the mission was not to search for a wounded NVA solider, but rather help Golf Company.

Don swiftly put the platoon back in its tactical formation and started towards Golf's position. They only walked a couple hundred feet when the radio once more broke the silence. It was the commander of Golf wanting to know if the platoon knew what the firing was from behind them.

He explained the platoon had encountered some NVA troops and had killed six of them. Apparently, according to the commanding officer of Golf, when 1st platoon shot the enemy, the NVA realized reinforcements were on the way and broke off the fight; therefore, they no longer needed the assistance.

Don was actually happy about the situation; one successful fire fight was enough for him today. He had the platoon set up a defense position so they could take a ten-minute break.

Doc Smith wandered over to Don, sat on the ground in front of him and said, "How are you doing, lieutenant?"

He grinned, laid down the map case, took a deep breath, and said, "I'm sure my situation is not any different from what the troops have been through. I have been in Vietnam a week, three days moving from 3rd MAF, 1st Division, regiment, battalion, the company, and finally to the platoon. Been in the bush two days and one night, trying to remember thirty some men's names, positions, evaluate their skills and abilities. I sat in a night ambush, momentarily finished a fire fight with the enemy, have traveled by foot with a hundred-pound pack on my back over many very hot and humid clicks on the ground. I feel physically and mentally exhausted and best thing, I only have twelve months and three weeks to go before I rotate. God, you have to love it!"

Doc smiled and said, "Well, I have only been here about a month longer than you and from what I have seen so far it's not going to change. Learn to accept it and enjoy it, if possible."

He thought, "Accept, probably—enjoy, not!"

Don received a call from the new company commander to report to his position. They trudged through the heat and humidity to the company's new position and made it without incident.

Once the company was inside the perimeter First Lieutenant Vallence, the executive officer met Don, showed him where his platoon was to man and guard the perimeter, and then told him to report to the company commander, Captain Frank McCarthy.

Before reporting to the company commander Don said, "Lieutenant Vallence, I thought you had already left for the states?"

"No, It turned out I still have a couple days to go."

Don made his way to the company headquarters and when he arrived he noticed an individual talking on a radio. He was clearly animated, talking loudly, flailing his arms around, and jerking on the hand set cord when he reached its end, much like a chained animal trying to break lose.

He stopped a lance corporal and asked who the individual was on the radio.

The lance corporal looked over towards the radio, smiled and said, "That's Captain McCarthy, sir, the new skipper. He arrived here a few hours ago."

"Thanks." He headed toward the new skipper.

The skipper was about five ten, muscled, red-headed and no doubt tenacious in manner. Mumbling something, the captain walked directly toward him then said, "Who the hell are you?"

"Lieutenant Garrett, 1st platoon commander, sir."

The captain stopped in his tracks and, with a gracious and pleasing smile, said, "Well, well, the only platoon to fight, beat, and kill the enemy before I can get a full day in as company commander. Congratulations! Now, why did you let two enemies escape and how come it took you so long to get here?"

Startled, Don momentarily stared at the CO and slowly said, "Well… uh, thanks. My mission was to go to Golf's aid rather than look for fleeing enemy. The platoon did cover a good distance of ground in full combat gear at a rather fast speed to help Golf. So, when Golf notified me we no longer needed I gave the troops a break. When you radioed me to move here, we moved in a tactical manner so we could make it here alive and you wouldn't have to come out and rescue us, or police up our dead bodies, sir."

The captain made a few facial movements with his lips, then rolled his eyes, smiled, and said, "Okay that sounds logical to me."

Feeling better, he could not pass up a comment about the radio conversation. "So sir, were you making new friends over there on the radio?"

The skipper turned toward the radio, chuckled and said, "Those nit-wits in the rear think they have all the answers." Now starting to become a little excited, he pointed his finger toward the rear and continued to say, "When a unit is assigned to me they are under my command. Their *former* commander loses his tactical command over the unit when it's attached to another unit....dumb bastards."

Don, feeling a little more chipper, mumbled, "I'm sure they understand now, sir."

"Are your Marines in their positions on the perimeter Lieutenant…"

"Garrett, sir."

"Right, Garrett."

"Yes sir, well the platoon sergeant with the company gunny was settling them in when I came up to see you."

"Great, let's go for a walk and take a look at *my* 1st platoon. Tell me, how long have you been with the platoon, lieutenant?"

"Two days and one night, sir."

The captain stopped walking, looked at him, and began laughing and said, "You're kidding me, right?"

"No sir!"

"So I guess all my officers and staff NCO's are all new to this company?"

"It would appear so, sir."

The captain stood silent with his head bent down for a few moments in deep thought. He then raised his head and in a much softer voice than he had been using before said, "Lieutenant you have a slight accent, where are you from?"

"That's funny, I thought you had an accent. I am from Oklahoma, sir."

The skipper grinned and said, "Nope, you have the accent. I am from the Bronx in New York and we certainly do not have an accent."

Don looked the captain right in the eyes, trying to figure out if he was serious or not. When it appeared to him the skipper was serious Don, slowly muttered, "Right sir."

Sensing this conversation was going nowhere, the captain said, "Well I guess we can both agree we are from different backgrounds and both a long way from home."

"Absolutely, sir."

The captain started at the far end of the platoon's perimeter and stopped at each position and briefly talked to each Marine, and it appeared he had an instant rapport with each of the troops.

After discussing a few non-important subjects, the skipper said, "In my opinion you have three strong squad leaders and good disciplined troops, but where is your platoon sergeant?"

Don looked out and noticed Lippy coming across the perimeter towards them. "Here he comes now. He's probably finished with the gunny setting in positions."

The two turned toward Lippy as he came close to them and Don said, "Captain, this is Corporal Lipsky. Corporal Lipsky, this is Captain McCarthy."

The captain frowned and said, "You don't have a staff sergeant for a platoon sergeant?"

"No sir, I don't even have a sergeant in the platoon. I have five corporals, thirty-three lance corporals, and four private first classes and one corpsman."

The captain's face began to turn red and he slowly said, "Damn, the good news seems endless. So, you're short one staff NCO, five sergeants, and, what, two or three corporals?"

"Well… kind of, that count also includes the gun and mortar sections I have from weapons too."

"Lieutenant, do you know what a Marine Rifle Platoon rates in personnel?"

"Yes sir, according to what I was taught at Basic School one officer and forty-six enlisted."

"That is correct. So taking out your weapons people, you're short about eighteen or twenty personnel and ninety percent of those are your senior enlisted?"

"I would say that was very close, sir."

The skipper's face became even redder, if it were possible; he then stomped off toward the company CP shouting, "SON OF A BITCH!"

The next morning the company moved off the hill they had been sitting on for a couple days. Battalion had sent down a new position to move to, which originally came from regiment.

The skipper put the company in a tactical spread-out formation. 1st platoon was in the middle, with the other two platoons, on it's left and right. Jersey's 3rd squad was the lead element of the platoon.

Don looked to his left and right. His platoon was on line and stepping off into the second-to-last rice paddy from the objective. They stepped off into water, about six to eight inches deep, and sloshed to about one hundred feet from the last paddy dike when he looked up to see Jersey and his squad reach the last rice paddy dike, about two hundred feet from their objective.

Suddenly, SWOOSH… SWOOSH… The sound of mortars coming out of tubes. "INCOMING!" Someone yelled across the line of Marines, who now were wide-eyed, looking up to see if they could locate the mortars now falling from the sky.

Don turned his attention quickly to Jersey and his men when a plume of water shot up right in front of Jersey, knocking him off the dike.

Don froze for a second then without warning there was an explosion right behind him, knocking him forward. Half running and floundering, he managed to stay upright and yelled, "MOVE TO THE DIKES FOR COVER!"

The platoon reached the dikes at the same time Pizza and Frenchy were pulling Jersey over to dike to the Marine's side. Doc Smith was beside Jersey when he slid to the bottom of the dike, looking him over for wounds.

Don jumped up and ran to Jersey and Doc. With a great deal of concern, he said, "How is he, Doc?"

Doc Smith methodically and, it seemed, unhurriedly finished his exam, then turned to him and said, "Well, he was lucky as he wasn't hit by shrapnel but the blast may have caused a concussion. I can't really tell. We should medevac him."

Jersey glared at Doc then the lieutenant and shouted, "I'M NOT GOING TO BE MEDEVACED!" He quickly leaped up and started mumbling profanities as he headed back to his squad.

Don immediately got on the radio and called for mortar support; he wanted the mortar rounds dropped on the back side of the hill. Rathbone's squad climbed the front side of the hill to secure it for the company.

Rathbone and his squad moved cautiously up to the top of the hill and secured it. He called in artillery fire on a tree line approximately five hundred meters behind the hill where he figured the enemy shooting the mortars were hiding.

The arty rounds blew up trees, sending large chunks of timber and limbs high into the air, leaving little hope for those who might be hiding in the tree line. The rest of the platoon moved on to the hill and called for the rest of the company to join them.

Captain McCarthy brought the rest of the company on the hill and surveyed the area and hill, and then commented, "I really don't like this hill. Marines have been here before and 'Charlie' may have booby trapped it. We need to be very careful."

The skipper had a quick meeting with his platoon commanders and gave each an equal section of the company perimeter to defend and informed them to be especially careful because the hill might be booby trapped.

Don started to take his pack off and the skipper reached over to help him get it off and said, "What the hell happened to your pack?"

After getting his pack off, he looked at what the skipper was referring to and he was shocked. A one-inch-wide and maybe six-inch-long piece of metal was embedded into his pack. It must have happened when the mortar went off behind him in the rice paddy, almost knocking him over. The pack had saved him from having the shrapnel bury itself in his back. He was very lucky!

He hurried back to his platoon area and met with Lieutenant Tom Baumgartner, 3rd platoon commander, to discuss tying the two platoons lines together to make sure all avenues were covered, when suddenly a thundering blast went off, sending them both to the ground. When they looked up, the lieutenants were horrified. On Tom's helmet was human skin.

Don's eyes widened and with a quivering voice he said, "Tom… you have a human scalp on your helmet."

Tom hesitantly reached up and felt the skin then flung it off and jumped back screaming, "Hell NO, THIS CAN'T BE HAPPENING!"

Both men quickly stared at each other, both horrified. Although their training was the world's best, it did not prepare either for the shock or realization of instant, grotesque death. However, both were trained to respond to such situations and without any signal leaped up and started running to where the explosion had gone off.

Don crawled over a mound of dirt and was horror-stricken to the point of being temporarily paralyzed. Laying in front of him was a Marine. His skull was stripped of facial skin and the scalp was gone, his head was barely attached to the torso, and the legs and torso were completely separated. Blood sprayed from the torso. He screamed, "CORPSMAN UP, CORPSMAN UP," as loud as his voice would allow.

After yelling for the corpsman, he noticed another Marine screaming, holding his stomach area, and another holding his right leg, and one holding his left leg and moaning, and yet a fourth one laying on his back, eyes wide open with blood spurting out of his skull.

Immediately, Doc Smith zipped past him, took a quick look of the situation and, without hesitation, leaped to help the Marine with blood spurting from his skull. Other corpsmen were equally as fast as Doc Smith and rendered aid to the other victims of the explosion.

He turned from the hideous scene only to be met by the captain asking what happened. Swallowing hard to keep from vomiting, he quickly wiped his hands across his eyes to clear away the tears and he looked down to the ground. "We have one KIA and at least four WIAs. I think they all are from 2nd platoon."

The captain remained silent for a few moments then yelled, "LISTEN UP, listen up! Stop whatever you're doing! Do not dig, do not dig! Lieutenants up! Gunny, get a medevac here ASAP!

"Lieutenant Baumgartner, you have a squad over there on the hill to our left, join them and secure the hill. Garrett, secure an LZ below the hill for the medevac. Lieutenant Gerhardt, get your wounded down to the LZ and make sure you get your KIA wrapped up... covered as much as possible.

"Lieutenant Baumgartner, once you have secured the hill let me know and I will move the weapons platoon over there. Lieutenants Garrett, Gerhardt, join us after you complete the medevac. You guys understand the orders?" All three lieutenants shook their heads in agreement and set off to accomplish their missions.

The medevac was completed and new perimeter established on a nearby hill. Then Captain McCarthy called in one arty strike after another on the old position, like an angry man repeatedly beating his fist against a wall. There would be no more booby traps killing Marines from that hill!

CHAPTER 8
TRIPLE CULVERT

The platoon spent another two days with the company. The company moved every day, only staying one night on each hill. All three platoons ran squad-size day patrols and night ambushes.

On the second day with the company, Captain McCarthy informed Don his platoon would operate solo from the company. The platoon was to conduct squad-size day patrols and night ambushes. He would submit the locations of the platoon's patrols, and ambushes, to include check points, pre-planned arty fires, and company mortar support. The platoon would operate within one to five clicks of the company and be ready to support the rest of the company if it came under attack.

Don was extremely happy to be working away from the company. It gave him more uninterrupted time with his men and allowed him to better evaluate each Marine's skills and how they operated as a unit. Much to his surprise, he was still amazed how mature and responsible these young Marines were, especially considering their young ages.

Bright and early on the fifth day of operating from the rest of the company, Don received a radio message from the skipper to move his platoon to the Triple Culvert, about eight clicks from his current position, by foot. The rest of the company would be moving to the Rock Crusher, about three clicks from the Triple Culvert.

Once again, 1st platoon would be operating by themselves. This did not go unnoticed by Don or his troops. There was a platoon sense of pride shared by all about being "good enough" and trusted to handle the situation. There was no bitching or gripping about moving, only smiles and comments like, "That's us, we can do!"

By 0800 hours the platoon had been on the move toward the Triple Culvert for over an hour. The humidity was stifling, causing the heat to feel like a blast furnace. Each Marine's pack weighted over a hundred pounds, not counting the weight of the flak jacket, helmet, and cartridge belt.

Don noticed his blouse was almost entirely wet from the sweat. He also was aware that several of the men had almost permanent salt marks on their blouses and trousers, especially where the pack straps crossed over the shoulders.

The Triple Culvert Bridge was merely that, a bridge made of three culverts lying side by side, at least ten feet tall, and had dirt piled on them to form a bridge over a stream which was mostly used by local farmers to get their produce to the market.

The Marines were guarding the bridge because the local Viet Cong liked to destroy anything the American or pro-American forces built. This position was not a highly military tactical bridge but rather a bridge of some political importance. It also gave the Marine Corps a place to put a platoon which needed a slower pace and to do some resting and regrouping, and after Hill 953, Hotel's 1st platoon was a perfect candidate for the bridge.

While the stream separated the platoon, the bridge also served to connect them. The wire around the perimeter appeared to have had little maintenance for some time and this concerned Don. He also noticed several unused roles of concertina wire lying where previous platoons had used as their CPs.

He studied the situation for some time, then Lippy came over and said, "This perimeter could use some cleaning up and new wire, don't you think, lieutenant?"

Don grinned, looked around, nodded in agreement, then said, "There are some roles of concertina wire over there. If we take those roles and place them across the road inside the existing wire and place our machine gun here next to the bridge and slightly off the road we will have a great field of fire. Well, at least for our single machine gun.

"Now we have nothing across the road running onto the bridge to stop or even slow the enemy down. The new concertina placement will at least slow the enemy down. Granted we will have to take it up every day to let traffic cross the bridge, but it sure will help at night."

Looking across the far side of the bridge he said, "We need to move the fighting position on the east side of the perimeter next to the road. It needs to be moved over on that piece of higher ground about twenty feet off the road. Once the current fighting position is moved, it gives the machine-gunner a much better view of the entry into the perimeter and less chance of hitting the Marines manning the position."

Lippy closely followed what he was saying, then smiled and quickly agreed and said he would get the squads and weapons section working on the new plan.

Don went from working party to working party explaining why the new positions were being built or moved. The Marines appeared to understand and agreed it was a good plan, but continued to complain about having to build the new machine gun position, especially with its new three-sandbag wall. However, he noticed the complaining was now more cheerful in nature. Well, it sure seemed that way to him.

Satisfied the work was going smoothly, he headed for the CP area to see how Poor Boy was doing in setting up the new CP. As he approached the CP area he saw four people dressed like PFs (Popular Forces, local militia) carrying rifles coming into the perimeter by way of the east road entry. Two Marines were escorting them. Don signaled for the Marines to hold the four up and he went to them.

The PF leading the others was much taller than the other three. Two of the four were women. The leader spoke understandable English and informed Don they were from the village located about a half of a mile north of the bridge. He told the lieutenant he was in charge of the local militia and his name was First Lieutenant Phan.

Right behind him was a girl, lieutenant Phan's sister and a second lieutenant. The second male was Third Lieutenant Phan and the last person, also a woman, was Fourth Lieutenant Phan. Don had never heard of a third or fourth lieutenant. He thought being a second lieutenant was tough enough but a third and forth lieutenant must be pure hell.

Lieutenant Phan told them the local VC was going to attack the bridge that night, and Lieutenant Phan and his three officers wanted to stay the night at the bridge. Poor Boy had cautiously walked up next to Don and when he heard the four wanted to spend the night he gave him a "not-a-chance-in-hell" look. The guards gave each other a quick glance and rolled their eyes then stared at him.

Don asked Lieutenant Phan how many men were in his militia.

"Maybe fifteen… maybe twenty… maybe twenty-five," Lieutenant Phan responded with a gigantic smile across his face.

"Okay, so you have an undetermined number of people in your force. But why do you want to spend the night here?"

"Some in militia don't want fight VC. Have family members in VC," Lieutenant Phan slowly explained, then swung his arm around toward the other militia members and added, "We ready to fight."

Don looked at the group. He especially eyed the third lieutenant. He looked very shifty and had a sinister smile. "Not one to be trusted," he thought. He raised his eyes to the sky and thought, "What the hell. I have a group of people who want to help fight the enemy that's supposed to hit us tonight, yet they admit to having family members in the enemy unit. Do I want them inside of my perimeter tonight during an attack? Not only no, but hell no!"

He reached over and placed his hand on Lieutenant Phan's shoulder and steered him off to one side and said, "Unfortunately Marine Corps regulations will not allow me to let you stay here tonight because we are in immediate danger. However, you and your brave militia members can be of a great service to us by getting your men together, however many that might be, and on my signal attack the enemy from outside the perimeter… you know, a sneak attack on them while they are busy fighting us."

Lieutenant Phan's smile faded for a moment then he smiled an even bigger smile, one Don thought not possible, and said, "I like plan. We do!"

Lieutenant Phan turned to his group, immediately began speaking Vietnamese. They all broke out in laughter and began slapping each other on their backs, then headed out of the perimeter back toward their village. The two escorts which had brought the militia group to the lieutenant followed the Vietnamese group out of the perimeter and then turned toward the lieutenant and gave him a thumbs up.

Don turned to Poor Boy and asked him to get the platoon sergeant, squad leaders, and weapons team leader up for a quick meeting. "But first get me the S-2 on the radio," he said.

The lieutenant started the meeting by saying, "Gentlemen I have received word that we are going to be attacked tonight by the local VC according to battalion intelligence's. The local VC unit is a sapper unit, about twenty to twenty-five members strong. No doubt their mission is to destroy the bridge, and here is our plan."

He hesitated a moment, making sure he had everyone's attention, then said, "Squad leaders place the concertina wire on the road, about twenty feet inside of our perimeter. This will trap the enemy at three places with only one place to run, back where they came from. We also want concertina wire strung across the stream. Put trip flares in the concertina wire so when the enemy hits the wire the flares go off."

Turning to his weapons squad leader he said, "Corporal Alcala, your signal to fire the machine gun is when the trip flares in the concertina wire on the bridge are set off. It is also the signal to shoot four illumination rounds of M60 mortar rounds about 300 meters past our perimeter in all four directions for illumination. The next rounds will be your call, unless I over ride you. Once the machine gun fires, fire at will."

Pausing once more he said, "At 2400 hours we go on fifty percent. Until then we will stay on regular watch times. Encourage your Marines to get as much sleep as possible until then. I want you all to go back and brief your Marines so that each one of them understands what is happening. I also want you to understand I will be going around later to talk to them. Any questions?"

"What about pre-planned fires?" Lippy inquired.

Don smiled and said, "Oh yes, good call, platoon sergeant. I have already called in our pre-planned fires. Here are the positions and call signs. Please pass these out to everyone." He then handed Lippy his notebook containing the pre-planned fires notations.

It was almost 0400 hours in the morning; the fifty-percent watch had been implemented about four hours ago and Don had made several tours around the perimeter checking on his Marines.

He settled down into his fighting/CP position and inter-crossed his fingers as he placed his hands behind his head and looked up at the night sky. The monsoon clouds were still prevalent except for a small hole which allowed three stars to shine through. He looked and wondered, if in fact, he might know which stars they were, but then decided probably not, since they were in the Southern Hemisphere. He was nervous and as he thought about his plan, he wondered if it would work. He loved tactics and truly enjoyed the subject... but was *this* tactical plan going to work?

Poor Boy started his radio checks, calling all three squads and weapons, getting the "Roger got you loud and clear" response.

Don stopped staring at the stars and looked over at Poor Boy and said, "What do you think of the situation?"

Poor Boy slowly turned toward the lieutenant in the darkness and quietly said, "Well the guys really like your plan, especially the trip flares in the concertina wire, and we know from experience the gooks will attack the first night in a position or after the third night in a position. And since the local militia thinks the VC are going to attack tonight, I think they will pretty soon."

The night was very dark. There were no artificial lights here and Don couldn't see Poor Boy, only a few feet away, because the small dim green light on the radio was covered. Through the blackness, Don sensed a real conviction of honesty and openness from Poor Boy.

Without any warning, the trip flares on the road leading into the perimeter from the west, burst into flames sending up a glowing light silhouetting the intruders. Almost instantly the M60 machine gun opened up, manned by Lance Corporal Billy Baker, who could be heard over the repeating machine gun fire in his heavy Texas accent yelling, "NOW THIS IS THE REAL DEAL!"

The five intruders spun and jerked as the machine gun fire tore through them; they fell to the road and lay motionless.

The "SWOOSH" from the M60 mortar rounds could be clearly heard as they left the tube and traveled through the darkness. They exploded, spreading the burning magnesium flames and instantly illuminating the night sky as their parachutes slowly, and gently, allowed them to float back to the earth's surface.

Don nervously called for his pre-planned supporting artillery fire. Simultaneously, on the north side of the perimeter, a barrage of semiautomatic weapon fire broke out. Four VC were in the stream approaching the bridge with satchel charges strapped on their backs. The M60 illumination reflected knee-deep water, and the thundering volley of fire from the Marines on the perimeter proved to be instant death for the sappers.

After a few minutes of silence, except for the supporting arty fire he had previously called for, Don quickly said, "This is Hotel 1, cease fire, cease fire." The battery acknowledged "cease fire." Don, sweating and possibly shaking a little, said in the calmest voice he could muster up, "Poor Boy, get a report from the squad leaders."

He then crawled out of the fighting position toward the machine gun position and asked how Baker was doing. Billy Baker, in his usual spirited mood said, "Locked and loaded, bring 'em on."

Don took that to mean he was okay. He then moved toward the mortar position. They were fine and ready to fire too. Don told them to stand by and on his order, be ready to fire additional illuminations rounds.

Crawling back to the CP fighting position Don caught a glimpse of a figure coming toward him from the bridge. He quickly reached for his pistol then heard Lippy quietly and softly saying, "Lieutenant, lieutenant."

Don relaxed his grip on his pistol and said, "Over here!"

The two met about three feet from the CP. They quickly moved to the CP and slid in. Once in the fighting position, Lippy slapped the lieutenant on the back and said, "Welcome to your first 'seven-minute war.'"

Don, somewhat bewildered, looked at Lippy and said, "What do you mean, seven-minute war?"

"How long do you think this attack lasted?" Lippy inquired.

"I don't know, maybe fifteen or twenty minutes. It seemed like an hour. I really don't know. Do you know how long it lasted?"

Grinning, Lippy said, "Actually, less than five minutes."

Don was shocked… under five minutes. He looked at Poor Boy; he could make out his facial features in the green light from the uncovered radios and he was shaking his head in agreement with Lippy.

Poor Boy then informed them the squad leaders had reported back. "First squad had five gooks dead on the road, no friendly casualties. Second has no casualties and heard screaming from one of the pre-planned fires that landed in the tree line west of the platoons position. Third squad has four dead gooks in the stream, no casualties."

He thanked Poor Boy for the info and was extremely thankful and happy his Marines were not hurt… only the enemy!

He welcomed the darkness; his hands were trembling and he was afraid he was going to throw up and he wasn't sure what to do next. He could hear Lippy and Poor Boy going over the events. "Timely… didn't have a chance… sitting ducks and couldn't been drawn up any better."

Lippy slid over next to him and said, "Lieutenant you were calm and collected during the fight, did they teach you that in basic school?"

He chuckled nervously and said, "Maybe a little." But after some thought, he said, "I think my brother-in-law, David Callison, may have helped too."

Lippy turned to him and asked, "How did he help you?"

Don grinned. "Well, David got his pilot license before he graduated from high school and he also needed to keep up his flying hours so I went with him any time I could and let's say he had no limitations as to what he would try."

Lippy thought for a moment and finally said, "You mean he was one of those 'Barn Stormers'?"

Don smiled and said, "Let me tell you a couple of true stories about David and you make up your own mind about his 'barn storming.' He would always fly out to my parents' house in the country and dive bomb the place. I swear there are airplane tire marks on the top of their roof."

Don chuckled. "One time, we were flying down the Arkansas River chasing coyotes on the sandbars, when I looked up and there was the Kaw Bridge. The bridge was an old steel gartered bridge with three sections. David flew under the middle span, between the bridge and the river, it scared the hell out of me."

He paused, smiled, and said, "I remember when we flew under the bridge there was a young boy, maybe ten or eleven years of age, looking over the rail right at me. We made eye-to-eye contact and his eyes were huge. I have often thought he will tell that story a thousand times, only I am sure that kid will say, 'And that co-pilot eyes were as big as saucers!'"

Laughing, Don said, "One final story. I was at a family reunion and several family members were standing around talking. David and my sister, Terry, walked in and someone in the group asked if I had ever flown with David. I said, "Sure, lots of times."

They all stepped back and said, almost in unison, "YOU... FLEW WITH HIM MORE THAN ONCE?"

CHAPTER 9
TRAGEDY FROM THE VIETNAMESE VILLAGE

Don appreciated the chance to take his mind off the current situation, but he quickly realized where he was and the circumstances. He then closed his eyes and thought of the silent darkness; like a warm blanket wrapped around him, it was comforting and it was his friend.

"Lieutenant…lieutenant." The mood was suddenly broken by Poor Boy telling him Hotel 6 was on the net.

He took the hand set and said, "Hotel 1, over." After Don explained the situation as best he could, the commander thanked him and insured him he would take care of notifying battalion of the details. Don thanked him and hung up.

He then turned to Lippy and said, "Corporal Lipsky, I'm not sure what to do now."

The CP area became very quiet. The silence lasted for what seemed a long time then Corporal Lipsky said, "Well, lieutenant, it will be light in about an hour. I would keep the men where they are for now and when it gets light I would get the dead off the road and out of the stream. I would have a squad check out the tree line west of here. That's what I would do, lieutenant."

Don looked at Lippy through the dark green light from the radios, and with a quivering smile said, "Thanks, that's what we'll do."

He checked and rechecked his troops, as he couldn't sit in any one place very long. He was burning off excessive nerviness, or energy, or both, he really didn't know. He did know the entire platoon reeked of excessive nervousness; they were all restless and jittery.

Finally he returned to the CP, but couldn't find a comfortable position in the cramped fighting position. Poor Boy, hoping to offer some type of help to his platoon commander, said, "It will be light in about ten minutes, lieutenant."

Don looked toward the east. He wasn't sure if it would start to get light in a few minutes, mostly due to the clouds. He thought, "God I pray you are right, Poor Boy." Last night the darkness was his friend; now he wanted so much for the sunlight to shine, brighter than it had ever shone before.

He sat silently looking toward the east for several minutes as the morning light slowly began to push the darkness away. Then, suddenly, through the dim morning light he noticed movement to the northeast, along the trail leading to the village.

He quickly alerted his Marines on the east side of the perimeter and had them hold their fire while he tried to determine who and what was coming up the trail. They were not trying to sneak up the trail, in fact one wore what appeared to be a white or near-white dress. He now could see the group carrying a stretcher.

He called for Doc Smith, the platoon corpsman, who came running up with Lippy hot on his tail. The perimeter watch was locked, loaded, and ready for a firefight. The clicking of the rifles' safeties could be heard in the still quiet morning air, sounding like a rolling *click* across the perimeter.

A lone figure slowly approached the perimeter, stopped, and tensely said, "Marine lieutenant. Lieutenant Phan need help!" Don recognized the voice of Second Lieutenant Phan, the sister to First Lieutenant Phan. She then started speaking in French so emotionally at first that he had difficulty recognizing it was French.

Lippy yelled over his shoulder, "Frenchy, get the hell up here!" The cry echoed across the platoon area and in a matter of a few seconds, a young Marine appeared standing next to the lieutenant and Lippy.

Lippy turned to Frenchy and said, "Find out what the hell is going on."

Frenchy began speaking in French to Second Lieutenant Phan and the woman in the white dress. After several minutes Frenchy told the lieutenant that the commanding officer of the village militia had been shot and they brought him here for medical treatment.

Doc Smith, with his B-1 bag hanging from his shoulder, said he would see what he could do for the Vietnamese lieutenant.

Don motioned for three Marines who had joined the group at the CP to pull back a roll of concertina wire so the Doc to get out and check the wounded man. The three Marines also acted as a security force for Doc and moved out ahead of him toward the stretcher lying on the ground.

Don started walking toward the group outside of the perimeter then turned to Lippy and motioned for him to stay there. He then looked at Frenchy (Lance Corporal Charbonneau) and said, "Frenchy, come with me." As they neared the stretcher holding Lieutenant Phan, Doc looked up at them and rolled his eyes, but continued to work on the wounded man.

He quickly told Frenchy to ask the female lieutenant, the sister-in-law of the woman in the white dress, how the Vietnamese lieutenant got shot.

Frenchy promptly began talking to the sister and several times stopped and looked very puzzled. The conversation went on for several minutes, Don looking back and forth, turning his head from side to side as if he were watching a ping pong match. Finally, he held his hands between the two and said, "Okay, enough, what the hell happened, Frenchy?"

Frenchy took his hand and placed it on his face and slowly brought it down to his chin, cradling his chin in his hands and said, "Where to start? Well sir, it appears this stream separates the village, not only physically but politically too. The people living in the villages on both sides of the river are related to each other. However, the people that live on the left side of the stream are pro-communist, while the ones on the right side are not."

"The VC we killed this morning lived in the village on the left side and twelve of them failed to come home this morning. We certainly know where nine of them are. Anyway, a brother-in-law of Lieutenant Phan, who favors the communist, accused Lieutenant Phan of informing us of the pending attack, causing half of the VC unit in the village to be wiped out and he was so angry with him he shot him in the head."

Don stared at the ground in silence. He thought, "Maybe this village is symbolic of the war." He felt sorry for the Phans, but did not know what he could do under the circumstances. Suddenly, a long and very loud shriek shattered the morning solitude; the wife, the female in the white dress, had learned her husband was dead.

The Vietnamese group remained outside the perimeter for over an hour, wailing, crying, and throwing their arms into the air, and finally the procession gathered itself together and headed back to the village.

The Marines had long returned to the perimeter and Don informed the squad leaders he wanted the bodies of the VC to be taken to the rice paddy dikes, about two hundred meters to the north of the perimeter, and for those bodies to be laid out carefully, *not dumped*, on the dikes. He told 2nd squad to see if they could find the remains of any missing VC in the tree line, where the artillery rounds had landed, and if so, to take those remains and lay them out with the other dead VC.

The Vietnamese had barely cleared the perimeter when two US Army OH6 Loach helicopters suddenly appeared about two hundred feet to the South of the perimeter.

These helos were very small compared to others used in the war. They appeared to have a glass "bubble" large enough to hold a pilot and co-pilot with a round pole sticking out the back which held the rear rotary blade.

They were fast and agile, and had a machine gun under the bubble, making them extremely effective for quick strikes. One of the helos held a hovering position about a hundred feet from a place along the stream which formed a pool of mostly mud and stagnant water and contained a very healthy growth of tall grass. The other helo flew down right above the top of the grass, which was forced flat against the mud and stagnant water because of the force of the wind from the helo's rotary blades.

The Marines watched in total wonderment. Don walked over to where Lippy and Jersey were standing watching the helos.

"What are they doing anyway?" he asked.

Lippy slowly turned toward him and said, "Well the helo over the grass is knocking the grass down so the other guy in the other helo can see if anyone is hiding in it and if there is someone he shoots them."

Don and Jersey slowly looked at Lippy with concern on their faces and asked, "What happens if the person, or persons, hiding in the grass has an RPG or some other type of weapon and shoots the helo above them?"

Jersey, not waiting for an answer, quickly replied, "Well, I guess his ass is grass!"

The army pilots finished their mission, waved at the Marines, and flew down the stream, apparently, looking for more grass to knock down.

"I wish they would have sprayed that spot," Jersey said.

"Sprayed for what? Don inquired.

"For the millions of mosquitoes that come up out of there every night. It's like a black fog rising out of that place each evening and those bastards attack you with an attitude!"

That reminded Don that he needed to see Doc Smith and get a couple more bottles of bug juice to strap on his helmet; he did not want to run out of the stuff. The mosquitoes, he feared, could suck all the blood from one person in a night's time here in the Nam.

"When I get back to the CP I will call the rear and see if they can't send us something to get rid or at least half-ass control the mosquitoes."

Much to his surprise, at about noon three Marine trucks of engineers and equipment arrived. They were loaded with wire, post, a flame thrower, and other engineering items. Ten trained Marine engineers also accompanied the trucks.

The engineering unit was sent from regiment to help refortify the positions around the bridge. Don could only figure that if you were successful in repelling an attack, the Marine Corps felt you worthy of immediate help, and therefore the engineer unit was quickly dispatched. In all honesty, he was very happy to see the engineers, and especially eager to get the weeds out of the wire and, hopefully, to cut down on the millions of mosquitoes.

Warrant Officer O'Malley was in charge of the unit, and as his name indicated, he was Irish, with a heavy accent. He was also rather loud and continuously waved his arms around as he talked, or semi-yelled, whatever his manner of speaking could be classified as.

O'Malley thought he would be through in two days with one night in the bush, and then back to the rear and beer. Don figured O'Malley would miss one night, but certainly not two, from the rigorous events of the O Club.

Don spent the rest of the day walking around talking to his Marines and learning more and more about each one of them. He either learned or relearned. What he had trouble with was trying to keep the all the names, faces, and nicknames of the members of 3rd squad straight. He began to think maybe he left someone out and then he heard vehicles coming down the road from the direction of the Rock Crusher.

He crossed the bridge and made it about half way to the edge of the perimeter when he saw two Marine Corps jeeps coming down the road. The first jeep had a mounted fifty caliber machine gun on a ring mount. Standing behind the gun was the machine-gunner. It pulled off the road right outside of the perimeter and set up in a defense position with its rear backed up to the perimeter wire.

The second was the skipper's jeep, which stopped at the edge of the perimeter. He stood and surveyed the area, remaining quiet for a few moments, then looked over toward the bridge and saw the engineers burning some weeds and grass in the perimeter with a flame thrower and asked as the lieutenant approached him, "What's going on over there?"

Don immediately began explaining how, and why, the engineers were there and how he had requested the work the day before and guessed because the platoon had killed the VC's, regiment must have thought them worthy of the request. The captain chuckled and agreed with his assessment.

Captain McCarthy, spent almost two hours with the platoon talking to the Marines and carefully checking almost all the fighting positions. He drank two cups of Poor Boy's coffee and said it was the best he had ever had, in Vietnam.

He finally told the first sergeant to load up in the jeep. As he walked to his jeep he stopped and told Don not to get too comfortable; the platoon would more than likely be moving to Pagoda Valley in the next few days. He smiled at him and drove off.

The next morning, the sun was beginning to come up as Don returned to the CP after checking the lines. Poor Boy was asleep when he left to make his rounds and Lance Corporal Larry Ballew had the radio watch.

Larry Ballew was from North Carolina—another soft-spoken, always-smiling young man—and Don was fairly sure he was from a farm family, like himself. Ballew had demonstrated to be a responsible, tactful, cooperative and hard-working individual; in other words, a damn fine Marine.

Upon reaching the CP, Don saw that Poor Boy was awake and in the process of making his "famous" coffee. Don rubbed the stubble on his beard and said to Poor Boy, "Since you're awake, I think I'll go down to the stream and shave, maybe even take a quick bath. Can you handle things if I let Ballew go back to his squad?"

Poor Boy assured him he had everything under control and that Don could enjoy his shave and bath.

Don chose a heavily-pebbled bank below the bridge. This area of water was about three to four feet deep; the engineers had pulled dirt from here because it was a clay deposit, which was preferred for the surface of the bridge. The pebbles made it possible to get a bath without getting muddy as he dressed.

He sat his pack down and took out his C-ration field stove, put a heat tab in it, then took his canteen cup and filled it from the clear mountain stream water. He lit the tab and placed the canteen cup on the stove; the water could heat while he bathed. He checked the bridge to ensure it had not been opened yet for traffic; he had time to take a quick bath.

He then laid out his green towel, wash cloth, and bar of soap from the plastic soap container that he had brought from the states. The soap not only served as soap, but shampoo and shaving cream too. Hastily, he removed his clothes and slowly started into the water. It was cool, shit, no, it was cold!

He dipped the wash cloth into the water and began rubbing the soap into the cloth, making soap suds. After making a large amount of suds, he wiped them with the cloth over his body, then into his hair. He thought about how cold it was and how happy he would be once his bath was over with as he vigorously scrubbed his body with the cloth. Without hesitation, he dropped, forcing his entire body into the three feet of cold water to wash the soap from his body.

He then sprang from the cold mountain stream and grabbed the towel and dried off. He swiftly dressed, putting on his shorts, utilities, and green t-shirt. He folded the towel and placed it on a flat rock rising about six inches from the bank; it made for a perfect place to sit and put on his socks. He reached into his pack, took out a pair of green, thick, cushioned socks, and put them on; they were clean and warm. After putting on his boots, he washed the socks he had worn down to the stream and laid them on his pack. The rule of the bush: Always have one clean pair of socks on, one on your pack drying, and one clean, dry pair in your pack.

He placed the tip of his finger into the canteen cup of water heating on his field stove and quickly jerked his finger back; the water was extremely hot. He gazed at the water in the cup then at the stream. It seemed to him in the short time he had been in Vietnam things were always extreme: the water icy cold or drastically hot, situations outrageously funny or tragically sad, actions either demented or performed with thoughtful concern, decision-making ranging from intelligent and discerning to senseless or idiotic. Maybe the troops were right when they said, "Nothing makes sense in war."

He finished shaving and was completing getting dressed when Warrant Officer O'Malley came down to the stream and in his usual loud Irish voice said, "Top of the morning to you, lieutenant. How is the water?"

"Cold unless you heat it, then it's damn hot," he said with a big smile.

"Well that sounds perfectly logical," the warrant said with a frown. "By the way, lieutenant, who are those little people running around with the rifles?" He pointed to three ARVNs on the bridge.

Don glanced towards the bridge and said, "They are from the ARVN district headquarters. Five of them came in late yesterday. They are here to investigate the citizens of the village which attacked us.

O'Malley leaned down and gently splashed a handful of water on his face. He looked at the lieutenant and said, "You know the group of trees west of the perimeter, where the pre-planned fires may have killed the VC yesterday?"

"Yes, what about the trees, gunner?"

"I have a truck bringing out a chainsaw today and I am going to cut them down. Do you need the trees for anything? If not, what do you want me to do with them?"

"I'll check with the platoon sergeant. If we don't need them, why not saw them into twelve-to fourteen-inch long sections."

The gunner looked at the lieutenant and asked, "Why short pieces?"

"Maybe the locals can use the wood for cooking fires, and by the way gunner, I wouldn't wash my face in the water right now."

The gunner looked at the lieutenant with a puzzled look and shrugged his shoulders. Don pointed to the bridge. Standing on top of the bridge, next to the edge, was one of the "little people" calmly urinating off the bridge into the stream, which flowed down toward the gunner.

The gunner raised up, stared at the ARVN, and in a bellowing voice screamed, "YOU BLOODY BASTARD, I'M GOING TO KILL YOU!"

He then charged up the hill and onto the bridge, handily grabbed the ARVN by the scuff of the neck and belt, and unceremoniously tossed him into the stream. The ARVN sailed through the air, still smiling and, strangely enough, never letting go of his private part as he slammed into the water.

CHAPTER 10
NEW ARRIVALS

As predicted, a truck arrived from LZ Baldy, regimental headquarters, with not one but four chainsaws, two passengers, and three bright red bags of mail. The gunner was happy and soon forgot the bridge incident, but not before he had cursed every Vietnamese in miles of the bridge and earned the nickname, "Yak, Yak."

The first passenger was a slender, well-muscled Marine. Don thought he might know him, he wasn't sure. Upon closer examination, he recognized Sergeant Loerzel, the sergeant who had ridden down in the trucks from division to LZ Baldy.

"Sergeant Loerzel, welcome to Hotel Company, 1st Platoon. I hope you're not here to head up a working party but rather to join the unit."

Sergeant Loerzel scrutinized the lieutenant and contemplated where he knew him from, then realized where he had met him before. "Yes sir, so I see you got the rifle platoon you were looking for."

"Yes, and I am in need of more outstanding NCOs to go with the ones I currently have."

"Well, I don't know about outstanding, but Captain McCarthy told me to get on the truck and get out here and help the platoon."

"I bet he was real subtle about it, too, right?"

"Not really!" Loerzel said, sarcastically.

Don escorted Sergeant Loerzel to the CP and asked who the other Marine was that came with him on the truck. He informed him it was Private First Class Bates a 0331, machine-gunner. The lieutenant then handed Poor Boy his little green notebook and asked him to go over and welcome Bates to the unit and get his info and put it into the notebook, and also to let him know he would be with him as soon as he got through talking to the sergeant.

Poor Boy smiled and took the notebook and set off to find Bates.

Don explained to Sergeant Loerzel that he had only five corporals and twenty-six lance corporals, and five, no, now six, private first classes. The five NCOs he considered to be outstanding; the problem was, three were going to rotate back to the states in the next three months, so by around New Years the platoon would lose most of its current seasoned NCOs.

For now, Sergeant Loerzel was the platoon sergeant and Corporal Lipsky would be the platoon right guide, a billet not filled until now. Sergeant Loerzel was concerned about how Corporal Lipsky would take it, being demoted down to platoon right guide instead of platoon sergeant.

Don assured him all would be okay. In fact, Corporal Lipsky was now coming across the bridge toward the CP. He called Lippy over and introduced Sergeant Loerzel to him. Explained the situation and left the two to talk as he went over to introduce himself to Private First Class Bates, the "newbie."

As he reached for the green notebook from Poor Boy, he said, "Welcome to Hotel Company, 1st Platoon. I am Lieutenant Garrett, Platoon Commander. I understand you are a 0331, a machine gunner. Tell me about yourself."

Private First Class Larry Bates was from the state of Pennsylvania, Pittsburgh area, where his father worked in the steel mills. The same steel mills Larry planned to work after his service to his country. However, he joined the Marine Corps because he could get a two-year enlistment instead of a three or four year, what the other branches of the military service offered. Right away in the conversation, it became clear Larry's grasp of the spoken English language was above the average high school graduate. He also came across as a clever, very knowledge, self-sacrificing, and dependable young Marine.

Don had to inform Larry he, unfortunately, would not be getting a machine gun until the platoon was able to get another one. In the meantime, he would go to 3rd squad, Corporal Howard's squad and serve as a rifleman.

He then took Bates over and introduced him to Jersey and explained why he was getting Bates. He then left, giving the squad leader and the newbie a chance to know each other.

Private First Class Larry Bates visually scanned Jersey. He was slender and olive-skinned with a big black mustache and piercing blue eyes, and he spoke with a New Jersey Italian accent, which he thought odd, since he had the last name of Howard. He did, though, look "salty," probably from all the time in the bush, or at least Larry Bates hoped that was the reason.

Jersey slowly squinted his eyes and carefully inspected Bates and made a mental evaluation of the newbie. Then in a rather deep voice said, "Bates, if you want to live and not be sent home in a body bag, you will listen to me and the Marines in the squad. It's a tight squad; we take care of each other. Be assured we will teach you the skills for you to survive, if you pay attention. Understand?"

Larry Bates readily agreed because he in fact did want to learn the skills they could teach him. Jersey then called the squad together to allow for introductions to the new guy.

The squad "bunkers" were sunken rooms approximately ten by fifteen feet in size. The rooms were dug about three and a half feet in the ground with filled sandbags coming up another two feet from the sides, making the rooms about five and a half feet high inside. The ends were open and the roof was made of sheets of metal which lay across the side walls with another two feet of sandbags piled on top.

Each of the squads had such a bunker, which provided shade in the day, kept the Marines dry during the rain, and gave those not on watch a relative safe place to sleep. This was a welcome benefit when providing security at a stationary position. In the bush you slept on the ground next to your fighting position, rain or shine.

The 3rd squad had a day patrol earlier in the day and now only had perimeter watch, which required two people at a time. Bates squeezed into the squad bunker and listened to Cherry tell of his wild and explicit escapades while on R&R (Rest and Recreation) in Bangkok.

Cherry had left the platoon to go on R&R the day the squad returned from the night ambush Don was on and he had just returned. He had managed to smuggle a fifth of Jim Beam whiskey back to the squad area.

He was now sharing it sparingly with the squad. Bates took a small splash in his canteen cup and mixed it with a Coke he had been saving since he joined the squad.

Bates had the 0200 to 0400 morning perimeter watch and didn't want to get drunk, miss his watch, and possibly be court-martialed. Besides, Jersey had the 0400 to 0600 watch and he sure didn't want his new squad leader catching him asleep on watch.

"Being caught could be worse than being court-martialed," he thought.

Once it became dark, the squad members quickly fell asleep one by one; it had been a long day on patrol and they all were exhausted.

Jersey, fresh from the "Hill 953" disaster, continued to imbibe in his friend's contraband. He had not had a break from the consistent, demanding daily pressures of a Marine squad leader in combat since he'd stepped off Hill 953.

The previous day's attack had not helped; it only brought to the surface those feelings he thought he had so skillfully hid from others. The more he drank, the more the pain became duller, and despondence and apprehensions began to ooze from his mind like molten lava flowing from a volcano. The tough, no-nonsense, unemotional, fearless, battle-tested Marine squad leader slid gently and without struggle into oblivion.

Private First Class Larry Bates was wakened for his 0200 watch. He gathered up his weapon, magazines, flak jacket, and helmet, then headed for his post. He crawled into the fighting position and got as comfortable as he dared. If he got too comfortable he might fall asleep; however, he felt wide awake and ready to do his part.

He liked 3rd squad, got along with the other members, and was pretty sure Jersey was more "bark than bite," but saw no reason to test his new-found theory. Private First Class Bates was a little nervous and yet felt somewhat empowered because many people were counting on him.

The watch was uneventful, except for the platoon commander coming by checking the lines and asking how he was getting along in the squad. However, when the next watch switched men, he became a little anxious. He wondered where Jersey was. After a while he told the Marine next to him he was going to get his relief. The Marine nodded an "okay" and Bates slipped out of the fighting hole and headed for the squad bunker.

He found Jersey and the empty bottle of Jim Beam, and after several failed attempts to wake him and after smelling alcohol, a rather frustrated Bates headed back to his post.

He didn't know what to do, but above all he knew the post had to be manned, so he assumed Jersey's watch. He was very concerned though; what would he tell the lieutenant if he came around and found him still on watch? He sure as hell wasn't going to tell him his squad leader was too drunk to stand his watch.

It seemed he agonized over this for hours and then suddenly, in the dim light provided by an artillery flare shot off from LZ Baldy, a lone figure headed his way from the bridge. He prayed it wasn't the lieutenant.

"Is everything okay here Marine?"

Bates knew the voice. It was Sergeant Loerzel. He was ecstatic with joy, cleared his throat, and said; "Great, just great!"

As the sun started to peek into the morning's sky, Bates' head came closer and closer to the sandbags, which encircled his fighting position. Finally, when the sunlight pushed the last of the darkness away, Bates' head slammed into the sandbags; the "sleep monster" had won the battle.

A few seconds later, Corporal Olsen and his squad, returning from the night ambush, approached the perimeter and notified the watch that he was entering the compound, where Private First Class Bates slept like a baby. The watch next to Bates threw a stone, about the size of a golf ball, and struck Bates in the helmet, causing him to leap up in total bewilderment. Once Bates collected his senses he motioned for Corporal Olsen to bring his squad in.

Olsen let his squad pass by Bates but remained staring at him, not saying anything until the entire squad had passed, then he asked Bates if he was sleeping on watch. Bates, embarrassed, sheepishly confessed he had fallen asleep. Olsen began, in a typical NCO manner, chewing on Bates and informing him of the importance of staying awake on watch.

Jersey was woken by the commotion and got up to investigate. Squinting, trying to adjust his eyes to the bright morning light, he stumbled out of the bunker, lurched over to Bates and Olsen, crossed his arms, and demanded to know what all the noise was about.

Olsen, without looking at Jersey, said, "I found this Marine asleep on watch."

Jersey glanced at Olsen then turned his blood shot eyes upon Bates and with a perplexed expression on his face said, "I'll take care of this matter; he's my Marine."

This time Olsen turned to Jersey and in an almost threaten manner said, "Okay, see that you do."

Jersey's eyes and head hurt. It felt like someone was inside his head hammering on the inside of his skull; his patience was nonexistent and he didn't appreciate Olsen's comment. Jersey snapped at Olsen, "Get the hell out of my area. I told you I would take care of it and I will. Now get the hell out here and go tend to your bunch!"

Olsen shrugged his shoulders and without a word walked off.

Jersey gazed at Bates and finally asked, "Why didn't you wake me up for my watch?"

Fearful, Bates whimpered, "I tried and tried, but I couldn't get you to wake up so I stood your watch."

Jersey kicked the dirt with the toe of his boot, then the other one. He began looking around and realized half the platoon was keenly observing the situation. He returned his attention again to Bates and asked him, "Why didn't you tell Olsen you stood two watches?"

In a defiant declaration, Bates yelled, "I'M NO RAT!"

Jersey, in a loud voice for the benefit of those so intently watching the event, yelled, "NO ONE STANDS MY WATCH! If you can't wake me up, then you drag my ass to the post! You got that?" He then leaned over with his hands on the sandbags and with a smile and a low soft voice said, "Bates, you are going to do fine in this squad. Now go over to the bunker and get some sleep."

Loerzel and Lippy stood by the bridge and observed the encounter between Jersey and Olsen. They both heard enough to know what had happened and decided to go over to Olsen's bunker and see where things stood between the two squad leaders.

They met Olsen coming out of his bunker, putting on a utility jacket. He informed them he was headed over to see the lieutenant. After a slight pause he said, "To brief him on the night ambush and nothing more."

Sergeant Loerzel smiled and asked, "Is everything okay with you and Jersey?"

"Hell yes, I would have told Jersey the same thing, if it were one of my men."

"Okay. What happened on the ambush?"

With a serious expression on his face, Craig Olsen said, "Nothing. It's almost like after we kicked those VC's butts, the VC and NVA want to give us a wide berth. We never even heard a mouse rustling around."

Both NCOs thought that might be possible and told Corporal Olsen they would turn in his report and to get some sleep. He thanked them and they left headed for the CP.

Don crossed the bridge and was stepping off it, headed to Olsen's bunker, when his platoon sergeant and right guide met him.

They briefed him on the ambush and about the enemy giving the unit a wide berth. As they talked, Don reached in his breast pocket and pulled out a cigar, removed the wrapping and started chewing on the end of it. Loerzel offered a light and the lieutenant smiled and told them he mostly chewed rather than smoked cigars.

"Now," he asked, "what was the yelling about?"

The NCOs looked at each other and Sergeant Loerzel told the lieutenant that the squad leaders had effectively handled the situation and that it didn't require the lieutenant's attention.

Don glanced from one to the other NCO several times and finally said, "Okay."

Poor Boy came scurrying down the road shouting, "Lieutenant, lieutenant, Hotel 6 wants you on the net."

Don shook his head and said, "I wonder what's up now?"

After the exchange, the lieutenant handed the handset back to Poor Boy and joyfully said, "We are going to LZ Baldy today! The trucks will be here between 1300 and 1400 hours."

The three stared at the lieutenant without any expression.

"What? Okay, I can't promise the trucks will be here on time… maybe not even today; however, I want every squad ready to load up at 1300 hours. I will conduct a police call at 1230 hours and I don't want to see as much as a cigarette butt lying on the ground.

Corporal Lipsky, make sure the trash pit is burned. Sergeant Loerzel, the squads won't leave their positions until the replacement squad is standing right behind them ready to assume their positions. The order of march will be 1st squad, CP group, the 2nd squad, and then 3rd squad. Sergeant Loerzel, go with 3rd squad and do another inspection of the entire platoon area before you leave."

Noticing the platoon sergeant and right guide looking at him, he said, "You may think I am overdoing this inspection thing, but I guarantee you, if anything is out of place, the CO of the unit coming in will call Captain McCarthy or McCarthy will call him and ask him what condition the positions were in. I guarantee it. And we don't need the crap which will follow if it's messed up."

The trucks arrived late in the afternoon. The turnover of the platoons went smooth. Don did a walk through explaining each position purpose and responsibility. Finally, the platoon loaded up and headed for LZ Baldy where hopefully the troops would be able to acquire the much-needed gear which was always promised but seldom obtained.

CHAPTER 11
STACK ARMS

After a successful turnover of the Triple Covert, Don's platoon quickly mounted onto the trucks to be taken to the Rock Crusher, where they would meet with the rest of Hotel Company.

As the trucks rambled through the countryside, Don thought it was good to be riding rather than walking the three clicks.

Upon reaching the Rock Crusher, the trucks actually drove past it about a half mile, on highway 535. Highway 535 was really a narrow rock-covered road which ran to the Rock Crusher and back to LZ Ross, then on into LZ Baldy. Here they found 3rd platoon in a tactical position setting on a small rise.

A guide from 3rd platoon met them and informed Don he was to set his platoon next to 3rd and lock in with them, making their circle even larger.

Don, while checking the lines, looked up and saw Poor Boy striding towards him. He knew there was message traffic or he was wanted on the radio.

"Lieutenant, the CO is going to have a company commanders meeting in fifteen minutes. He desires your attendance."

Don quickly glanced at his watch and said, "Thanks Poor Boy. Where is the meeting at and what's about?"

"Not a clue what it's about, but it's being held at the single culvert we passed over about a quarter of a mile down the road."

Don was not surprised about the meeting; the question was where were they going and what were they going to be doing?

He walked over to 3rd platoon and found Lieutenant Tom Baumgartner. "Hey Tom, how is it going?"

Tom had a serious look about him, shrugged his shoulders, and said, "It's going, how about with you?"

"Actually, not bad. I have been able to get to know my troops a lot better and this break has helped me get my body a little more used to the weight of the pack and odd hours. Have any idea what the meeting is about?"

"No, other than we are going someplace. I guess we'll find out pretty quick."

Both lieutenants strolled toward the company meeting in anticipation of what the future might hold. As they walked up to the meeting place, they noticed the skipper sitting on a large rock, talking in a very low voice to Golf Company commander. The other two lieutenants had already arrived and were sitting on the ground cross legged. Once the two COs finished their discussion and the Golf commander left, the skipper said, "Well, I see we all are here. I might as well get started."

The CO stood up, cleared his throat, and said, "As you can tell, the company is moving off the Rock Crusher this morning. Trucks will be picking us up and taking us to Hawk Hill for a much-needed and welcomed in-country R&R for the troops."

There was a quick mumbling of joy among the Marines. Hawk Hill was located South of Da Nang and operated by the US Army as a Hawk Missile Base and R&R center.

The R&R facility offered hot food, cold beer and sodas, a movie at night, and places to play volleyball and flag football. More importantly, it allowed the men a dry, relatively safe and comfortable place to relax, rest, and sleep, which they had been deprived of for some time.

Gunny Dixon, Hotel Company gunnery sergeant, came down the hill and informed the CO the turnover was complete between Golf and Hotel Companies. Right behind the gunny was the last of Hotel's troops coming off the Rock Crusher perimeter.

Captain McCarthy pointed to the two lieutenants sitting on the ground and said, "Get your Marines and march them down to where Garrett and Baumgartner Marines are at and tie in with them."

As usual, when the rest of the company reached the designated place, the trucks were not to be seen. The CO established a company defense position on a small hill not far off Highway 535, then got on the radio and, in a tenacious manner, ripped into those responsible for not having the trucks there on time, earning the company gunny's admiration and saying, "The skipper loves a good fight!"

Captain McCarthy gathered his officers and Staff NCOs once he was off the radio and informed them of his plans. "The XO, Lieutenant Vallence, and Gunny Dixon will leave in the XO's jeep. The two will head to Hawk Hill as fast as they can. I don't want any screw-ups. I want hot chow and cold beer for the troops as soon as they get off the trucks."

Lieutenant Vallence and Gunny Dixon gave the CO a swift, "Yes sir."

"There are two six-beys for each platoon with a ring-mounted, fifty-caliber machine gun on the truck. You platoon commanders, tell the Marine on the gun he is under *your* tactical command if we hit the shit, not the damn convoy commander. Got it?"

The lieutenants all quickly expressed they did in fact understand. The skipper further stated, "The order of movement will be my jeep, 1st, weapons, 2nd, then 3rd platoons. 3rd, you will have a convoy armed six-by behind you bringing up the rear guard."

Don smiled, his platoon wasn't going to be last this time. He knew if he had to tell his troops they were going to be last he would have heard the normal complaining. He knew this because in OCS his platoon had been last several times and he and others in the platoon voiced the same idle threats. It's a known fact in the Corps that all Marines have earned the right to complain and they do it with perfection and gusto!

He then heard the gentle sound of trucks in the distance coming their way. The skipper turned toward the distant noise, then to the group and, with a frown, said, "I want an *orderly* and *tactical* movement to the trucks. I don't want this command looking like a bunch of screaming girls running to a Beatles concert. Got it?"

The CO, XO, and company gunny walked down from the hill to the road and waited for the convoy to get turned around and back in formation.

The CO and XO's jeeps arrived in front of the truck convoy and were immediately pulled to the side, where last-minute instructions were given, and the XO and gunny jumped into their jeep and sped off to Hawk Hill.

The CO stopped the convoy commander, a gunny sergeant, and laid out his "basic and unquestioned rules on how things were going."

Troops loaded in the prescribe manner and the lieutenants made liaison with the Marines manning the fifty-caliber machine guns all within a very few minutes. The captain walked down the side of the convoy, carefully checking every detail, and as he neared 1st platoon's position in the company convoy yelled, "Lieutenant Garrett, get your gear and come down here and ride with me in the jeep."

Don, somewhat stunned, murmured, "Yes sir."

The Marines of the platoon quickly looked at each other, then him. Not a sound was made and the only motion made by the troops was that of their eyes following his progress getting off the truck.

Don threw his pack in the back seat of the jeep with the captain's and then jumped into the seat beside the two packs.

The captain, who had been holding the front seat up so the lieutenant could get in the back, put the seat down and climbed in and sat down, looked over at the driver, and in a whimsical tone said, "Marine this jeep isn't going to break down on the way to Hawk Hill is it?"

The Marine stiffened in his sitting position, looked straight ahead, and in a loud voice responded with a, "No sir!"

The jeep bounced down the rough gravel road past LZ Ross and LZ Baldy, then turned north up toward Da Nang, and more importantly, in the direction of Hawk Hill.

The captain sat quietly in the front seat, taking in the sites as the jeep steadily left the grueling and gruesome requirements of war behind. It was a cloudy warm day but not stifling hot like it was in the jungles or the valleys inland, which were cut off from the ocean breezes due to the hills and mountains that engulfed them.

Fortunately, it was not raining, nor, was the sun bearing down on them in the open jeep and trucks, which made the trip even more enjoyable.

As the convoy made its way around a curve in the road, Don turned in his seat and looked back at the truck behind him carrying part of his platoon. He squinted to see how his troops were reacting to the trip. He was surprised to see how solemn their frozen-like silhouettes were merely staring out over the countryside.

He immediately wondered what was going through their minds. A few hours ago they seemed so excited to go on this R&R. What, if anything, had changed? Maybe nothing; these young men were likely so spent from the demands of war, coupled with a high level of excitement, that they finally gave way to exhaustion and fatigue.

The convoy slowly lumbered into the R&R center where the XO and company gunny stood waiting in the middle of the road. The convoy came to a jarring stop, and the CO, XO, and gunny went into a quick conference. After some head turning and hand pointing, the conference broke up with the XO instructing the platoon commanders to dismount the trucks and turn their platoons over to the company gunny.

The CO instructed his driver to drive down the road a short distance, then turned and said, "Stop driver!" Then, pointing to the hard-back hooch to his right, said, "Lieutenant, take our packs and secure this building for the officers' quarters."

Don took the packs and dropped them off the side of the jeep then jumped over the side and said, "You want your own entrance, sir?"

"Yes, this end of the building."

"Yes sir."

He walked up the three wooden stairs and into the hooch. It had several cots with thin mattresses laying on them with a wire strung across from side to side about a fourth of the way into the hooch where military blankets hung from the wire, enabling one to pull the blankets across the room, creating a curtain partition.

He immediately decided this part of the hooch would serve as the captain's quarters and placed the CO's pack on a cot. He walked down past the room divider and carefully considered where he wanted to sleep, then placed his pack on a cot.

The wooden screen door of the hooch jerked open and three individuals immediately entered. They were loud and it was obvious from their speech they had been drinking. The one in the lead, looking at the lieutenant, said, "Hey, what the hell are you doing in here? You're in the Senior Staff NCO Quarters."

Don recognized the person who spoke, it was Hotel's First Sergeant Knight. The other two he had no idea, probably rear echelon pogues.

First Sergeant Knight was a tall barrel-chested man with very short red hair, maybe even a little bald, which sent the lieutenant wondering if all captains, gunnys and first sergeants in Vietnam were all red-headed.

"I'm Lieutenant Garrett, 1st Platoon Commander, First Sergeant Knight."

The first sergeant, trying to steady himself, staggered toward the lieutenant and said, "Well, *lieutenant*, this is the SNCO's quarters. We got here first and claimed this hooch, so go find yourself another one." He looked over his shoulders and grinned at the other two as if to say, "I guess I told him."

"Yes, first sergeant I can tell you probably have been here for some time judging from your speech. However, as to who will be sleeping in this hooch, it is not your, or my decision, but the CO's. He told me to put his pack in this building because he desired it for his quarters and his officers'."

The first sergeant slapped the CO's pack off the cot and said, "I'm telling you to get your pack out of here!"

Don stepped closer to the first sergeant, glared into his eyes, and in a low stern voice said, "First sergeant, your subornation is about to put you in a situation you can't win. I highly recommend you find a place to regroup before you piss me off."

The two SNCOs quickly grabbed the first sergeant and began pulling him out of the hooch, warning him he could get into serious trouble.

Don quickly jerked his helmet off and violently threw it across the room, where it slammed into the wall of the hooch. He sat down on the cot behind him and rubbed his hands through his hair and thought, "Shit! You come out of the bush to get away from the fighting and killing only to have a run-in with the senior NCO of the company."

Out of pure frustration, he began processing the situation and said to himself, "This guy never stays overnight in the bush, has a hooch to sleep in every night, a warm dry bed, three hots a day, then comes to the R&R center, slugs down a few beers, apparently before the company even arrives, then believes he should have first choice as to where he is going to sleep. UNREAL!"

He did a slow burn as he once more thought over the situation with the first sergeant, finally coming to the conclusion that the first sergeant was no different than any other pouge who suffered from the disease…me, me, me! The captain walked into the hooch and strolled over to the blankets serving as a divider and pulled it about half way across the room and said, "Nice. Good work, lieutenant. Are you and the other lieutenants staying in this end of the hooch?"

He took a deep breath and mumbled, "Unless you don't want us to, sir."

"No, it's fine. In fact I would prefer you guys stay here too. By the way, whose packs are those over there along the wall as you come in?"

Don glanced to where the captain was pointing; it was the first time he had noticed the packs and slowly said, "I think they may be the first sergeant's and his NCO buddies'."

The captain quickly turned to the lieutenant and said, "First sergeant? What the hell is he doing here?"

"I have no idea but I can guarantee you he is here, and, well into the 'relaxing mode.'"

The skipper frowned, ran to the door, stuck his head out, and yelled to the driver to come and take these three packs over to wherever the first sergeant was staying. He then turned to Don and said, "Come on, we have to go over to the Stack Arms Ceremony at the reception center."

Before the official R&R began, the army conducted an Official Stacking of Arms Ceremony where several M16s were stacked together in a teepee formation. The stacking worked well with the M14s but the M16s had a much shorter barrel and larger magazine slots and therefore these rifles were harder to stack, as witnessed by the company when it took four tries before the drill was completed, much to the dislike of the not-so-patient Marines of Hotel Company. Finally, however, the command, "commence stack arms," was given and the Marines cheered! However, the cheer quickly melted away when the troops learned they had to turn in their individual rifles into the armory.

They felt naked without their mechanical extensions of their bodies, not to mention having to rely upon someone else for their personal safety.

The troops, after repeated guarantees they would be safe, gave up their weapons and took to the mess hall where they gorged themselves on steaks, French fries, hot bread, fruit, desserts, and cold beer or sodas until they were beyond stuffed.

The Marines slowly wandered back to their quarters where most fell into their racks and slept. They dreamed of far off homes, families, and certainly girlfriends. The few who did not fall asleep were busy writing letters home, most while nursing a beer or soda, and others found whatever they could find to read.

Every member of the company, though, was anxious for the movie to start. Most had not seen a movie in months, but all hoped the movie was about beautiful girls.

Don finished writing letters home to his folks and his fiancée. He walked over to the center where there was a mailbox, posted his letters, and then checked on his troops.

He peeked through the screen door into the hooch where his CP group was staying. Poor Boy was lying on his stomach in his rack with his head on a blanket he had wadded up to form a pillow, both arms draped over the sides of the rack and his legs sticking out about a foot over the end of the rack; Lipsky was curled into a ball on his cot; Doc Smith was lying on his back with one arm over his face—all very much asleep.

He silently walked in and through the hooch. Members of the weapons, Ray Alcala, Al Brown, and Richard Anjlo were also asleep. Ed Cruz and Billy Baker, both from Texas, were sitting on the floor leaning against the wall looking at magazines while sipping beers.

From his position in the hooch, he could clearly see to the end of it and all he saw were bodies in many twisted forms lying on cots and sound asleep. He smiled and left.

CHAPTER 12
A CESSATION

Don walked back over to the hooch about an hour before night falls to see how many troops might be going to the movie; after all, the weather was good, no rain, though lots of clouds. Upon arriving at the barracks, he found no one, not a single Marine.

Someone had left a radio on and "Hi, love! This is a date with Chris Noel," was playing. He didn't listen to the end of the song and headed over to the mess hall in hopes of finding his Marines.

Again, there were no Marines, his or anyone else at the mess hall. "Only place left they could be at was the outdoor movie theater." he thought. "What was the title of the movie? Oh yea, *Where Eagles Dare*," he mumbled.

He thought it was really early to go over to the theater but, they had to be there. As he entered the outdoor theater, he surveyed the facility. The entire facility was fenced with wire and mesh wire gates at the entry. The screen was four large posts in the ground with a fifty-by-fifty-foot board painted white. The bleachers were made of wood, like those found throughout the United States at every small high school football stadium, well at least in the Midwest where he grew up. The projector booth sat at the top and in the middle of the bleachers. The bleachers were packed with Marines.

He slowly walked across in front of the bleachers, looking for his Marines when he saw Poor Boy waving his hands, and then he quickly saw Lipsky, Loerzel, Doc, Jersey, Pizza, and Lujan. He quickened his pace toward them.

They were sitting almost in the middle of the bleachers, a couple rows up from the first row, where he now saw the skipper and first sergeant sitting. Looking at Sergeant Loerzel, he said, "How long have you guys been sitting up there anyway?"

Loerzel, grinning from ear to ear, said, "The entire platoon came over about an hour ago. We wanted to be sure to get the best seats."

Don gave them thumbs up, and then spoke to the skipper. "Evening sir, I guess rank does have its privileges. Those are excellent seats you have. Is that real buttered popcorn you have?"

"Yep, got it right outside the gate, to the right. They also have cold beer and sodas, if you are interested."

Don could smell the popcorn. It smelled exactly like the popcorn back home at the theater; he definitely wanted some. "Is it as good as it smells, skipper?"

"I think may be better."

Don rubbed his hands together and returned a few minutes later with an extremely large box of buttered popcorn and two Cokes.

Jersey saw Don returning and poked Pizza in the side, pointed and said, "Damn lieutenant, where in the hell did you get that bushel basket of popcorn?"

"It's not merely popcorn, it's *buttered* popcorn. I also got two sodas, all located right outside of the gate to the right."

The platoon members had been listening to the conversation, and without a word half of the platoon leaped up from the bleachers and headed for the theater gate.

As Jersey went by Don, he said, "Thanks lieutenant. Cherry, Frenchy, save the platoon places; we will get you some popcorn too."

The captain watched as the Marines tore out of the bleachers, past where he and the first sergeant were sitting, then looked at Don and said, "Well I guess that's no longer a secret. There won't be any left the way your guys are going for it."

"Maybe so sir, but you have a giant box of popcorn and I don't think between the two of us there is going to be a shortage."

The captain held his box of popcorn up, looked at it, and chuckled then said, "Yes, I guess you are right. You might as well have a seat next to me… in case I run out of popcorn."

Don sat down and acknowledged the first sergeant, who in return gave a low gruff "Evening." He sat down on the other side of the skipper, putting the captain between him and the first sergeant.

When 1st platoon came back with buttered popcorn, it made the entire facility smell of it. In a few moments the rest of the company jumped out of the bleachers to get buttered popcorn. The showing of the movie was delayed a few minutes so those getting the popcorn could get settled.

Fifteen minutes into the movie, the first sergeant leaned over and picked up a canteen cup and a fifth of Jack Daniel's Kentucky whiskey. He filled his canteen cup half full of whiskey then Coke. He then offered the CO some whiskey.

The skipper poured a little whiskey in his can of Coke.

The first sergeant then leaned out past the skipper and offered the bottle to Lieutenant Baumgartner, who was sitting on the other side of Don. Baumgartner poured the whiskey into a cup he was drinking from then passed the bottle to the man on his right, who also poured himself a splash of whiskey.

When Baumgartner passed the bottle to the out-stretched hand of the first sergeant, Don intercepted the bottle and poured a generous amount into his Coke can then tipped the bottle up and took a long slug of the whiskey. He smiled and handed the bottle to the first sergeant.

The first sergeant stared at Don, then the bottle, then back to him. He then slid back on to the bleacher seat, looked straight ahead, and then leaned forward again and glared at the lieutenant.

Don continued looking at the screen, pretending not to notice the first sergeant. His throat was on fire and he was about to cough his lungs out, but with a tremendous amount self-discipline he managed to maintain his composer.

The captain glanced at the first sergeant then Don and smiled as he turned his attention back to the movie.

When the movie stopped, lights came on, and the skipper stood up and stretched, saying, "What are they showing tomorrow night?"

The first sergeant quickly blurred out, "One of my favorites, *Fixed Bayonets*."

The captain frowned and, shaking his head, said, "Hell, that movie is twenty years old. Can't they find newer release?"

Since no one knew the answer, they all remained silent and slowly started walking back to their quarters.

The first sergeant looked at Don for a short moment then muttered voice, "You are a pain in the ass, lieutenant, but you're gutsy and not a blabber mouth." He then looked him in the eyes and in serious tone said, "We okay?"

Don stared at the first sergeant for a few moments. He knew this was about as close as he was going to get in the form of any apology, so he immediately broke into a big smile and said, "This time first sergeant… this time."

The next morning turned into another lazy day for the troops mostly sleeping and writing letters. However, after the noon meal, as the officers returned to their quarters, laughter, cursing and debates about if the ball was in bounds or not could be heard from the football field and volleyball court.

Once in their quarters, the skipper slid a cooler from under his cot, which contained ice and lots of beer.

"Gee, skipper where did you get the cooler and beer?" Baumgartner inquired as he peered into the ice chest.

"Never fear, skippers have their sources." And with a gleam in his eyes pointed to the cooler and offered them cold beer.

They sat around talking of the military and political situation of the Vietnam War and drinking beer. After a few minutes of silence, the skipper started a story of when he was at 8th&I.

"I was coming to the end of my rifle drill where I tossed the rifle in the air and was supposed to catch it before it hit the ground. Unfortunately, I missed and it came straight down and the bayonet, sharp as hell, went through my shoe and split my big toe from my other toes by two inches. I quickly reached down and pulled the rifle up, slapped it on my shoulder, and finished the drill. Of course blood was smeared on the bayonet and more blood was gushing out of my shoe… but I completed the drill."

The lieutenants believed every word he spoke because, after all, he was a Marine.

After the skipper finished his story, a loud knock at the door broke the silence. The captain turned and yelled, "ENTER!"

Sergeant Loerzel opened the door and entered the room and slowly said, "Lieutenant Garrett, may I have a word with you?"

"Sure, what's up?"

Loerzel squirmed a bit then stepped back to the door and in a very low voice, almost a whisper, said, "The platoon, as a group, is going to the movies tonight. It's *Fix Bayonets*, and hardly anyone in the platoon has seen it. The troops would like to know if you would come too?"

Don was briefly caught off guard then quickly felt exhilaration and stammered, "I... I'd be honored."

From the hooch doorway he watched Joe Loerzel briskly walk down the road where he met up with Lippy, Jersey, and Rathbone. Don turned, a faint blushing on his face and returned to the group.

Finally, after a few moments of silence, the skipper said, "It sounds like you have a date tonight, lieutenant."

Don's face grew even darker red and in a low voice uttered, "Well... uh... the platoon is going to watch the movie together and they asked if I would join them and I told them I would... it would be an honor."

The skipper smiled and tried to remember the title.

Don told him it was *Fixed Bayonets*, and that most of the troops hadn't seen it before. The skipper snorted and said, "I can believe it, it was made about the time they were being born." They all laughed and took gulps of their beers.

Don left the group an hour later and watched the platoon members play flag football, and volleyball, for a couple of hours then wandered around the area, mostly wanting to be alone to do so some thinking. He had only been with the platoon less than a month and things seemed to be going smoothly, but something was nagging at him and he couldn't put his in finger on it. What was it?

Having no other place to go, he drifted back to his quarters and found the skipper alone, writing a letter using a wooden box as a desk.

"Want a beer, lieutenant?"

"No sir, I'm about 'beered' out."

The skipper gently laid down his pen sat up straight looked up Don and said, "What's bothering you?"

Don glanced around the room, slowly walked over to an empty cot across from the skipper, and sat down, wrung his hands, cleared his throat, and hesitantly said, "That's part of the problem I can't pin point it."

"Okay. Is it a home situation?"

"No, no nothing like that… it's… I don't know."

The skipper reached down, picked up his pack, and placed it behind him then leaned back on it. He crossed his arms and was quiet for a while and finally said, "I have noticed you have a very good connection with your troops. I also have noticed it appears to be on a professional manner too." The captain paused for a moment, then looked Don in the eyes and said, "Tell me about your Marines."

Don paused for a moment then chuckled and said, "The first time I saw them I couldn't believe the way they were dressed. To me they had certainly earned the name Horrible Hogs. There wasn't one of them in the same uniform and, quite honestly, it's still that way."

He stood up and slowly began to pace back and forth as he talked. "They are uniquely different in sizes, shapes, accents, education, places they come from, ethnic backgrounds, you name it. But, sir, peel all that away and you have solid, young, *responsible* men. There is not a one of them I wouldn't stand shoulder to shoulder or back to back with. You know the platoon even has a platoon song? 'The Fightin' Side of Me' by Merle Haggard… great choice."

He now stopped and stared at the skipper and said in a stern voice, "Now you may think that is a bold statement to make, considering no longer than I have known them, but I stand behind what I said." Lowering his voice almost to a whisper, Don said, "You know what is so ridiculous about this whole situation is these guys are in a foreign land fighting for their country, laying their lives on the line, and the most valuable material thing they own in the states is probably a rock and roll record collection. Don't you think it's ironic those who have the least to lose are the ones doing the fighting?"

The captain said nothing, merely sat with his arms crossed and finally in a very deliberate manner said, "You bring up some interesting points… don't know that I agree with all them but they are worthy of consideration nonetheless. Now tell me, do you have real close friends back home?"

"Yes sir, five of us grew up together we, are like brothers."

"I think I see your problem. I believe you are wrestling with the fact you are becoming close to your platoon members and are having a problem as to where to draw that 'line in the sand.' Don't be; it will work out for you because of one thing."

"What's that, skipper?"

"You and your platoon members have already developed mutual respect for each other. Mutual respect is the key element in all successful leadership positions. You should be honored your platoon invited you; it may be the only time you will ever have an opportunity to do something like this with them and don't worry about getting too close or 'buddy, buddy.' It will work out, because you, and they, have respect for each other… go have a good time."

Don felt he had a ton lifted off his shoulders he felt great and managed a smile and as he got up to leave then stopped and turned to the skipper. As an afterthought he said, "Are you going to the movie?"

As he rubbed his stomach he said, "No, too much buttered popcorn."

Don inquired, "So you have seen this movie several times, what it's about anyway?"

"Several times? A million times. Well maybe not a million, but, a lot."

He paused and a serious look appeared on his face and with some deliberation he said, "It's ironic, strange, odd, whatever you want to call it, but the movie is about a military platoon in which all the leaders get killed and a corporal has to take over the command. It's a lot like when Corporal Lipsky took over your platoon, so as the movie ends, your story starts."

A chill ran down his spine as he thought about what the skipper had said; he hoped it wasn't an omen. It couldn't be, as he no longer had those nagging feelings, and he believed what the skipper had told him. "It would work out."

He thanked the skipper for his time and insight then left the hooch in high spirits; after all, he was anxious to go be with *his* platoon.

CHAPTER 13
PLATOON BONDING

Don had a lively step to his gait as he entered the outdoor movie theater. In the front row in the middle of the bleachers sat Joe, Lippy, Jersey, Rathbone, and Olsen, his squad leaders, along with Poor Boy and Doc Smith.

There was an empty seat between Lippy and Joe. Behind them was a cooler; in fact, as he scanned the bleachers, he noticed several coolers spread throughout the platoon, no doubt filled with beer and stronger spirits. The place reeked of buttered popcorn, and beer. Despite the gentle ocean breeze flowing through the facility, making it noticeably comfortable.

Don sat down between Lippy and Joe. They offered him a beer, which he gracefully accepted, and a ham sandwich they made at the mess hall.

While eating and sipping his beer, he once more scanned the bleachers. There were a few Marines and corpsmen from 2nd and 3rd platoons and couple soldiers from the army, but most were from 1st platoon, the entire platoon, and this made him feel especially good.

The facility lights were turned out and for a few moments the theater was dark. Then the white-washed wooden screen exploded with light, and sound from the speakers on both sides of the screen blared. A news reel came on and three beautiful women in bathing suits appeared on the screen. After an instant of silence, a burst of cheers, whistles, and loud lewd catcalls erupted. Eventually the troops calmed down as the news continued, including politicians and movie stars expressing their nonsupport of the war, which was mostly ignored by the troops.

Suddenly, Jane Fonda's face appeared on the screen and the lull was instantly broken by flying beer bottles, cans, canteen cups, anything that could be hurled at the screen then blood curling screams of, "TRAITOR… DIE BITCH… PIECE OF SHIT… BURN IN HELL… I WANNA KICK YOUR ASS!"

The projectionist, an army specialist, quickly turned off the projector and the facility once more fell completely black and silent. He then turned on the facility lights, came out of the booth, and announced to the audience if discipline couldn't be maintained the movie would be canceled for the evening.

The audience, almost at the point of uncontrollable rage, stood and glared at the projectionist. Some stepped onto the stairs leading up to the projection booth, but stopped when a single, crystal-clear and very angry voice shouted, "Better get the movie started before that projector gets shoved up your ass!"

The projectionist eyes darted from person to person as he saw the same built-up frenzy, anger, and gnashing of teeth in each, all on the verge of uncontrollable rage. He gulped and swallowed a lump in his throat, leaped into the booth, and in a flash the movie was back on. Don thought, "Shit, this is not good."

Most of the audience members sat back down and after a few minutes began to relax and watch the movie with an occasional voice threat flung at the projectionist and, Jane Fonda.

About twenty minutes into the movie Don slid forward on the bleacher seat and looked back over the bleachers. Since there were only about a fifth of the people in the theater that it would normally hold, the Marines had spread out over the bleachers. Some were lying down, others were leaning against the bleacher behind them. All were drinking and eating, in general simply relaxing and enjoying the movie. Some had fallen to sleep while others were beginning to doze off. Everyone appeared relaxed and at peace. It was a very a very serene picture. The platoon commander shifted back into his seat, glanced at Joe Loerzel, smiled, and whispered, "All is quiet."

Suddenly, without warning, the movie stopped again. Don jumped up, turned toward the projection booth, and immediately saw the men in the audience starting to sit up, looking around and murmuring. In hopes of avoiding a repeat of the last situation, he leaped up the stairs to the booth and found the projectionist sitting there shaking.

"Did the film break?"

"No… no, sir. I have to turn the film off here because of the bayonet attack. They feel it could have a psychological effect on the Marines."

"They… psychological effect… listen, the only effect this action is going to have is those men are going to get really pissed off again. Hell, there is nothing on that film you are going to show that they haven't seen in *real life*! Now turn on the film!"

The projectionist quickly squirmed past Don, shot down the steps, and raced toward the facility gates with his arms over his head, under a hail of beer cans and shouts of, "Run you little bastard, run before we get ahold of you!"

Don thought, "Damn it, damn it to hell!" He swiftly composed himself, held his hands up, and in the best command voice he could muster yelled, "AT EASE, at ease! It seems we have lost our projectionist… so, does anyone here know how to run a projector?"

An unease silence fell over the group, then Lance Corporal Ed Cherry of 3rd squad stood up and indicated he thought he might be able operate the projector.

Ed took only a few moments and started the movie once again, much to the delight and relief of Don. The movie goers started settling in, relaxing, and watching the movie… with an expected amount of grumbling and swearing.

Don sat on the step next to the projector booth and rubbed his hands over his face and thought, "Jesus, does this crap ever stop?"

After reflecting on all the things that had happened in the short time he had been in Viet Nam, he came to the conclusion it probably would not change. He glanced up at Cherry and asked, "If he was okay?"

Cherry gave him a nod and mouthed, "Yes sir."

Don, in a procrastinating manner, rose and started down the steps to once more join his CP group, when about three-fourths of the way down he noticed a motion past the theater gate. He strained to see what the movement was through the dim half-moon light; all of a sudden he couldn't believe his eyes and stammered, "Christ, this couldn't be true. It was impossible. Shit!"

Plainly outside the gate was a squad of army military police slowly advancing toward the theater. He took a deep breath, in almost total exasperation, hastened down the remaining steps, and shot past his seat and NCOs, staying parallel to the bleachers, hoping few would notice his exit of the theater. He then approached the MP squad, identified himself and inquired of their business.

The sergeant in charge of the MP squad of nine stood about five eleven and was thick-bodied with a very "bull dog" appearance. Holding a billy club in his right hand, gently slapping it into his left palm, he said, "I understand there's a riot in the theater."

Don looked over his shoulder toward the theater then back to the sergeant and said, "Riot? I walked out of there only a few seconds ago and there certainly isn't a riot, or anything else, going on. I think someone gave you bad information, sergeant."

The sergeant glanced over the lieutenant's shoulder toward the theater and said, "Well, my men and I will go in there and determine if there is a riot or not."

Don was starting to get perturbed with the sergeant. He quickly held his hand up in front of the sergeant and said, "Sergeant, wait one minute. Those Marines in the theater are watching a movie. Yes, they are drinking beer, but I believe they were sent here so they could. They certainly have earned the right to. Those men have been in the bush for months fighting the NVA almost every day. I don't think it would be wise for you, and your men, to go in there. You would only upset them and really start a riot. They out number you nine to one and that's not good odds for your men, plus those men are special trained professional killers, they do it every day… your boys ever killed any enemy?"

The sergeant didn't say anything. He simply looked over the shoulder of the lieutenant again toward the theater.

His men, however, shuffled around a bit and then one said, "Come on, sarge. We can see from here there's nothing going on, why risk a big fight?"

The MP sergeant now became irritated because his men were backing down, and he turned to them and angrily said, "I'm in charge here and *I'll* decide if we go in or not!" He then turned and faced the lieutenant, looked him in the eyes, then rolled up his eyes over the lieutenant's head and stopped, focused on one spot.

Don slowly turned and saw Lipsky, the squad leaders, and Tiny. Tiny was not tiny; he was over six three and had been described several times as "looking like the genie that came out of a bottle," except he wore a sleeveless Marine uniform, and his arms were as large as Don's legs. Tiny was a sergeant and was currently acting weapons platoon commander; he was not one to trifle with.

The sergeant once again focused on Don and started to say something when he was interrupted by Tiny, who said, "Sergeant, you had better watch your mouth and start adding some 'Sirs' when you talk to the lieutenant or you and I are going to have a personal problem and that night stick might get shoved in a real uncomfortable place."

The sergeant righteously stared at Don, and then in a low snarling voice said, "*Sir*, I am going to hold you responsible if anything happens here."

Don smiled. He knew he had won this battle and said, "Sergeant you don't have the authority to hold me to anything." Scowling, he continued, "But I am telling you to leave and it's not a request but an order… now move!"

The sergeant swung around and yelled, "Come on, you cowards!"

The group watched the MP squad leave and could hear the sergeant for some time cursing his men as they all faded into the night.

Don turned to his Marines and said, "Thanks guys. Not sure how things would have turned out if it wasn't for your support."

They began mumbling "No problem… no one messes with us… assholes…" and so on. As they started through the gates, Don said, "Let's close them to keep the riffraff out."

The lights came on and Cherry came out of the booth and said, "Lieutenant, I found this metal drawer and it kind of came open."

"Okay Cherry, you broke into the drawer, what's in it?"

The Marines in the bleachers laughed.

"Films, several and this one," he held the reel up, "is *The Dirty Dozen*."

A cheer went up from those in the bleachers.

"So I guess we could have an all-night film festival?"

More cheers rang from the Marines.

Then someone stood up and said, "No, let's have a *beer* and film festival!"

Then someone else jumped up and yelled, "Hell no, let's have an *all-night* beer and film festival!"

A thunder of cheer went up and they began chanting, "BEER... BEER... MOVIES...!"

Don slowly opened his eyes; they hurt, as did his head, back, and butt, and his stomach was somewhat queasy. He gradually rose as pain shot through his body. He finally sat up then stood up and stretched. Through blurred eyes, he saw, what looked like hundreds of beer cans, bottles, popcorn boxes, paper sandwich wrappers, and a few canteen cups strewn over the grounds of the theater facility.

He then noticed Joe and Lippy lying on the ground in front of him. Next to them was Jersey and Rathbone, who were curled up holding open cans of beers. Looking around more, he saw Olsen lying face down with his arms hanging over the bleacher seat. And Tiny took a cooler and propped it up against the bleachers and used it as a back rest and was in a setting position. They were fast asleep or passed out. "Probably passed out," he thought.

Don nudged Joe with the toe of his boot, nothing; he nudged him again only harder, still nothing; he finally reached down and shook him violently. Joe's eyes popped open and, after a few moments, he sluggishly sat up and scanned the entire bleachers then said, "Think they're alive?"

"I hope so." He looked around then said, "Wake the squad leaders and Tiny. They can get the troops up, then hold a good police call, this place is a pig sty. And take the whole bunch to breakfast, no exceptions. I'll check on Cherry up in the booth."

Don, half walking, half staggering, climbed the stairs occasionally kicking a beer can or two out of his way until he found Cherry sitting up with his head slumped over, resting next to the projector. He gently shook Cherry until he woke up, "Cherry, you alive?"

Cherry moaned, sat up, stared at the lieutenant, and finally said, "Shit sir, I think it got drunk out last night."

Don chuckled and said, "What do you mean 'It got drunk out last night'? You think an alcohol fog rolled in here last night and got everyone drunk?"

Cherry laughed then said, "Shit it hurts to laugh. Yep, that's what happened, lieutenant."

"And I suppose you didn't drink any of the beer in those empty beers cans at your feet? Crap—there must be thirty of them."

Cherry leaned his head down to look at the cans. "Well, they're not all mine; Pizza and Cox threw a bunch of them at me, telling me to hurry up as I changed reels last night."

Don snickered, "You need some help to get this place squared away?"

Cherry felt he was able to clean up the area, providing Pizza, and Cox, were kept away.

The cleanup went well, especially considering the circumstances. Tiny picked up Lance Corporal Lynn Stroop, a small lightweight young man from Virginia, and had him tighten his legs and feet together so he could use him as a human tamping rod to tamp down the trash in the fifty-five-gallon drum trash cans.

On the way to the mess hall, they dropped off trash which wouldn't fit in the drums at the movie theater.

Once they lined up to enter the mess hall a couple people got sick from the smell of the cooking food. Naturally, cat calls and crude remarks were made most indistinguishable to the lieutenant, except when Albert (Speedy) Gonzales pointed to two men vomiting and said in an extremely heavy Hispanic accent, "Hey man, they're serving hot food. Don't need to go in the mess hall."

That, of course, brought out even more and, if possible, even cruder remarks. Don hung around the mess hall for a while and then told Joe he was going to his hooch to get some much-needed sleep.

A few hours later Captain McCarthy and the other officers entered the hooch, waking Don up with loud talking and slamming the screen door several times.

"Have a nice nap, night owl?" the skipper asked as he stood over the lieutenant grinning. "I have heard about your movie adventures from all over the camp."

Don, twisting his face, sat up very slowly and said, "Skipper, I have no idea what you have heard, but I am reasonably sure whatever you heard was exaggerated and far from the truth."

The skipper chuckled and in a more serious manner said, "I need all of you officers to clear the cobwebs from your brains and listen up. I have an important announcement and word on where we are going.

"As of today, Lieutenant Colonel A. E. Folsom, has taken over command of the 2nd Bn., 7th Marines. I personally do not know anything about the CO. However, I have been told by people I know that he is a damn fine officer."

The skipper slowly paced the floor for a few minutes then said, "Tomorrow we will be leaving this place. Its been good but now we need to get down to business and it starts with having the troops ready tomorrow. Each of you need to hold some informal inspections to insure each of your Marines has all their gear. It's possible we can make a run to division supply and pick up a limited amount of gear. The company gunny will make the run with your right guides; make sure you have a list ready when he leaves tomorrow morning."

The captain paused and, with a very serious expression on his face, continued to speak. "The Company will be moving to LZ Baldy for a couple days and we need to make the most of it. After the couple days at Baldy we are going to Pagoda Valley. Intelligence has many reports of heavy NVA/VC activities. It appears the next month could be rough, but I know we will stand up to the test.

"It's 1400 hours so you don't have a lot of time to make your inspections and determine what, and how, much gear you will need, so let's get busy. That's all."

The lieutenants hurried to their respective platoons and began setting up their inspections and compiling their list, which went well into the evening hours.

The next morning Don rolled over and sat up on the edge of his cot, looked around, and decided the sun would rise in a few minutes. He patted his cot and said very softly, "You are way more comfortable than the theater bleachers."

He slowly and very carefully dressed, trying to be quiet so he wouldn't wake the others. As he tied his last boot string and stood up to stretch, the blanket curtain was gently pulled back a little ways and the skipper stuck his head out.

In a low voice, the skipper said, "Morning, going to the mess hall?"

He whispered, "Yes sir."

"Good. Hold up a minute and I'll go with you."

While the captain was getting dressed he went over and picked up his pack, helmet, and cartridge belt, and laid them on his cot. He fumbled around in the pack until he found the package of Swisher Sweet cigars, which he opened, and took one out. He then pulled his K-bar out of its sheath and cut the cigar in half. He put half in his mouth and the other half back in the package and returned the package to his pack.

The captain stuck his head around the corner of the curtain and said, "You ready?"

The sun was coming up and quickly bathed the camp in warm light as the two exited the hooch. As they walked toward the mess hall Don lit his half cigar, took a couple drags on it, then took it out of his mouth and gently put the flame out.

The captain glanced over at him and said, "You barely lit the damn thing and now you put it out. Why?"

Don chuckled and said, "First of all, I don't smoke them, I chew on them. I light them to burn the ends smooth, which helps stop them from unraveling while I chew on them. Secondly, you don't smoke cigars in the bush because it only puts a great big target on you and believe me, I have enough targets on my back. Did you know the North Vietnam Government has a fifty-thousand-dollar, American dollars, reward for each Marine lieutenant killed or captured?"

As the skipper started to answer the lieutenant, two large explosions, one right after the other, rang out through the hill. Small arms fire erupted sporadically around the perimeter too.

Both officers jumped down on the ground. The captain slowly rose, turned to the Don, and said in a hurried manner, "Get your men down to the armory and get your weapons. Also, get the other two officers up and have them get their men to the armory too."

Don jumped up and as he ran toward his men's barracks, yelling back to the skipper, "Yes sir, on my way!"

Reaching his men's barracks, he saw Joe, Lippy, and a couple of his squad leaders outside looking around. As he ran up to them, he cried out,

"Get the men down to the armory in their fighting gear! I'll meet you at the armory!"

He then tore off to the officers' quarters to inform them of the captain's orders and to pick up his own fighting gear.

Upon reaching the armory, two sentries met him and asked him what was going on.

Don said, "I don't know. But in a minute or so there is going to be a company of Marines coming here to get their weapons and I need to get the armory open."

The tallest of the two sentries went over and took his rifle butt and banged it against the steel door to the armory several times while screaming, "Bill, get this damn door open. NOW!"

The door flung open and two armors exited the building with pistols drawn. The first one looked at the sentry and quickly asked, "What's up?"

The tall sentry pointed to Don and said, "This Marine officer has a company of Marines on their way here to draw weapons and he needs the armory open."

The armor looked toward the lieutenant, frowned, and said, "Sir, I don't have any authority to give your unit its weapons."

Don threw his hands up in the air and in a commanding voice said, "Did you hear the explosions and small arms fire going off right now?"

The armor stammered, "Well... yea."

Don, a little frustrated, said "Damn it, man, this hill is under attack. Let me tell you—if and when the enemy comes through the wire their first target is not going to be the theater or the mess hall. It's going to be this armory. So tell me, do you want these two sentries protecting you, or would you rather have over a hundred fully-armed combat marines?"

The armor glanced at his partner, then at the sentries and back to the lieutenant, and quickly said, "Where are your men?"

Don sighed and said, "They will be here in a minute. What's the fastest way to get the men in and out of the armory?"

As Sergeant Joe Loerzel arrived, the armor explained there were doors on each side of the building, so the men could enter on the right and exit the left with their weapons and ammo. The armor then asked for two Marines to help hand out the weapons so the process could go faster.

The captain arrived at the armory and told 1st platoon that once the platoon was fully armed to go on a patrol outside of the wire perimeter around the entire hill. He gave them call signs and frequencies to use.

It took 1st platoon a little over an hour to complete a detailed patrol. They discovered many spider holes, some new, and a pile of large rocks from where the enemy launched rockets.

For the rest of the time on the hill, a valiant logistical effort was put forth by all hands, but in the end, it did little to resolve the bulk of clothing shortages, weapon repairs, and manpower issues. However, through his dogmatic and persistence, the captain did get a promise from regiment that all these issues would be dealt with and resolved to the captain's satisfaction once they got to LZ Baldy.

CHAPTER 14
GRUESOME DISCIPLINE

The trucks, as promised by regiment, did arrive late in the afternoon and the company was loaded by platoons and headed to LZ Baldy.

The trucks carrying 1st platoon rolled past the gates of LZ Baldy and snaked through the camp until they stopped at the designated troop billeting areas. The buildings were wood framed with plywood sides which, half way up, became screen wire windows until the metal roofs. Each building was designed to hold a rifle platoon of three squads.

The open style squad bays had cots lined up on both sides for the troops to sleep on. The cots were wooden framed with canvas stretched over the frame with a bar running across the center of the cot which was very annoying and painful when laid upon and which most men took out. At the end of the 1st platoon buildings was another building which held the platoon weapons section and CP group, with the same torturing cots.

The next few days were filled with troop movement to supply, where they were able to get clean, not necessarily new, but clean utilities, then to the armory to get weapons repaired and the barber shop for haircuts. However, the most important things, to the troops, were showers, hot meals, and lots of sleep.

Don awoke early as the sun was coming up, but it was still fairly dark because it was early November and the monsoon season was in full swing. He finished dressing, except for his boots. He walked through the barracks in his socks because he didn't want to wake the CP group, who were sound asleep.

He walked to the screen door with his jungle boots in his hand and stepped out on the steps leading up the barracks. After reaching the bottom step, he sat down and put on his boots, laced them up then leaned back on the steps, and thought what he had been through the last three weeks or so.

He was extremely happy with the platoon. He had been right in selecting the 1st platoon; it was perfect fit for him. His tactics had worked, which he was very grateful for, and he seemed to have a connection with the Marines in the platoon.

He was enjoying the solitude when suddenly Captain McCarthy came around the end of the barracks. He immediately jumped up to attention.

The skipper smiled and said, "Lieutenant Garrett, how are things going with you and your platoon? Getting everyone squared away?" The captain motioned for him to stand at ease.

He informed the skipper all had gone well, as the troops were enjoying a needed break from their other break.

The captain chuckled and said, "Have you had breakfast?"

"No, sir, was thinking of it when you came by."

The two officers walked over to the mess hall, where they enjoyed a hot breakfast of roast beef in gravy on large fluffy biscuits, sunny-side up eggs, and steaming hot coffee for the captain and orange juice for the lieutenant.

After finishing their breakfast the captain stretched and said, "We are going to conduct a joint operation with the Korean Marines. So, I thought I would go over and talk to their operations officer and if possible the commanding officer. Want to go with me?"

Don eagerly agreed to go and they both set off to notify their respective command post.

Captain McCarthy came out of the company office as Don arrived. A jeep was parked in front of the office with a driver sitting in it waiting for them. Don crawled into the back seat, and the captain was in the front as they drove off to the Korean Marine Base.

As they drove north on Highway 1, which Don figured was the only highway and doubted if there was a Highway 2, he took in the sights. It was a beautiful day with a little sunshine for once and the closer they got to Da Nang, the more farmers he saw out working in the rice fields.

Several times they saw small children, sometimes as many as five or six at a time, sitting on the backs of the giant water buffalo. These water buffalo easily weighted a ton and yet seemed extremely gentle.

Once they reached the Korean Base they were directed to building 8. Inside they found Major Sun, the battalion operations officer. He was most cordial and was very excited Captain McCarthy had come to talk about the upcoming operation.

After about thirty or forty minutes, the major suggested they call on the battalion commander, Lieutenant Colonel Lee. Lee was rather tall for a Korean, had a slender build, and spoke in a loud voice, and his English speaking abilities were good. He did come across as being a proud and "stuffy" individual and maybe a little arrogant.

Colonel Lee invited the captain and lieutenant to witness an office hours he was about to conduct. The major quickly suggested the two American officers had other obligations and needed to leave. The colonel was not "suggesting";he insisted they stay for the office hours.

The colonel's office was small, so small; to get to his desk he had to slide sideways along the wall to reach his chair behind the desk. The walls were white washed and very bright with a bank of windows on one side of the office. The other walls were empty of any pictures or decorative items; it was merely a plain white wall.

The colonel took his seat behind the desk and explained in great detail how the office hours were to be conducted. Much like the American office hours or nonjudicial punishment, the commanding officer, and only him, would decide the guilt or innocence of the individual.

Then a young Korean Marine, undergoing the office hours, was marched into the office. He stood attention in front of the colonel's desk, and reported to the colonel.

The major, captain, and Don stood against the plain white wall facing the windows. The young Korean stood between them and the windows. The young man's first sergeant and commanding officer stood at the back of the room on both sides of the office door.

The young Korean Marine was trembling as he reported to the colonel. His eyes wildly glanced from person to person then back to the colonel.

The colonel screamed in his native tongue at the young man and slammed his fist on his desktop, causing an extremely loud and sharp *CLAP*, which echoed off the walls of the small room.

Everyone in the room immediately tensed up as the colonel became even more enraged. He jumped up from his seat, his face dark red, his voice growing louder then roaring. He appeared to have lost control of his emotions. He had become a shrieking wild man. He then reached down to his side and pulled out his pistol, aimed it at the young Korean standing directly in front of him, and pulled the trigger.

The noise from the gun blast was deafening in the small room. The young Korean slammed back against the closed door behind him. Dying, he slowly slid down to the floor, leaving a large bright red blood smear on the white washed door.

Don stood dazed and immediately went into a semi-shock as he could not believe this horrible act had been committed. He didn't feel the captain pulling him out of the office. His jolt of reality came as he stood next to the jeep with the captain shaking him saying, "Lieutenant!… lieutenant! Snap out of it!"

Don slowly focused on the captain then stammered, "What… what the hell happened back there?"

The captain, looking back toward the building, said, "I have no idea what that son-of-a-bitch was trying to prove. Are you all right?"

Slightly trembling, Don said he thought so, but that he would like to sit down. The captain and driver helped him into the back seat and the captain jumped in beside him and told the driver, "Get us the hell out of here!"

Don appreciated the open-air drive through the country back to LZ Baldy. He began to steadily gain his composure and tried to make some sense out the horror-stricken mess. His efforts proved to be futile.

The captain turned to him and said, "How are you doing?"

Don glanced at the passing countryside and then looked at the captain and said, "You know skipper, I have seen more violence in the past few weeks than I have my entire life. This war business can really suck."

The captain placed his hand on the back of the lieutenant and said, "Unfortunately, this is the face of war and it's only going to get worse. You have to be both mentally, and physically, tough or it will eat you up. To lead Marines you need to control your emotions. Do you understand?"

Don thought about what the captain had told him and after a few minutes said, "I understand and will not let this happen again…I promise."

Once back at LZ Baldy, Don went to the company office and buried himself in the records of his troops, checking promotion eligibility, pay records, anything he could come up with to occupy his mind and keep it off the indecency at the Korean Base.

After a couple of hours and now completely composed, he went into the captain's office, thinking this might be a good time to bring up the subject of another machine gun for his platoon.

The captain listened carefully to his request for another gun then said, "Well, you are right you need another gun. In fact, if you don't get a second gun, I am going to take the one you have, leaving you without any guns. Therefore, I highly recommend you get another one…lieutenant."

Stunned for a moment, Don stared at the captain. He quickly glanced toward the first sergeant, who was setting in a chair in the admin office chuckling under his breath.

The first sergeant's actions pissed Don off. He glared at the first sergeant then smiled and said, "Well, I guess I will have to find a gun. It's obvious our senior staff NCO hasn't been very successful. Yep, leave it to a second lieutenant if you want results."

The first sergeant quickly wiped the smile off his face and saw red. He didn't care for lieutenants and especially this "smart ass" second lieutenant.

The skipper said, "You know, first sergeant, he has a real good point."

Don left the company office with the first sergeant staring a hole through him. He headed for the barracks; he knew it was unwise to provoke the company first sergeant, but it was irritating, and unacceptable, since he had done nothing to obtain a gun. A second machine gun could save the lives of his Marines.

Where was he going to get another machine gun and within two days?

He walked into the hooch and found Joe Loerzel and Lippy sitting on the edge of their racks looking very bored. "You two want a hard mission which will really help the platoon?"

The two looked at each other then the lieutenant and smiled. Joe said, "What do you have in mind?"

Don explained to them both that he wanted, no, *needed* a second machine gun or the platoon would lose the one they currently had. He needed an M-60 Machine gun with bag, extra barrel, tripod, traversing rod, and cleaning gear... a complete gun.

"Do either of you have a valid military driver's license?"

Joe indicated he did.

"Good, I'll go get a jeep out of the motor pool for you. Then I want you two to drive down to LZ Ross and see Corporal Mount at the battalion armory. He owes me."

The two looked at each other then Joe raised his eye lids and said, "Owes you?"

Don smiled and pulled out his pistol. He explained to them about teaching the corporal how to completely strip, and put, a 45 pistol back together.

Don and Joe were returning from the motor pool with the only jeep available, the captain's, when they met the skipper walking down the road.

He yelled for them to stop and said, "Lieutenant, that's my jeep, what are you doing with it?"

Don, grasping for words, finally said, "Well sir, I am on a mission assigned to me by my company commander."

"Very funny lieutenant, you better not tear up my jeep."

Don motioned for Joe to drive on and as they sped off they yelled, "YES SIR!"

Joe and Lippy drove down to LZ Ross and found Corporal Mount at the armory and explained their situation.

Corporal Mount not only agreed to help, but seemed eager to help accomplish the mission. After much in-depth thought, he came up with a plan, a great plan. It did require them to drive to Marble Mountain and someone to forge an army colonel's name, which Lippy was more than happy to do.

The next morning Don lay in his rack facing the wall, then slowly rolled over on his back and looked up at the metal roof. He smiled and thought it was the same type of metal used in almost all barns in the Midwest. Great, he had graduated from college and was now living in a barn.

He chuckled as he sat up in his rack, throwing his legs over the side, when his foot suddenly struck metal. Lying next to his rack was a brand new M-60 machine gun with all the "extras" he had requested.

He quickly dressed and went to the NCO's quarters where both Joe and Lippy sat on the edge of their cots with mile-wide smiles.

He started to say something when Joe held up his hand and said, "Don't ask. And by the way, Corporal Mount said he was more than happy to help. However, in thirty days NIS (Naval Investigative Services) will be looking for the gun."

Poor Boy walked into the room, froze, sensing something, and glanced at the lieutenant then the two NCOs and said, "I didn't hear, see, nor do I know anything and it will stay that way… okay?" The other three smiled and agreed.

All four of them walked back into the lieutenant's quarters and marveled over the new gun.

Finally Don looked at Poor Boy and said, "Go get Larry Bates, it's time he got his gun. Don't tell why I want to see him though."

Poor Boy grinned and said, "Yes sir!"

Bates stopped at the door to the lieutenant's room, and waited until he was told to enter. He then heard Don yell, "Get in here Bates!"

As Bates entered the room, he immediately saw the M-60 machine gun uttered, "I have never seen a new M-60 before."

The others all laughed and Don said, "Join the crowd, we all said the same thing."

Don paused a few minutes while Bates closely examined the gun in detail then said, "Well, I promised you the first machine gun and here it is. It's all yours. So get your stuff out of the rifle squad areas and move into the weapons section with this gun."

Don was anxious to share the fact he had a second machine gun with the skipper and maybe a little too eager to let the first sergeant know. Upon entering the company office he acknowledged the first sergeant, who was standing next to a bookshelf looking through a thick reference book.

He then spoke to the admin chief and asked if any messages came in concerning promotions for his troops. The chief said they hadn't had any new messages but was expecting one later in the day.

He slowly walked toward the captain, who was sitting in a chair behind a field desk in the office and said, "Oh sir, by the way, did I tell you we procured a new M-60 Machine Gun for the platoon?"

The first sergeant dropped the reference book, causing a loud *thud* as it hit the wooden floor.

The captain glanced at the first sergeant and said, "Procured? Is that a fancy word for stole? You better not have 'procured' it from one of the sister Marine Company's or any other Marine unit."

Don put on a defense of being totally insulted and said, "Sir, I am an officer and gentleman, how could you even suggest such a thing?" Then in a whimsical manner said, "No, we procured it from the army."

The captain smiled, and said, "Well, that's good. Good work! I'm proud of you." He then paused, appeared to be in thought, then continued, saying, "In your short time in Nam you have demonstrated good leadership traits, tactical savvy, and combat sense. A real warrior. I should call you… I know, you are from Oklahoma, Indian country… I'm going to call you Geronimo and, by the way, how's my jeep?"

Don returned to his quarters and felt magnificent. Things had been going great with the platoon. He knew they were coming together as a platoon and therefore he was sure they had accepted him as their platoon leader. This was one of the most important things to him right now; secondly, he wanted the skipper to accept him as a sound, reliable leader, which he sensed was coming along fine too.

Wallowing in his good fortune, he laid down on his cot and immediately fell asleep. His rest was not without his recently acquired demons haunting him, but it was, nevertheless, rest his body yearned for and to some large degree demanded.

He awakened to a sharp knock on the outside door of his room and sluggishly said, "Yea… what do you want?" Lippy opened the door and stuck his head into the lieutenant's room and said, "You got a minute?"

Don, now more aware of his surroundings and quickly reaching complete control of his mental cognizant, glimpsed toward the entry and said, "Come on in, Lippy. I must have fallen asleep. What's up?"

Lippy slowly climbed the steps, entered the room, and said half apologizing, "Sorry to bother you, lieutenant, but I really need to talk to you."

Don motioned to the only chair, a folding chair, for Lippy to have a seat. Lippy gradually sat down and after some nervously twisting said, "Well I have a couple of things I need to talk to you about."

Somewhat concerned now, the lieutenant said, "Okay, Lippy, what is the first thing you want to talk to me about?"

With some hesitation Lippy finally said, "Well, the platoon members want to know if they can call you LT?"

Don rather puzzled said, "Why, sure they can, it's short for lieutenant. I have no problem with that." He looked at Lippy, who now was frowning, and after a few moments he said, "Am I missing some point here, aren't most lieutenants called Lt.?"

"No, I mean, yes they are but, Lt. is an abbreviation for lieutenant. Capital LT is different from Lt. It's kind of hard to explain."

Both sat very quietly for a few awkward minutes when, finally, Lippy once more took a stab at trying to explain the difference. "Okay, there are gunnys, and then there is *the* gunny. So, there are Lt.'s and there is the LT. But you're the platoon's lieutenant. They respect and trust you. They know you will do your best for them; therefore, you are the LT and that's what they want to call you… okay?"

He sat staring at Lippy, not sure what to say, but finally said, "I think I understand what you are saying. And I would be honored if the men called me LT."

Lippy smiled and said, "Great, I will tell the men." He then started to rub his hands together and looked around at nothing in particular, then glanced at LT as his face became pale and his smile disappeared.

LT looked at Lippy, slid closer toward him, and said, "And what is the second thing you want to talk to me about? You look rather serious; this is not the 'good, bad news' talk is it?"

Lippy jumped up from his chair and blurted out, "I have orders for home. I leave this evening for Da Nang!"

The news hit LT like a bolt of lightning. He merely stared into space. This was a tremendous blow. He was on top of the world and now he felt as if he were knocked down into a deep black pit. In somewhat of a stupor, he slowly rose from his rack and walked a short distance toward the entryway to the squad bay, stopped, turned to Lippy, and forced a slight smile on his face.

After clearing his throat he said, "Well, that's great. You certainly have put in your time in this hell hole." Becoming more composed, his voice strengthened and his mind became much clearer. "I want to thank you for helping me. And I especially want to thank you for being the bridge for me between the platoon… you will be missed, by all of us."

"One more thing LT, I recommended Corporal Larry Ballew replace me as right guide."

LT nodded and with that, the two shook hands and Lippy quietly and unceremoniously left to catch his ride to Da Nang.

As the evening light faded, LT began thinking about his immediate situation. For several hours he had been mentally debating his current situation, with some success. He knew for sure change was always going to happen and he merely had to roll with it and make the most of it. He, and Joe, along with Larry Ballew, Poor Boy, and Doc Smith could handle any situation that should rise within the platoon. He was confident of it.

His train of thought was broken by a knock on his screen door. He walked over to the door and opened it. There stood the skipper with a smile on his face and he quickly said, "How's it going Geronimo?"

LT looked at the skipper for a moment and said, "Not especially good, since I lost my right guide. But, hopefully things will get better. Please come on in to my humble quarters."

The captain stepped into his room and, chuckling, said, "Yep, yours are about as lavish as my quarters." His face then became serious and he said, "Look, there is no easy way to put this, but all three platoons have lost people today and I had an emergency leave from my CP. I lost my radio man and I need another one. You said you have one man in your platoon who is married… I believe Mosher is his name."

LT gradually turned and looked the captain in the eyes and said, "Jesus Christ! You are kidding, right? Damn, we are going on an operation in the morning. I will have a new right guide and now have to find a new platoon radioman… this is crap."

The captain shook his head and said, "Well, believe it. Hey, you do have a new machine gun and therefore will be able to keep both of them, so it's not all bad."

LT sluggishly walked into the CP part of the billeting area and found no one. He knew he had to get on with solving the radioman problem. Stewing and going through hours of mental debates would be futile. He needed to find Joe and the squad leaders and get the dilemma resolved.

As he entered the weapons billeting area he saw only one person, Larry Bates. Larry was sitting next to his brand new machine gun and gently wiping it down with oil. He really hated to bother Larry; he was so engrossed with his gun. However, important matters were at hand and require immediate attention.

"Larry, I need for you to find the platoon sergeant and the three squad leaders, it's really important. I need them pronto. They are probably at the movie."

Jumping to his feet, Larry came to attention, started to walk toward the exit of the squad bay, and suddenly stopped, turned to the lieutenant, and said, "Well, sir I'm on fire watch and security duty. I'm not supposed to leave my post."

Almost totally exacerbated from the recent crappy news, LT rolled his eyes and consciously took a deep breath then said, "Yes, you're right Bates, but as your platoon commander I now relieve you of your duties."

Larry once more started for the door then stopped and glanced at the lieutenant then around the room, clearly concerned over who would take his place.

LT started to lose his patience and said in a loud voice, "WHAT… you don't think I have the abilities to assume your responsibilities!"

Becoming embarrassed, Larry stuttered, "Yes sir… no sir… I mean…" He then turned and darted for the exit, wishing only to put as much distance between him and the lieutenant as possible.

LT, Joe, and the three squad leaders met in his quarters. Ballew was promoted to platoon right guide. A replacement for Poor Boy proved to take much longer. None of the squad leaders wanted, understandably, to give up someone from their squad, especially since they would not get a replacement.

However, after much discussion on the logic of getting the best radioman for the position, they all agreed only one person could fill the post. Lance Corporal Lee Graff. Lee was not your typical radioman; he was tall and very slender, making him appear somewhat fragile, and it seemed it would be impossible for him to carry all the extra weight required of a radioman. Yet time would prove different. Lee owned a continuous smile, was quiet, attentive, intelligent, hardworking, always ready to help, and possessed an enormous amount of energy.

LT's platoon was ready for Pagoda Valley; he had Ballew for right guide and Lee as radio operator. He had earned two nicknames today. One, Geronimo, from his skipper and, more importantly, one, LT, from his troops. He would sleep well tonight.

CHAPTER 15
PAGODA VALLEY

Pagoda Valley lay about seven clicks due west of LZ Baldy. The valley was about four or five clicks long and one click wide. Both sides of the valley were bordered by high steep fingers from the Que Son Mountains. At the southwest end of the valley, the narrow end tied into the mountain chain, where large boulders about the size of a two-story house were naturally piled. The ground shot almost straight up into the mountains from there.

The mouth of the valley opened out into an extremely large area. Rice was once grown in the Pagoda Valley but with mountain fingers on both sides, the NVA living in the mountains would come down and steal the rice from the farmers. For this reason, rice was no longer grown in the valley.

The valley served as a route for the NVA/VC to get to the many villages in the Quan Queson District, which lay out in front of the valley. This offered the enemy the ability to liberate rice and conduct their heavy-handed recruiting.

The platoon set out for Pagoda Valley after three days of rest, good food, weapons repaired, and a resupply of fresh ammo. In addition, each Marine carried five days of food, which made each one appear much like a beast of burden. The platoon was trucked out of LZ Baldy up Highway 1, towards Da Nang, about three clicks, then unloaded. This put them about four and a half clicks away from, but right in front of, the mouth of Pagoda Valley.

The rest of Hotel Company had been helo lifted the day before behind Hill 110, which crossed about half of the mouth of Pagoda Valley next to the vast rice fields.

The main part of the company was acting as a blocking force by establishing ambushes at the mouth of the valley, while 1st platoon spread out over the numerous hamlets and rice fields in hopes of driving the enemy into the traps.

Additionally, 1st platoon had with it an engineer section, primarily explosive experts and two Vietnamese "Chui Hoi's," Kit Carson Scouts, Tau, and Quoc.

The Chui Hoi Program was established to get NVA and VC soldiers to turn themselves in and surrender. Propaganda with "Safe Conduct Passes" were air dropped into contested areas to help persuade these enemy soldiers to surrender.

Some of those who surrendered where recruited for the Kit Carson Scout Program. These people were taught English and their function was to act as interpreters with the Vietnamese civilians and point out potentially dangerous situations to the commands they were assigned to.

There was a matter of trust though. The NVA and VC considered the Kit Carson Scouts traitors and many of the Marines looked upon them short of being the enemy. As a result, they were under-used and mostly ignored… men without a country.

LT went over the tactical plan in his head once more as the trucks rumbled down the highway. The platoon would be spread out on line. To the left, 1st squad under the short, get-in-your-face Corporal Eugene Rathbone; in the center, 2nd squad would be the calm and expressionless Corporal Craig Olsen; and to the left, the no-nonsense Jersey 3rd squad.

Rathbone had the Kit Carson Scout Quoc and Jersey had Tau. The engineers and weapons would stay with LT's CP group and move right behind 2nd squad in the middle; this position provided the best place to control the squads.

The area was so flat they would not have any problem seeing people in front of them a good mile away. The spread-out squad members would produce a long line of Marines sweeping across the rice fields toward Pagoda Valley.

The trucks finally slowed, then stopped on the highway. 1st platoon exited the trucks in the dark and began to get organized to start the movement at daybreak toward Pagoda Valley.

LT once again slowly and methodically eyed each Marine in the platoon, checking on equipment, their enthusiasm, and mental alertness; he was most impressed with each of his Marines. He was especially impressed with the three rifle squad leaders and his weapon leader.

He recalled a situation when Jersey had given a class on how to break down C-rations necessary in the bush. At about the time he finished, a Marine from another platoon, who had finished filling his pack, tried to stand up, then fell forward, running headlong about fifteen feet and did a nose dive into the ground. His platoon members quickly relieved him of some of his C-rations and several items not needed in the field.

Jersey leaned over to Bates and said, "That's why we lighten our packs, Bates, you don't want that happening on a mountain. And remember, you can eat a can of chicken, pork slices, or eggs when you get up in the morning but only have a can of fruit for lunch. Have your big meal at night. Long humps are never easy until you get into the swing of eating right and also remember, only carry what you *need*."

Jersey, along with the other squad leaders, were great mentors, teaching each new recruit the rules for survival in the bush.

LT looked up to the east, where the morning light was very faintly starting to show. He walked over to Lee and asked if he had completed his radio checks. LT then glanced toward the engineers who were moving about, tugging on straps, mostly venting their pent-up nervousness because they normally did not go on sweeps.

Once more he looked down the line of Marines spread out along the road. He could now see the last man on each end of the long line of Marines and gave the word to "move out."

Their movement, though slow, still surprised many of the local Vietnamese farmers. Most gave the Marines short silent stares then went back to their work. It was obvious, though; several hundred yards ahead of the Marines, a few of those "working" in the fields began walking away from the advancing Marines, toward Pagoda Valley.

The platoon had crossed about half the distance from the highway to Pagoda Valley when Jersey called LT to ask him to hold up the line of advancing Marines. Tau, the Kit Carson Scout, had found a booby trap on a rice paddy dike.

LT informed Jersey he was on the way to his position with the engineers and wanted them to take a close look at the booby trap. Upon arrival, the engineers did a close inspection of the booby trap and discovered it was a "Daisy Chain."

Sergeant Luck, the engineer section head, found the booby trap actually consisted of five more explosives on each side of the dike.

The explosives were about fifty feet apart and it was designed so when the front man tripped the device, all the rounds went off at the same time, causing the "Daisy Chain effect," killing the lead man and all the other troops about two hundred feet behind him.

Sergeant Luck fastened a one-hundred-foot rope to the trip wire and detonated the entire booby-trap with one pull of the rope, causing no injuries to any of the Marines.

Tau pointed out he knew there was an explosive device in the area because none of the farmers working in the fields were within two hundred feet of it.

1st platoon had a new appreciation for the Kit Carson Scouts.

After sloshing through the rice patties for several hours, the platoon finally reached an old abandon railroad berm which also crossed the front of the mouth of Pagoda Valley. The berm was about a click from the mouth of the valley. The platoon stopped and took a lunch break on the back side of the berm. LT contacted Captain McCarthy to let him know where the platoon was at and to ask when he want the platoon to push to his position.

Captain McCarthy told him to take a well-deserved rest and when he was ready to move to the hill left of the mouth of the valley. He also informed him they had captured a dozen rice carriers, five political officers, and a ton of North Vietnam's communist propaganda.

LT, Joe, and Ballew moved through the squads, insuring each Marine took off his wet socks and put on dry ones. There were no more rice paddies or standing water from the berm to the hill top.

He then plotted a route to the hill and decided they would travel basically in wedge formation. Rathbone would lead out since he was on the left end of the platoon and closest to the hill. He called the captain on the radio and gave him his route and time when the platoon would leave their current position. He then called the squad leaders up.

"Gentleman, we are going to leave this position in forty-five minutes. Order of march is Rathbone, Olsen, and then Jersey. The CP group will travel between Rathbone and Olsen.

"Rathbone, go to the west side of the hill. We will tie in with second platoon on your left and third platoon on your right. We will have one squad on perimeter watch, one on day patrol, and one conducting night ambushes. Any choices as to what you'd rather do first?"

Jersey slowly looked at the other squad leaders and since no one said anything he said, "Does the first ambush go out tonight?" LT nodded yes. "Okay, I'll take the ambush tonight. Does that mean my Marines won't have to dig fighting positions, once we get with the rest of the company?"

Once again, he shook his head yes.

Rathbone shifted from a kneeling to a sitting position and asked, "When does the day patrol go out, today or tomorrow?"

"Tomorrow."

Rathbone quickly said, "I'll take the day patrol."

"Good," LT said. "And by the way, your squad will help Olsen's squad dig the perimeter fighting holes."

Rathbone, who had been pouring a handful of dirt from one hand to the other one, threw down the dirt and said, "Crap, thought I might have slipped that by you, LT."

They all laughed and the other squad leaders pointed their fingers at Rathbone in mocking fun.

"Any questions?" LT asked. "Okay, get your troops informed. We move out in forty minutes."

The company gunny, Gunnery Sergeant Pat Dixon, met the platoon at the perimeter and informed LT the captain wanted to see him. Dixon was a tall red-headed, chiseled out-of-rock Marine. His facial expression looked as if he was about ready to chew someone out, yet LT found him to be a man with a quick smile and a very pleasant and polite personality. He did run a tight ship and was the typical no-nonsense Marine gunny.

"Where can we put the platoon while I'm talking to the captain?" LT inquired.

"With your permission, I'll get with your platoon sergeant and we will take care of the platoon, lieutenant."

"Thanks gunny," he said as he started walking towards the captain.

He found the captain sitting on the ground cross-legged and leaning up against a boulder with a map case lying in his lap. The captain was intently studying the map when he looked up and saw LT, smiled, and said, "I see you made it all right. Your platoon did a great job today. So tell me, was it a Daisy-Chain booby-trap?"

LT explained it was and that Tau had found the device and how the engineers blew it in place. The captain listened with great interest and finally said, "Well, we owe Tau a great deal of thanks and I'll see he gets the credit he deserves in my report."

"Thanks sir, and do you have new orders for my platoon?"

"Oh yes," the captain said as he glanced at his map case. "I want you and two of your squads with a machine gun to conduct a recon patrol up the valley. Go up one side and down the other. I want you to be on the lookout for trails, signs of military activity, and places to for us to set up night ambushes. I also want you to leave the other machine gun and M60 mortar with the weapons platoon commander."

LT, who had been standing, sat down next to the captain and said, "Will I get the tubes, guns, and crews back?"

The captain looked at the map case smiled and said, "Well, I did tell you if you got another machine gun you could keep both of them. However, the mortar tubes are another story. Do you want *that* tube or *that* crew back?"

"Both, sir!"

"Oh, you want a specific tube and crew, why?"

LT relaxed and leaned against the rock and said, "When we were at the Triple Culvert, I worked with the mortar section. We shot up two and a half pallets of ammo; by then the mortar team was really good. When we were in the rear, we took the tubes to the armory and had them worked on. They put in new pea lights and tightened up the bevel rings on the tubes. The tubes are in great shape now and the crew is the best."

The captain turned to LT, chuckled, and said, "You think they are better than my tubes and crew?"

LT could smell a challenge brewing. He thought the matter over for a few moments then said, "I have never seen your Marines shoot their tubes, but I believe I have the best M60 mortar crew in Vietnam."

With that the captain immediately said, "I'll bet you a hundred dollars my crew will beat yours in a shoot-out."

LT, somewhat caught off guard slowly, said, "All right sir, and if I win I get to keep the tubes and crew too."

They agreed and shook hands on it. The captain said a helo would be arriving within the hour to pick up the prisoners, rice, and propaganda, and after that they would have a shoot off.

LT then left the captain and hurried over to his platoon to inform them and especially the M60 crew of the challenge.

Regiment sent out helos and picked up the prisoners, rice, and propaganda.

1st platoons mortar section completed digging their circular pits, which were about eight feet across and lined with two layers of sandbags, creating an eighteen-inch-high wall around the pit. The tube was carefully seated, and positioned; they were ready for the competition to begin.

Captain McCarthy walked to the edge of the perimeter and gazed out into the valley and finally said, "See the lone tree out there about six hundred meters?"

LT's eyes followed to where the captain was pointing and said, "The one with the perfect cone shape that looks to be about thirty feet tall with small and light green leaves?"

The captain nodded and then said, "You will shoot first. You will call the firing mission and I'll call mine. You only have two rounds; a good mortar team only needs two rounds and that second one should be on target. Don't you agree, lieutenant?"

LT smiled and walked over to his team and said, "Sure, captain. My team will be on target by the second round, if not the first."

He then glanced down at Lance Corporal Romano Aglaia, the team leader, and asked, "Are you ready to win this event?"

Romano, a California boy not short on confidence, chuckled and said, "Yes sir. Those guys over with the captain are good but not, as good as we are."

LT called out a firing mission, giving the direction and distance, with one round of "Willie Peter," phosphorus round, which creates a blast and plum of heavy white smoke on a windless day. There was no wind in the valley so the phosphorus smoke would go straight up in the air, easily marking where the rounds landed.

"Fire!" The round climbed high into the sky as he watched it and noticed it drifted slightly a little to the left; probably an ocean breeze a thousand feet up or so causing the drift. The round hit slightly left and behind the tree. He quickly looked through his binoculars and mentally calculated a correction.

"Right twenty, up ten."

Agula repeated the correction as he made them then said, "Ready to fire!"

LT took a deep breath and calmly said, "Fire for effect."

Once again, the round leaped into the sky and as it hit its highest point seemed to momentarily freeze in midair then drove toward earth, gaining speed with each foot it traveled downward. The round hit the ground, exploded, and the phosphorus gently engulfed the lone tree, causing a burst of loud cheers and yells of joyful accomplishments from 1st platoon.

The captain smiled and offered a hearty, "Well done lieutenant." He turned to his crew and said, "We can beat them!" The crew gave out a loud cheer of enthusiasm and echoed the captain's words.

The first round landed much where 1st platoon's first round landed. The captain made his correction and his crew fired the second round. The round came in line with the tree but about ten meters short of actually hitting the tree, and therefore didn't engulf it in phosphorus smoke.

The captain, however, declared the event to be a tie. As a token of his good character, though, he agreed to let LT keep the machine guns, 60MM tube, and the crews. He also decided he did not win the wager of a hundred dollars because it was a tie.

Today was Thanksgiving. The troops waited very impatiently for the helos to bring the vat cans of turkey, mashed potatoes, green beans, and cranberry sauce. Mouths began to water as the birds landed, and the men quickly unloaded the prized cargo.

Gunny Dixon expeditiously organized a buffet assembly line, allowing the company of Marines to be fed quickly.

Within 1st platoon's perimeter was the company trash pit. Jersey walked over to Bates, who had just exited the buffet line with a full plate of food, and said, "Bates I know you're not on hole watch but how about you go up and sit on the trash berm and keep an eye open for the enemy."

Bates, in his agreeably manner, hurried off and sat down on the small berm and began eating his Thanksgiving dinner.

Speedy, who had just come out of the chow line, looked around and saw Bates on the berm and climbed up to him, sat down, and said, "Mind if I join you?"

Bates immediately welcomed Speedy.

Both young men sat in silence for some time eating their meals when Bates broke the quiet by saying, "Speedy, you know I grew up in Pennsylvania, around Pittsburgh, where my dad worked in the steel mills. We didn't do a lot of traveling and you're the first Hispanic I have ever known. I was wondering what do Hispanics have traditionally for Thanksgiving dinner?"

Speedy stopped eating, turned to Bates, frowned, then smiled and pointed at Bates' plate, and said, "Turkey and the other stuff on your plate. Tell me, what do you gringos have?"

Both youths simultaneously slapped each other on their backs and burst out laughing.

CHAPTER 16
KIT CARSON SCOUTS

That evening the company was still abuzz about the shoot off; naturally some felt 1st platoon won, others felt it was a tie, but all agreed it was great shooting by both M60 teams.

The machine gun team of Larry Bates and Al Brown, Larry's assistant gunner, was billeting in the 1st Platoon CP area since they would be going out on patrol with LT in the morning.

Bates ambled over to where LT was sitting, carefully going over his map before he lost the evening light. "LT, have you talked much to the Kit Carson Scouts?"

He glanced up at Bates and slowly said, "No, I can't say that I have. Why are you asking?"

"Well, I have. Did you know Tau was once an officer with the VC?"

He quickly glanced back at Bates then over to where Tau and Quoc were sitting, about fifty feet away and said, "No. I had no idea." Still staring at the two scouts, he turned to Bates, waited a few moments, and then said, "Do you like sardines?"

Bates looked at him with a very puzzled look and slowly said, "Yes... yea I do, come to think of it, but what has sardines have to do with Tau and Quoc?"

"Do me a favor. Go over and invite them both over for dinner with you, say in about fifteen minutes. Will you do that for me?"

Bates, even more puzzled, wondered what he had gotten himself into. In boot camp the drill instructors told the enlisted men to stay away from the officers, maybe he had really screwed up; however, he hesitantly agreed and strolled over to the scouts.

At the prescribed time, Bates, and the scouts, arrived at LT's CP. He stood up and greeted them and offered everyone a seat on the ground. They formed a circle and sat down.

Bates became more aware of his situation and quickly glanced around to see if he was being watched by his fellow Marines; after all, he did not want to be known as a kiss ass.

The scouts were all smiles and appeared to be most pleased with the invitation. Lee, who had been brewing up some of his famous coffee, he thought more famous than Poor Boy's, brought over C-ration cans of hot coffee.

After a few minutes of small talk and a round of congratulations and toast to Tau for finding the booby-trap, LT reached over and opened his pack and produced several cans of Beach Cliff Sardines in mustard sauce, which he had received from his parents' care package.

The guests' eyes lit up and they swiped their tongues across their lips in anticipation of the feast. He also produced several opened cans of salted C-ration crackers, known as "John Wayne Crackers" by the Marines.

Larry, becoming less suspicious and more at ease, produced a huge smile said, "You know how many holes are in each one of those John Wayne Crackers?"

LT smiled and said, "Let me make a wild guess… fifty-four?"

Bates couldn't believe his ears; how could the LT have known such facts? He acknowledged the lieutenant's correct answer in a frozen, laudatory smile.

After consuming the sardines, crackers, and coffee, and after some more small talk, LT asked if Tau and Quoc would mind telling the group about how they became scouts.

After several moments of silence, Tau, with a big smile, said, "In 1963 I married and lived in the village of Tam Ky. My wife and I, with my family members, built a new home. It was made from, as all homes in the village were, bamboo walls and a thatched roof. We had been married about a month when I had my parents over for dinner and we were visited by several members of the National Liberation Front.

"Two men entered the hooch and said, 'Greetings from the National Liberation Front. You are being given the privilege to fight against the puppet government. We are a democratic organization so you are free to choose, but if you don't come with us we will consider you a supporter of the Saigon government and execute you.'"

Tau said, after quickly thinking about it, "It seemed to be a very good idea to go with them. I was sent to a training camp in the Que Son Mountains. I was taught to be a sapper and instructed on how to crawl through barbed-wire entanglements."

Tau paused took a sip of coffee and said, "At the end of my long and intense training. I was told to report to the commander's hooch. The commander, in a very complimentary manner, informed me I was being recommended for the officers' program. I accepted the offer, feeling I had no other choice. After several more months of intense training I became an officer.

"I was placed in command of a VC sapper platoon and thought it was wonderful. I was given a pistol, a sign of great authority, and when I entered villages, the chiefs would bow and show me great respect. The villagers would give me and my men whatever we desired.

"I thought life couldn't be any better. Then one day I was called to a meeting of the VC Command Group. We were told the Americans were coming and they had very good weapons, artillery, and aircraft. The American infantry, however, had no stomach for a fight. They would flee the battlefield if attacked with determination.

"I carried this news back to my people. However, a short time later, on my way to see a VC tax collector, I spotted some American helicopters while crossing a rice paddy. I decided I would show the Americans my resolve and began firing at the helos with my newly acquired SKS rifle."

Tau took a long drink of his coffee, chuckled, and said, "Many rockets immediately came blasting back from the choppers, answering my challenge. I was knocked off the rice paddy and left totally unconscious. When I awoke I was being dragged through the rice paddies to a helo, by the biggest black man I had ever seen. I then looked around and saw the American soldiers were sweeping the entire area. I knew then the Americans had come to fight and I had been lied to. Joining the Kit Carson Scouts was my way of repaying the VC."

As the night swallowed up the evening light, the group said their good nights and headed back to their respective sleeping areas.

LT asked Bates to hold up a minute as he started to leave. "You looked surprised that I knew the answer to your question about the John Wayne Crackers."

Bates sheepishly stuttered, "Well… uh… I didn't think you officers would… uh… be involved with such trivia matters, sir."

LT grinned and said, "Bates, did you know all Marine Officers, unlike the other military services, are trained by enlisted Marines. The same ones that taught you in boot camp? Maybe, just maybe, we aren't much different from any other Marine… you think?"

Bates, not knowing what to say, smiled then headed off to his area and said a scurrying, "Yes sir."

The next morning 1st and 2nd squads, along with LT's radio operator, Lee, Tau, and Larry Bates with his new machine gun saddled up to recon the valley.

LT chose to go up the left side of the valley and come back on the right side. The temperature was about eighty degrees with eighty percent humidity and the sun shining. However, there was fog in some of the lower pockets in the valley.

As the unit moved up the valley, LT made detailed mental notes of the terrain and kept a sharp eye open for possible ambush sites, which he noted on his map. Close to noon, they reached the end of the valley where the large boulders were piled.

The heat and humidity was stifling at the end of the valley where breezes seldom reached. The unit found a well-worn trail that lead to the edge of the boulders then turned into what proved to be a very narrow, continuous trail past the large boulders and eventually into Antenna and Que Son Valley.

Tau confirmed the enemy was using the trail and in big numbers almost every day or night. LT marked this position on his map with a red circle; it was the number one place for an ambush.

He chose to follow the path they had discovered at the large boulders, which ran down the right side of the valley, on the return trip to the company area.

About half way to the company area the trail split, one continuing on the valley floor, the other farther up on the side of the valley wall where it crossed a finger which protruded out into the valley then dropped down to the valley floor. LT chose the trail leading up the valley wall.

He soon found this position allowed a person to be able to look both up and down the valley, giving a commanding prospective of the entire valley.

He sent a fire team up higher on the wall of the valley to check out three large boulders above where the unit stopped to visually recon the valley.

No sooner had the fire team reached the boulders when, using hand and arm signals, informed the platoon there were enemies coming up the valley on the lower trail.

LT dropped to the ground, as did the entire unit; he then crawled to the edge of the finger so that he could see the enemy. Tau crawled up beside him now; both could see three enemy soldiers.

Two were NVA and wore green uniforms while the other man in the middle wore the typical VC black pajamas; all three had AK 47 assault rifles.

The trail continued along the base of the finger paralleling a small stream which cut out across the valley floor before reaching the edge of the finger. The farmland, no longer being tilled, contained elephant grass about eight feet tall.

LT hoped the three would not try to jump in the grass and hide. He slipped back so he couldn't be seen by the enemy and very softly said, "Bates, you, and Al, move up and take a position with the machine gun."

He turned to the rest of the platoon and said, "Listen up: I am going to get Tau to try to get them to surrender. If they act as if they are going to fight, open up on them." He then gave them a thumbs-up and they returned the same gesture.

He then once more slid to the edge and asked Tau to try and talk them into surrendering. Tau quickly jumped up and in Vietnamese yelled at the three men. The three were startled and froze in their tracks. As Tau talked to them, LT stood up and had the machine gun move up, hoping the men could see there was a force to be dealt with if they did not give up.

The older man in NVA clothing was openly disturbed, the other was slightly quivering, and the VC became more and more appalled as Tau spoke.

Finally, the three looked at each other and simultaneously raised their rifles toward Tau and LT and began firing. Both men dropped to the ground as the Marines fired at the enemy.

The machine gun proved to be overpowering for the three. The VC dropped on the trail, dead. The older NVA stopped firing and leaped into the tall grass, leaving his sidekick alone to fight the Marines.

The NVA on the trail quickly figured he was alone so decided to run up the hill, apparently thinking it was a better choice than the elephant grass. However, he ran right into 3rd squad and was shot.

LT was watching the top of the elephant grass part as the NVA solider ran through it. He calmly turned to Bates and said, "Fire at will."

Bates immediately pointed the gun about three feet in front and about three feet off the ground in front of the fleeing enemy and opened fire, spewing death out across the valley floor, mowing down the elephant grass and the NVA solider.

LT told Corporal Rathbone to take his men down and check the enemy for papers, maps, anything they were carrying.

He then told Corporal Olsen to maintain a perimeter to cover Rathbone and his men. He told Jersey's squad to check on the Marines that went up to the big boulders above them, then he immediately started working up a situation report for Captain McCarthy.

"Do you think you can get the report done before the captain calls you?" Lee inquired.

"Not a chance!" was the immediate answer.

No sooner had he finished his reply to Lee when the radio came alive with "Hotel 1, this Hotel 6, over."

Lee, grinning from ear to ear, handed the radio handset over to LT. He informed the skipper the platoon had three enemy KIAs, no WIAs or any POWs, but had captured three AK-47's and two radios.

The captain was very happy and wanted to see him as soon as he returned to the camp site.

The four Marines who had gone to the side of the mountain returned carrying two radios and several cardboard C-ration shelves used to cover the C-ration boxes. The cardboard shelves had a lot of writing on them.

Tau told LT they were NVA/VC call signs and radio frequencies. Tau quietly said, in Vietnamese then English, "This is very good!"

Rathbone and his men searched the dead soldiers for any information and returned, showing LT the captured material.

As LT started to give the platoon the signal to move out, the radio came alive once more, squawking, "Hotel 1, this is Top Dog 2."

Lee quickly scanned his radio book of call signs and said, "Division Intelligence."

LT took the handset and said, "Top Dog 2, this is Hotel 1." After a few moments he told the caller he understood and would have an LZ set up in time.

He then called the squad leaders up and informed them division wanted the enemies' bodies laid out next to each other and that they were sending out a helo in twenty minutes to pick up the "spoils of war."

Once again Olsen reestablished a perimeter, and Rathbone and his men trekked down the finger to gather up the bodies and lay them out on the trail. They then knocked down the elephant grass and created a temporary LZ.

Sergeant Joe Loerzel glanced over toward LT, then motioned for the squad leaders to join him for a quick meeting. He said, "One of those AK-47 rifles is brand new. Let's strip it down, spread the parts throughout the platoon, and then we can give it to LT for a Christmas present." They all immediately agreed and the weapon parts were passed throughout the platoon.

Soon three Huey Helicopters appeared over the edge of the valley wall and swooped down to the temporary LZ.

A green smoke was popped in the center of the temporary LZ and a single helo landed. The other two helos circled the area with machine guns readied for possible enemy contact.

Without hesitation, a man dressed partially in military clothes and partially in civilian clothing leaped out of the bird, ran up to the three bodies, and snapped pictures of the dead enemy.

He then motioned for the Marines to bring the captured materials to him. He quickly gathered them up then sprang back into the helo, and it shot back into the sunny afternoon sky, leaving as they had arrived, without comment, explanation, or a word of gratitude.

On the platoons arrival back to the company area, Captain McCarthy met LT at the perimeter and enthusiastically congratulated him and his platoon on their military victory. Then, with a serious expression, the skipper said, "Before you brief me, how many rifles did your platoon capture today?"

LT turned to the captain and said, "Three. Why?"

"Well, I got a call from division and they claim there are only two rifles."

LT chuckled and said, "Well, maybe someone on the helo wanted a souvenir."

The skipper shook his head and said, "Yep, probably that's what happened."

LT briefed the captain on what he had found and explained he had some excellent places for ambushes. The far end of the valley was heavy with nightly enemy foot traffic.

Captain Frank McCarthy listened intently and finally said, "Can you plot on the map or describe to someone the exact place to set up this ambush?"

LT thought about it for a moment and then said, "Yes, but I really need to send someone out that was with us today or take it out myself."

Frank grinned and said, "I understand you went out on an ambush your first night with the platoon."

LT said, "Yes, I wanted to see how good the squad leaders were at setting up the ambush sites."

"Well, until I tell you different, you will no longer go out on ambushes, do you understand?"

"Yes, but why? Don't you think it is important that the platoon leaders know if the ambushes sites are being properly set up?"

"Sure, but you can do that right here inside of the perimeter by having each one of them set a mock ambush site, right?"

LT felt once again like a dumb shit and meekly said, "Yes sir."

"Your job is to control the platoon. That means you need to be with the majority of your platoon, not a fire team or a squad but rather the platoon leader. That is the reason you have squad leaders. Do you understand?"

LT swallowed a hard lump in his throat and thought, "How stupid can I be?" He said, "Now that you have painted such a clear and simple picture of my responsibilities, yes, it is very clear, and thank you, sir."

LT trudged back to his platoon area almost in a trance as he thought about the day and what had happened in such a short period of time since he had been in Vietnam. One moment of glory immediately followed by a rookie mistake. Damned if you do and damned if you don't. His final analysis: trying to be a responsible Marine platoon commander was challenging, to say the least.

He took off his pack, helmet, and flak jacket, and leaned them up next to a large rock in his CP area and sat down.

Lee carefully studied the lieutenant and finally, with a somewhat concerned look, said, "Want me to make you some cocoa, tea… or coffee, LT?"

The next morning LT sat leaning on the same rock in his CP after a cup of cocoa and can of ham and eggs, and gazed over the pure white fog which covered about fifty percent of the valley floor. The fog was so pure in color and in such a battlefield-torn nation; shouldn't the fog be pink or even bright red? In the morning quietness, the lieutenant failed to hear or see Captain McCarthy approach the platoon CP. "Morning Geronimo, caught up in your thoughts?"

LT, taken by surprise, attempted hastily to rise. The captain instantly motioned for him to stay where he was.

The captain then sat down next to him and also took in the view of the valley and its display of natural beauty. He glanced over at LT and said, "It's really amazing how beautiful this country is. It doesn't matter if a bloody battle was fought a week ago, yesterday, or an hour ago; it simply stays beautiful."

"Yes, the country and its people look so peaceful, friendly, and inviting. You are right, it really is hard to believe there is a raging war."

They both continued to sit in silence taking in the spectacular view when Lee interrupted them by handing the captain a C-rat can cup of his delicious coffee.

The captain smiled and thanked Lee for the coffee and sipped on it for a few moments then finally said, "I want you to send out a squad ambush to the far end of the valley where you said the giant rocks separate the valley and the trail into the Que Son and Antenna Valleys."

LT jerked his head toward the skipper and said, "Squad ambush! Sir, that trail looked like a damn interstate of foot traffic. A squad would be a suicide mission and I have no intentions of putting my people in that kind of position. Send a platoon, not a squad. A platoon would stand a greater chance of being successful."

The captain's jaws tightened and he glared at LT and said, "Did you not send in a report that stated the site at that place on the map would 'accommodate a *squad-size ambush*'?"

LT, who had risen to his knees to face the captain, slowly lowered his head and meekly said, "Yes, it was, sir."

"And also let me remind you, *lieutenant*, I am in charge of this company, which includes you and your platoon."

They both remained quiet for some time when the captain finally, in a low and somewhat consolatory voice, said, "Before you get my Irish red hair and temper to a boiling point, let me explain something to you. You sent the report in to me; I sent it into battalion. Battalion sent into regiment. Regiment, Colonel Codispoti, ordered the ambush put into place, which the battalion commander passed on to me and I have passed on to you. Do you get the big picture, lieutenant?"

LT gulped and in a low voice said, "It's perfectly clear, sir."

CHAPTER 17
A GOOD FIT

LT walked around the platoon area mostly thinking about what had happened between him and the captain. It was very annoying to him; he didn't want to send out a squad-size ambush. He felt he had messed up with his recommendation and had no alternative.

As he ambled through the area, he suddenly stopped to listen to a discussion going among several of 2nd squad members.

"She has beauty, men will kill for and she will do anything I ask her do. She can hum all night. She never disappoints me."

LT thought, "What the hell is going on here?" and quickly walked into the group and looked at what Lance Corporal Richard "Moe" Sabanos was showing them: a picture of a 1964 black Chevy Corvette.

LT, with great relief, chuckled and quickly attested to the fact "she" was a beauty. Lance Corporal Richard "Moe" Sabanos was about six foot two and well-muscled, not so much from Marine Corps training but more from the fact for his twenty-six years of life he had worked hard with his hands.

He had owned his own full-service gas station where he provided fuel for vehicles and had a full auto mechanics shop. He was the oldest member of the platoon; yes, even older than LT. Moe had been married; however, his marriage ended in a somewhat messy divorce.

Through their influence, his former wife's parents, rather influential in New York, where he was from, had managed to get Moe drafted. He, however, chose to join the Marine Corps. The Marine Corps, unfortunately for Moe, chose to send him to Vietnam. The only thing he was able to salvage from the marriage was the 1964 Corvette, which he doted over.

LT, after a few moments of listening to the squad members kid Moe for having a picture of a car rather than a girl, left the 2nd squad and headed over to 3rd squad.

He wrung his hands. He knew what he had to do; he knew what he and the squad leaders had agreed on back at the railroad dike. He now had to deliver the orders that he detested.

As he turned to go to 3rd squad he saw Lance Corporal Clyde Gillespie coming toward him with someone with him. LT had not seen the individual before and wondered who the person was. Clyde and the new person kiddingly pushed at each other, as if they knew each other.

Clyde looked up and quickly saw LT and said, "Lieutenant Garrett, this is Gary Weston, Doc Weston. He has been assigned to our platoon."

LT quickly studied Doc Weston. He looked to be about fourteen, had no shoulders or hips, looked much like a number 2 pencil, however, instead of a red eraser he had dark black hair stacked high on his head. LT smiled and said, "Welcome to 1st platoon Doc Weston. It appears you two know each other before coming to Nam."

Clyde grinned and said, "That's right. We went to school together back in Alliance Nebraska. I was a year ahead of him and stole his girl friend. However, Gary must have wanted to get even with me because he literally ran over me when he charged off the chopper." Gary chuckled and said, "Yea, and I owe you a lot more…you…you, girlfriend thief."

LT was amused. He once more welcomed Gary to the platoon and asked Clyde to take Gary over to the CP group where Gary would be assigned.

LT, then reluctantly entered the 3rd squad area, where he found the squad leader, Jersey, saying, "Remember you Pukes, if you don't listen and heed what I told you, you'll wake up some morning in some damn gook rice patty dead and rotting, got that?"

As he walked into the 3rd squad meeting, he said, "Well I guess that's about as clear as it can be stated." He then gestured for Jersey to join him. As they walked away from the meeting place he said, "You are going to take out the ambush tonight."

"Sure, I know, we all agreed my squad would take out the ambush this evening, LT."

"Well, listen very closely to what I am going to tell you. Remember when I first joined the platoon? What did I tell you I thought were the two most important things a rifle Marine platoon needed to do in a combat situation?"

Immediately Jersey stated, "First thing was for us to use supporting arms and be squared away on hole-watch, right?"

LT was amazed anyone had listened and actually remembered what he had said. "You are one hundred percent correct. Now look into my eyes, and listen to what I am going to tell you. I am going to send a machine gun team with you; they will be able to show you exactly where I want you to set up your ambush site."

LT looked Jersey in the eyes and slowly said, "Tau, and I, believe the place you are to set up the ambush is a regular highway for the NVA. What I am telling you is to use good judgment as to whether or not to spring the ambush, and to consider, instead, using supporting arms."

He paused a moment as if he was allowing the information to fully soak in like rain into the ground then said, "Additionally, rig up the machine gun so if you have to you can immediately destroy it. Your lives are more important than the gun; I can always get another gun... one way or another."

Peering at Jersey, he asked, "Now, based on what I told you about using your judgment and supporting arms, do you have any questions?"

Jersey thought for a moment and finally said, "Yes, which gun team am I taking?"

"You are going to take Bates and Brown. They know where the ambush site is located."

"LT, you know Bates has never been on an ambush before."

"I know and I know you will take all these very important issues into consideration.

That evening, LT met Jersey and his squad at the company perimeter and said, "Remember your supporting arms."

Jersey went over the call signs and laundry list of equipment: flak jackets, helmets, poncho liners, canteens, ammo magazines, grenades, and the all-important bug juice to keep the damn blood-sucking mosquitoes at bay.

LT looked at the machine gun and said, "What's that?"

Corporal Ray Agula said, "Well, LT, you said if they had to leave the gun you wanted it destroyed. So I took duct tape and wrapped it around the gun and grenade; this way all they have to do is pull the pin on the grenade and run like hell."

LT was truly amazed at what he saw and wondered where they found duct tape and if the grenade would actually explode with that much tape on it.

Jersey told Pizza to lead the squad out. They moved quickly, and quietly, up the valley floor, staying on the left side of the valley. Once at the ambush site, Jersey, without hesitation, moved everyone into place about hundred feet from the worn trail. He took out his compass and sighted on several objects, carefully writing down the information in his small notebook and then called in several pre-planned artillery fires down the trail.

"Bates, you put your gear right here next to me," Jersey said after recording his information. Jersey gave Bates first watch, a very desirable watch as you would have uninterrupted sleep afterwards, providing the ambush wasn't sprung.

Two hell box hand-squeezed detonators were within reach on either side of Jersey for the Claymore directional mines, which when detonated sent hundreds of ball bearings blasting down the trail, tearing through whatever was in their path.

Bates's watch was uneventful, only being disturbed occasionally by illumination rounds shot out of LZ Baldy, lighting up the night sky. Bates passed off the radio handset when his watch was over with. Worn out beyond exhaustion, immediately dropped off and slept soundly.

About 0230 he was abruptly and sharply awakened by one hand on the back of his head and another over his mouth, then he was sat up straight. "Beau coup gooks," Jersey whispered. "Don't move, stay quiet."

A distant illumination round from LZ Baldy burst high in the night sky, bathing the area in a shadowy white magnesium light, clearly exposing the long line of well-equipped NVA Soldiers.

A long line of NVA regulars could be seen moving from left to right on the trail heading into the valley. They were wearing new green uniforms and had high and tight haircuts. They were carrying 51 caliber machine guns, 82mm mortars, and RPG launchers. The riflemen carried new AK47's. It was a new enemy unit recently in from Laos. They were talkative and moving at a fast pace down the valley.

The squad members' hearts were beating like base drums and adrenaline was surging as over two hundred enemy passed by them.

After the enemy passed, Jersey immediately called in a fire mission. Followed by a 105mm round exploding in an air burst over where the NVA had gone. "On target. Fire for effect," Jersey said in a low voice.

Then at least five 105's began firing as fast as they could, walking the rounds down the valley floor toward the mouth of Pagoda Valley. The squad stayed alert, thinking some of the NVA would be driven back toward them, but, by dawn, all was quiet.

The squad saddled up and headed back to the company position, using a route that kept them away from the trail the enemy had used earlier in the morning. Jersey didn't want to take the risk that the enemy might set up their own ambush to get anyone trying to get a body count.

Once back at the company perimeter, the squad met Captain McCarthy, who pulled Jersey off to the side.

About the same time, LT came over the hill from checking his lines and saw Jersey and the captain waving their arms in what appeared to be a heated discussion.

LT quickened his steps; as he neared them, he heard Jersey saying, "Well, I was in charge and you weren't and I did what I was told to do by my platoon leader… CAPTAIN!"

LT walked in between the two and told Jersey to go take care of his men then turned to the captain and said, "Is there a problem with *my* squad leader?"

Captain McCarthy glared at Jersey, then LT, and said, "Who the hell gave you permission to dismiss the squad leader? Yes, lieutenant, there is a problem with *your* squad leader. In my way of thinking, he should have sprung the ambush, and what is this crap about 'doing as my platoon leader told me'?"

Honor Dishonored

LT looked at the captain and smiled his best fake smile and casually said as he turned and looked in the direction of Jersey, "I'm really proud of him, he did exactly what I told him to do. You see, captain, I have instructed all my squad leaders to use their heads and supporting arms. This will allow them to live and fight another day."

Realizing he apparently had the captain's attention he quickly continued saying, "Now you said you would have sprung the ambush. I'm somewhat confused; would you have done it with the front element of the enemy, thus allowing the following one hundred and fifty of them to attack your squad of nine from the left side?

"Or would you have waited until the middle of the unit, allowing seventy-five from two directions attacking you and your nine men?"

"Or maybe waited for the last fifty or so, therefore allowing the reaming one hundred and fifty to attack you from the right side?"

Feeling he was on a roll, LT said, "We all know the NVA do not run and will fight with a drop of a hat; therefore, I think I am being generous when I assume that you would have killed fifty of them before they wiped you out in less than thirty seconds."

Now feeling invincible, the platoon commander surged forth with his last argument by saying, "But wait, there is another option, the option Jersey chose: Wait for the enemy to pass and call an artillery mission on them, which, no doubt, since they fired over fifty artillery rounds, we can assume each round easily killed at least one enemy.

"So, let's see what we have in the final analysis: You kill fifty and you all die; Jersey kills at least fifty and he, and his men live, to fight another day. Did Jersey and I miss something, captain?"

The captain's jaw became even tighter and his red hair became possibly a little more red, it seemed to LT. After a few minutes of complete silence the captain's jaw slowly began to relax and the corner of his lips began to crack in a slight smile. He then said, "Lieutenant, your argument is logical and I commended you on it. And I think you deserve your platoon and in return they deserve you."

The captain started to turn to walk away but stopped and said, "Oh yes, one more thing, asshole: you really have the knack for pissing off people."

LT smiled and walked off toward the company CP. He had a light step, a tremendous amount of satisfaction, and a feeling of victory as he headed to his platoon CP.

Joe, Jersey, Lee, Larry, Al, and Tau had all been watching the events unfold, barely over the hill and mostly hidden from LT and the captain. Once they saw LT heading back to the CP area, they scrambled back to the CP as if they were there the whole time waiting for him to return.

As LT entered the CP, Lee asked, "LT, did he call you Geronimo?"

LT smirked and said, "No, I was called an asshole."

He then glanced over to Jersey, who was sitting with his arms crossed over his chest and still fuming. "Good job Jersey, you did exactly as I wanted you to do. Because of your brilliant thinking the enemy today lost at least fifty soldiers and you and your men live to fight another day."

Jersey quickly looked at the others in the CP group then the lieutenant and said, "Shit LT, the captain said I messed up today. He would have sprung the ambush."

"Yeah, I know but after I explained the entire situation to him he agreed you did the right thing. He also thinks I'm a perfect match for the platoon."

Joe looked questionably at those present and said, "What does that mean, LT?"

"Well, he thinks I'm an asshole, along with you guys, and he said he would never split us up because we deserve each other." The group glanced from one to the other and then broke out in laughter.

CHAPTER 18
THE MONK'S WATER WELL

A few days before Christmas the skipper decided to move the company to a new position. This move started many rumors within the company as to what was in store on Christmas Day. The Marines wanted a hot meal so badly they could taste the turkey. Their mouths watered as they made up stories as to what was going to happen.

The next morning, 1st platoon saddled up and headed for the first of six check points. Between check points two and three LT held up the platoon and formed a quick defensive perimeter.

"All right, listen up, we are not taking care of business today. It's obvious in the manner you are moving. Hell, a damn elephant could walk past you and most of you wouldn't notice it. Focus on this patrol, not on Christmas!"

There was a quick lowering of heads and some mumbling. After a few minutes LT asked, "Well, are we ready to patrol?" There was silence, then they moved, not as a group, but as a single coordinated entity.

He smiled and winked at Lee as he moved to his position in the patrol.

Lee stood up, shifted his heavy pack of radio, batteries, and his personal gear, looked to his left then right, quickly looked at the lieutenant, and gave him a "thumbs up."

Before check point five, Lance Corporal P. K. Rouse, the platoon point, held up his hand to hold the patrol up. The Marines went into an instant defense position ready for battle.

Corporal Rathbone, the squad leader, moved up to LCpl Rouse. Rouse pointed to Lance Corporal Bill (Country) Shellenberger, the right flank. Rathbone went over to Country then motioned for LT to move up to him.

LT silently but quickly moved to the squad leader. In a very low whisper Rathbone said, "Sir, Country thinks he found a buried vat, it may have rice in it."

After much probing and prodding, Country's find turned out to be a clay vat containing about two hundred pounds of unpolished rice. It probably belonged to the local VC or NVA that lived in the mountains because locals had left the valley and no longer farmed in Pagoda Valley.

The platoon was more than prepared for a situation like this as each squad carried empty sandbags and began filling them with the rice.

After collecting the rice, the platoon moved onto their objective and as they moved a safe distance from the buried vat, Lance Corporal Ed Cherry, Jersey's "back door man," dropped an M26 hand-grenade into the vat and ran like hell to catch up to the platoon. The grenade explosion rendered the vat useless.

The platoon moved on to the new position without further incidents. The new defense position was an abandon pagoda. It contained an excellent area for a large landing zone, which further fueled the rumor about Christmas.

Well aware of the buzz about Christmas, the skipper immediately reminded his Marines of past truces during holidays with the NVA and his SOP (Same Old Procedures) about perimeter watch at night. The SOP was simple and smart, and would be enforced to the max.

Should the unit be probed by the enemy at night, no one was to fire a round from their weapon unless they had an excellent target. No recon by fire. This was especially true for the machine guns. If you heard movement or saw movement you were to toss a grenade. It would do more harm than a shot or two and not give your position away.

The company commander's rules were tactically sound and life-saving, and if you failed to follow the rules and lived, you would face the skipper... that could be worse!

Captain McCarthy told his platoon leaders to get their men together, except those on perimeter duty. He gave each platoon leader a time he would be by his sector of the perimeter; he wanted to wish each Marine a Merry Christmas.

LT and Joe assembled the troops. The skipper arrived, told them he was extremely proud of them, wished them a Merry Christmas and then shook their hands. As he was leaving Joe said, "LT, the troops have something they want to give you."

LT stared at Joe then slowly scanned the men, turning back to Joe said, "What do you mean they want to give me something?"

Joe grinned, pointed to the middle of the semi-half circle, where the squad leaders and Ballew were standing out in front of the group. They then pulled a brand new AK47 rifle from behind their backs and handed it to LT.

LT was astonished, and after staring at the rifle for a few moments, he smiled then chuckled and said, "Well I guess the third rifle didn't make it aboard the G-2's helicopter after all."

The men roared with laughter. He repeatedly thanked his men for the present while bursting with pride. Joe explained how the weapon was broken down and that the platoon members had carried the parts in their packs until now.

When the skipper found out about the rifle he was happy for LT, but had the rifle sent to the rear to the battalion commander.

About a quarter of a mile from the new company perimeter was a large active pagoda where several monks lived, and worked. They wore very bright yellow robes, seemed friendly and had an outstanding water well—to the Marines thinking anyway, since most of their water source was from small streams (like the one CWO "Yak, Yak" washed from at the Triple Culvert) and rice paddies (which were fertilized by human waste.)

However, Halazone tablets (iodine water purification tablets) were put into the canteens and shaken up, to purify the water within a few minutes. The tablets would not remove any organic matter in the water (preferably you spit it out) but made it potable; not tasty, simply drinkable.

LT, Ballew, and Doc Smith had barely returned to the platoon CP from making rounds within the platoon area when Captain McCarthy appeared at the entrance of the CP with a big smile and a question. He wanted to know if the platoon still had the rice they had found in Pagoda Valley on the move to the company's new position. LT informed him the rice bags were lying in the corner of the platoon CP.

"Tell me Geronimo, have you met the head monk at the pagoda down the road?" "No sir."

Smiling like a Cheshire Cat, the skipper said, "I hear they have a good water well. Know anything about it?"

"No sir, but I do have someone in the platoon who I bet can answer your questions and a lot more. Corporal Ballew, please get Mr. Inquisitive."

Corporal Ballew looked at Lee, who sat in the corner monitoring the radios with a frown on his face, then suddenly grinned and said, "You mean Lance Corporal Bates?"

"Yes, that is correct. And Corporal Ballew, do *not* tell Bates why I want to see him."

Corporal Ballew chuckled, as did Lee, and he quickly left the CP to find Bates.

The captain turned toward the bags of rice and studied them a moment then started walking out of the CP and said, "Let's stand outside so we don't have to lean over, Geronimo."

In a few minutes Ballew and Bates came running up to the CP. Both stopped short of the where the officers stood and Bates said in a winded voice, "Lance Corporal Bates reporting as ordered, sirs."

LT smiled and said, "Stand at ease. The skipper wants to ask you couple of questions. Please give *short* answers… like maybe… yes, or no."

Bates looked at LT with a bewildering look, and then focused his attention on the skipper.

"Lance Corporal Bates, what do you do in the platoon?"

"Sir, I am a machine-gunner."

LT quickly cut and said, "Yes, Bates graduated number one in his class and should have been promoted at the school. You know, sir, we have talked about his case before."

The captain gave the lieutenant a quick look and held his hand palm up as to say "Stop!" Without looking at Bates, but staring at LT, he said, "Yes, I remember and we are working on it. Now back to my questions." Still looking at LT, he said, "So tell me, Lance Corporal Bates, have you met the head monk down at the pagoda?"

Bates' eyes danced back and forth from the captain to the lieutenant and finally he said, "Well... I uh... well maybe... met the head man... not for sure... I."

LT took a deep breath, turned to Bates and folded his arms on his chest, and said, "Bates, short, honest answers!"

"Yes sir, I have met the head monk. He speaks French and a little English. He has fifteen other monks that work in the pagoda."

LT once more took a deep breath. Bates stopped talking and focused on the captain.

The captain grinned and said, "I hear they have a water well with really good water. Know anything about that?"

Bates once more allowed his eyes to glance from the captain to the lieutenant and finally said, "Yes sir, I was ordered to go on a water run and got water from the well." Turning toward Ballew Bates, he blurted out, "Ballew has been down there too!"

Ballew quickly dropped his smile and gave Bates a dirty look.

Bates turned to Lee and slowly said, "And others from the platoon have gotten water there."

The skipper chuckled, looking at Ballew then LT and finally at Bates and said, "Great! Think the head monk would allow us to get water from the well?"

Bates remained silent a moment, trying to figure how to answer the question and not get into any more, what he perceived to be, hot water. Bates slowly and carefully said, "I am sure he would let us get water from the well, sir."

"Super! Lieutenant, could you put together a detail of your men to take the rice down to the pagoda? And make them look like a real Marine unit. You know, maybe if they could somewhat dress alike and, yes, I know we are the Horrible Hogs, but try, okay?"

"Yes sir. If the damn supply worked and we could get clothes and such it would really help. I notice they never have any problems getting us ammo or bags to fly out captured rice... and..."

Once again the skipper's hand went up as he chuckled and walked away saying, "Have the detail at my CP in fifteen minutes."

LT frowned, kicked the dirt, and said, "Damn it! I hate it when he does that damn hand thing."

He walked over to where the rest of the Marines were standing and with a sigh said, "Okay, Ballew, you, along with three men, one from each squad, go to hump rice, and a radio operator from one of the squads and Frenchy in case we need an interpreter, better yet Tau, if you can find him."

"Be sure they are dressed like Marines, rifles, full mags, helmets, armored vest, even if you have to take clothing and gear from members within the squads."

Then with a big smile and a low chuckle, he turned to Bates and said, "Bates, get a rifle and ammo, you are going too!"

Bates quickly scrambled off. LT smiled and under his breath said, "Mr. Inquisitive."

In a few minutes Corporal Ballew returned to the CP with his Marine detail. LT was truly impressed with how good the uniforms looked. His troops never stopped amazing him as to what they could do under such primitive conditions.

"Damn Ballew! Did you have to rob the entire company to get those uniforms?"

"No sir, only 1st platoon. We kept it in-house."

LT chuckled and said, "Great job. Okay, listen up men. Ballew and Bates will go first followed by the captain, Tau and me, then the rice humpers, followed by the last two as rear guards. Rifles slung on the left shoulder. Rice humpers carry the rice bag on your right shoulder. We well be in a route march. Any questions?"

With no questions asked, the Marine "diplomat detail" marched off to pick up the captain to head on down to the pagoda.

The senior monk, a small elderly man with a very big smile and dressed in a bright, almost dazzling yellow robe had two monks flanking him, and met the Marine detail in front of the pagoda. It was as if somehow the monk knew of the Marines coming long before they had arrived and had set up a welcoming group.

Bates made introductions. Tau proved to be of little value because the senior monk spoke rather "respectful" English. The senior monk was happy with the gift of rice and, in return, to the captain's surprise, offered the Marines water from his well.

Captain McCarthy gleamed with joy and satisfaction as the detail returned to the Marines position.

The platoons took turns sending details down to draw water from the monks' well. The water, tested by the corpsman, proved to be pure and was greatly appreciated by the Marines. Canteens of water gathered from the small streams and rice patties were immediately dumped, cleaned out, and filled with the cool well water. This water did not taste like Halazone tablets nor did it contain foreign objects to be spit out. It was cool, smooth, and delicious!

CHAPTER 19
A CHRISTMAS TRUCE

Lee handed the radio hand set to LT and informed him the rear wanted to talk to him. He hesitatingly took the hand set and with a very brief, three words of, "Yes, understand, out," handed the hand set back to Lee and walked out of the CP looking for Joe.

"Joe, need for you to get Bates, Brown, and their gun up here, and one more thing, get Pizza and his fire team up here to. I'll fill you in later."

Once everyone was assembled, he explained the gun team and Pizza's fire team were going to conduct a test. They were to move on to a small knoll down from the company perimeter; the gun and themselves were to be camouflaged so no one in the helo could spot them.

As the group moved out Joe walked over to LT and said, "So, what's really going on?"

LT quickly scanned the area making sure no one else could hear him. "NCS is on their way out here. They think a stolen machine gun could be out here." Pausing a few moments, he then said, "Joe, I don't want anyone talking to NCS. If they do have to talk to them, no one mention the second machine gun."

NCS Agent Forest Walker landed and was met by the skipper. The skipper took him from platoon to platoon. Upon arrival at first platoon, proper introductions were made and then the captain had to leave to take a radio call from battalion.

LT was relieved the CO left, because he was not sure how the machine gun was obtained and therefore felt more comfortable talking to the NCS agent.

Agent Walker was a tall, barrel-chested, good-humored man. LT instantly liked him even though he was conducting an investigation, looking for the very machine gun he was hiding. The two snaked through the platoon area. Agent Walker, not missing much, finally said, "Hey, thanks, lieutenant. I really appreciate your time. I hear the chopper coming back and I don't want to miss it."

Agent Walker raced down to the LZ, making it as the helo touched down. As he jumped aboard LT thought, "That could have been close, if not the warning from the rear. I hope it's the last time an agent comes out here."

That evening the captain called the platoon commanders together and informed them that the local VC commander was very unhappy with the monks who allowed the Marines to get water from the well. The VC commander did not want to put his popularity up against the senior monk in the pagoda; therefore, he decided it would be better to attack the Marines.

The troops were to be extremely alert and follow the Marine Corps SOP on night defense to the letter. However, the good news was the company would be getting a big Christmas dinner the next day, much to all of their delight.

It was about 0340 in the morning when LT returned to the platoon CP after checking the lines. Lee and Ballew were both sacked out right outside of the CP. He stuck his head under the cover over the CP and in the darkness could make out a figure through the tiny amount of green light put out by the radios. It was Joe.

"Joe."

"Yes sir, anything going on out there tonight?"

He took a deep breath and said, "Yep, I don't think the local VC commander is as brave as he indicated though. There is some movement out there, mostly probing. Don't think there will be any attacks. Go ahead get some sleep, I'll take over the radio."

Joe didn't say anything for a few moments then said, "LT, are you sure you want to finish the watch?"

"Sure, I am awake and can't sleep so one of us might as well get a little siesta and besides it's going to be light in an hour or so."

Joe mumbled a "Thanks" and crawled out of the CP to his sleeping bag.

LT did a quick radio check and began searching in the dark for a place to sit somewhat comfortable when suddenly a loud explosion broke the night silence.

He quickly leaped from the CP and headed toward where the explosion had come from. As he neared one of the machine gun positions, he knew from recently making the rounds that Bates was on duty here. "Bates… Bates are you all right?"

Bates responded in a shaky voice. "Yes sir, it scared the crap out of me though."

He smiled, mostly to know Bates was okay and asked, "What happened?"

"I think a chicom was thrown into the perimeter, probably trying to hit the gun. It went off about thirty or forty feet over there to my left."

He started to go where Bates had indicated when two more explosions occurred about a hundred feet to his right. He quickly changed directions and ran towards where the new sound had come from. Nearing the position, he heard the sound of someone else coming toward him and he stopped and said, "Who's there?"

The skipper in a low voice said, "It's the skipper. That you, Geronimo?"

"Yes sir, I think the last explosion came from one of the positions in front of us." He then slid over to a position in front of him and asked Speedy if he had thrown a grenade. Speedy told him he had not, but thought it came from 1st squad's position from his right, Country's fighting hole.

Lance Corporal Bill (Country) Shellenberger was a "Missouri country boy" and an excellent Marine, honest as the day was long.

As LT and the captain slid over to his position, Country immediately said in a nervous voice, "I threw the two grenades because they threw something at me and hit me in the chest."

The two officers looked at each other and the skipper said, "Where is the thing they threw at you?"

Country turned his head to the left then right and said, "I guess down in my hole because it hit me then fell down."

The captain told Country to get out of the hole and then slid into it and turned on a small flash light with a red lens (red lens would not let the light be seen at any distances or put off light from the hole) and after taking Country's pack from the hole, the only thing left was a single C-ration can of pound cake.

The captain and LT left the area together and on the way back to their CP's, the captain stopped him and said, "What kind of Marine is Country?"

He turned to the captain and said, "Skipper, he is as solid as gold. He always carries out his duties, is extremely responsible, honest, and most reliable."

"So you believe someone actually threw something at him?"

"If Country says someone threw something at him, then they did."

"Okay, then I think one of his buddies was screwing with him and threw a rock or something at him and hit him."

LT was quite for a few moments then said, "Did you find a rock in the bottom of his hole?"

"No! But I did find a can of pound cake."

"You really think a Marine would throw a can of pound cake away? Hell skipper, pound cake and peaches are like having a Christmas present every time you get it in a resupply... no way!"

The morning light was barely starting to glow over the land. LT walked over to the area where the first explosion had accrued and in the dim light he found several strips of shiny metal pieces. Picking one up, he found a piece of what appeared to be a side of quart-sized can.

On the piece he had picked up was stamped "Pineapple Juice." It was a USA can used in the mess halls in the rear. Apparently, the VC had acquired the can and made a chicom grenade then threw it into the perimeter, hoping to hit the machine gun.

Today was Christmas, and the battalion promised hot chow for the company. Some of the Marines had not eaten yesterday's dinner or the morning's meal of C-Rats, so they could stuff themselves with turkey and all the trimmings.

The captain called the officers up and told them he did not trust the Truce Fire and wanted the officers to ensure their troops did not let their guard down during the meals and church services. A priest would be coming out around 1000 hours.

LT, returning from the meeting, was stopped by Country. "What's up, Country?"

Country handed the pound cake can to LT and said, "Sir, look what I found this morning, when I went to open this can."

He inspected the can and instantly noticed when he turned it over the bottom of the can had been soldered shut. "So, this is can that hit you in the chest last night and fell into your hole?"

"Yes sir."

"Thanks Country. I need to take this over to the captain and show him."

As he approached the CO he said, "Skipper, remember the pound cake incident last night?"

The captain nodded and reached out and took the can LT handed him.

"Look on the bottom. I also found part of a large pineapple can in the area where the blast came from last night."

"So, your men were not screwing around with each other last night. I bet we get hit today and, if not, we damn sure will tonight. I am going to put the company on fifty percent alert starting right now. Damn truce is a bunch of crap!"

LT hurried back to his platoon and had a quick meeting with the squad leaders and informed them of the current situation. Jersey was not at the meeting; Pizza was the acting squad leader now. Jersey was at the Bob Hope Christmas Show. He'd had the "Thousand Mile Stare," which was not uncommon for those near the end of their tour. Everyone knew if LT told Jersey to go to the show he would put up a big fight. So a plan had been drawn up to trick Jersey into going.

Pizza had worked out a scheme with the other squad members to insure Jersey's name was drawn from a hat, the name drawn goes to the show: each man in the squad wrote Jersey's name instead of their own on the slips.

Now, Jersey was back in the rear enjoying the show.

About eleven helos arrived with the vats of hot food: turkey, mashed potatoes, gravy, stuffing, and the usual green beans.

The company gunny quickly established a serving line. The troops, in shifts, moved from their fighting holes, through the line, then back to their positions.

The only problem with this fine Christmas meal was it sat on an LZ for hours and when it got to the company it had spoiled and poisoned many of the troops. So the meal was immediately suspended and the food dumped.

The chaplain and his aid arrived by helo about forty minutes later. He immediately set about setting up a place for his services. His aid had just finished setting the pulpit up and the priest began laying out his notes on the pulpit when all hell broke loose.

Enemy machine gunfire, small arms, motors, and rockets bombarded the company area. The NVA charged the north side of the company perimeter, 3rd platoon's area, only to be met head-on by a wall of small arms, machine gun fire, and laws, stopping the attack before it really had a chance to succeed.

However, the chaplain lost no momentum; when the firing started he immediately conducted his own "one man onslaught" toward the helo, which the crew was trying desperately to get airborne.

The chaplain managed to cover the distance in record time and leaped into the bird before it completely lifted off, much to the surprise of the crew chief. In his haste, he left behind his conscious objector aid to fend for himself, and all of his equipment.

The 1st platoon CP was behind a single adobe wall, about six feet tall, probably once a small building with three-foot-piled rock fences running about ten feet both ways from the wall. The wall had two small one-by-two-foot slit windows and LT was using the windows to see and control his men.

Billy Baker, the machine gunner, was about twenty feet in front of the wall. LT was desperately trying to locate a sniper in the trees somewhere in front of Billy. Finally the lieutenant saw the muzzle flash in the trees slightly to the right and about half way up in the trees and yelled, "CRUZ... CRUZ!"

Ed Cruz, the assistant gunner, quickly turned to him and hollered, "What, LT?"

"TELL BILLY ONE O'CLOCK, HALF WAY UP THE TREE, SNIPER, GET THE BASTARD!"

Ed tapped Billy on the shoulder and leaned into him and relayed the message.

Billy turned towards LT grinning, then nodded, turned back and screamed his normal response to most everything, "THIS IS THE REAL DEAL!" and began spraying the area with a torrent of hot lead, turning the M-60 machine gun's barrel a cherry red.

All eyes were on the area being blasted by the machine gun. Billy, and the gun, had done their job, the sniper remained silent.

LT once more yelled at Billy, "HOW ARE YOU FIXED ON AMMO?"

Billy and Ed, almost perfectly in sync, yelled, "NEED AMMO!"

LT turned and began searching the CP area for more ammo. There, next to the wall, were four cans of machine gun ammo.

Louis Lujan came charging into the platoon CP area with the chaplain's aid in tow. "Sir, need to leave the aid with you, we don't have cover for him at our position."

LT looked at the aid, a tall, lanky, long-faced young man with eyes wide open and very nervous.

"What's your name?"

"Lance Corporal Peter Pure, sir."

"You have a rifle?"

"No sir, I'm a conscientious objector. But I'll help in any way I can, sir!"

LT looked at Louis, then glanced around at Joe, Doc, and Lee, then back to Louis and said, "Thanks Louis! Better get back to your squad."

Louis chuckled and gladly ran back to his position.

LT once more gazed at the aid and started to say something when Al Brown, Bates' assistant gunner, came running around the end of the rock fence and into the CP area.

Joe quickly said, "You after the gun ammo?"

Breathing hard, Al said, "Yes, sergeant."

Joe, pointing to the ammo, motioned for Al to grab a couple of cans of ammo as he picked two up himself.

LT held up his hands, and said, "STOP!" Everyone in the CP froze and stared at him. He turned to Lance Corporal Pure and said, "You said you want to help, right?"

"Yes sir!"

"Okay, I don't really know if I should ask or, order, you to do something. There are so many damn rules and regulations we have to deal within this war. Not that the other side is held to any standards. However, let me ask you, would you mind helping Al take those cans of ammo to the gun position?"

"No sir, I'd be happy to help him!"

LT turned to Joe and motioned for him to hand the cans to the chaplain's abandoned aid.

Joe hesitantly handed the cans to the aid.

Al looked at the aid, smiled, and said, "Well, come on, follow me." Both young men ran out of the CP in a single file to the gun position.

LT, grinning from ear to ear and looking at everyone in the CP, said, "Another problem solved by a command decision."

With a frown Joe said, "Yea, if the conscientious objector doesn't get killed."

LT's smile quickly turned to a frown and he said, "Oh shit!"

In the meantime, Jersey had returned to the platoon during the NVA attack. He seemed refreshed, eager to jump back in the saddle.

After the battle ceased, Captain McCarthy tore into the regimental staff because they refused to allow him to call in any additional fire missions or pursue the enemy due to the "Truce. He was one really pissed off company commander.

The chaplain's helo came back that afternoon, to pick up the aid. The company received new orders... move to LZ Ross for steak and beer. Most considered this a consolation prize for the total disaster—a poisonous Christmas meal and the fact that Hotel Company was the only American Forces to come under attack on Christmas.

LT looked toward Round Top, the main hill in Pagoda Valley. He thought of all the events that had happened with his Marines in the valley. The fog was starting to form once more in the early morning light, as, apparently, it did every morning. He once again noticed the fog was not red or even pink but pure white.

Pagoda Valley was a beautiful place and the monks had chosen a very special, and no doubt at one time a very serene place to build their pagodas. He smiled and thought the valley had been good to 1st platoon. No marines lost!

CHAPTER 20
ANTENNA VALLEY

The company was sent to LZ Ross, the battalion headquarters. After Pagoda Valley for hot meals, showers, and resupply, new orders sent the company to Antenna Valley. The entry into the valley was about six clicks west of LZ Ross.

The company marched tactically out of LZ Ross across Que Son Valley for about six clicks to the narrow gap which led into Antenna Valley. The gap was approximately four clicks long, with a trail only few hundred feet wide in most places, which separated the Que Son Mountains. The sides of the gap were extremely steep. On the right, at the top of the mountain, was 953, the highest point in I Corps. To the left, about three to four clicks up into the mountain, lay LZ Ryder, a Marine Corps artillery fire support base.

Antenna Valley was a long, narrow, V-shaped valley, the head or point of the V faced the gap and LZ Ross. Both sides of the valley rose steeply up into the Que Son Mountains. Running at the foot of the valley, vertical to the foot of the valley, was the Song Tranh River. The town of Hiep Duc was also built along the river's banks. The valley was home to some of the oldest and most beautiful pagodas in Vietnam.

Bright and early, the company left LZ Ross and started the trek to Antenna Valley. Once again 1st platoon led out. A few clicks out of Ross, in a tree, rested a tail of a Huey Helicopter with a US Army First Calvary logo painted on its side. Barely past the Huey, also in the tree, were the remains of several US Army tanks. All had large holes in and through them. The helicopter tail and tanks were all reminders to the Marines that this war was deadly, destructive, and still being fought.

The North Vietnamese had very good intelligence and were rarely surprised by the American forces field operations.

About two clicks out of Ross, 1st platoon was greeted by a new sign, attached to a bamboo pole, barely off the trail by the "tank graveyard." The sign was a cardboard sign made from a C-ration carton shelve with white hand painted words, "Hotel, you are all dead men." Word was passed back by LT, "Do not touch the sign."

LT realized the sign could be booby-trapped and also thought it could be considered a souvenir by a couple of his men and not worth the risk. He quickly glanced back toward Bates. Sure enough, Bates started making a beeline for the sign when LT yelled, "Bates, stay away from that damn sign and get back in formation!"

As the company moved through the gap into Antenna Valley everyone was on full alert. The steep walls of the corridor allowed for the enemy to have fire superiority and the Marines would have an extremely hard and surely deadly climb to make meaningful contact. However, much to everyone's surprise and delight, the enemy chose not to or failed to realize the opportunity.

Soon after the company reached their predetermined destination, which cleared the gap, Captain McCarthy set up a company perimeter. He called his officers together and told them they would be working the valley only four days, maybe a week at the most. The company was to patrol down the valley toward the river, then swing left. He did not know if the company was to walk out of the valley to the south then east, back up into Que Son Valley, or if they would be picked up by helo and put down somewhere else.

Captain McCarthy called up LT and told him to run a reconnaissance patrol along the right side of the valley. The patrol moved off the relative coolness of the hill the company occupied. However, very quickly they found themselves in very dense vegetation. The trail made a series of S turns until the unit searched an area of long-abandoned rice paddies. The rice paddies were now over-grown in elephant grass standing eight feet tall on either side of the paddy dikes.

The point motioned he had something he wanted LT to see. He carefully moved up to where the point was standing and pointing. About a hundred feet down the rice paddy dike was a five-hundred-pound bomb standing straight up, resting on its tail section. He immediately saw that the bomb was fire scorched and the fuse was missing. The enemy had heated the bomb, enabling them to remove its explosives. From the explosives, they made booby traps and hand grenades.

The bomb proved to be inert and not booby trapped, so the Platoon moved on. About twenty minutes down the trail LT called a halt and a perimeter was formed. He thought the platoon had gone far enough out and started plotting a return route when he suddenly saw something move in the grass.

In a couple of seconds, he realized the movement was caused by a very large snake. Looking over at Bates, he whispered, "Bates, look at that." He pointed down the trail about fifteen feet.

Bates stared at the snake and finally, with a great amount of authority, said, "LT, that's a reticulated python. Its coloring is perfect, dark brown with black diamond-edged markings with gray inside them. Shit LT, that thing's a good twenty feet long and look at its girth. It's as big around as a volley ball… you want me to shoot it?"

"Hell no, Bates, I merely wanted you to see it. He's big enough to swallow a gook, so leave him alone. Besides he is not wearing an NVA uniform, he's free to go."

The platoon returned to where the company had stopped. Not far away was what could only be described as a beautiful waterfall. The waterfall fed a small stream which snaked down the middle of the valley to the river. After a long march, the entire company was in need of a water resupply and 1st platoon was no exception.

Joe organized a water run and as he started to leave the platoon CP to prepare for the working party, he hesitated a moment, turned to LT, and asked, "Is Bates off limits?"

Questionably LT looked up at Joe and asked, "No… why did you ask that?" Then thinking real quick and suddenly realizing Joe was going to let Bates know his indiscretion over the sign was not going unpunished, he chuckled and said, "No… no he isn't."

Joe found Al Brown and Bates putting their machine gun together, which they had barely finished cleaning. Joe looked at Bates and said, "Bates, you are on the water run. Get your men's canteens and catch the guys going on the run, they are leaving now."

Bates hastily pushed the last part in the gun and told Al to grab his canteens, along with the rest of the crew. By the time Bates had reached the place where they were to depart, the others had already left. He hurried to catch up. Scurrying down the established trail, leading through the elephant grass to the bamboo thicket, he found the stream. However, no one else was there. In his haste to catch the group he had forgotten never use the same route more than once, to avoid ambushes.

Bates quietly and very nervously filled the canteens, well aware of his vulnerability. Once the canteens were filled he carefully and with some procrastination reversed his steps back to the company lines. As he approached the perimeter he softly called out to those on guard duty, trying to ensure he would not be shot.

Flushed, Bates dropped the string of canteens at Al's side. Al looked up and then scanned the area and said, "Wow, you left last and are the first one to return. How did you manage that?"

Bates took a deep breath and, trying to be very convincing, said, "Well we decided to split up, the water run was to big of a group."

Al grinned, stared at Bates, and said, "Got lost, didn't you?"

Bates slammed his body down next to Al and, shrieked, "Yes... I was scared shitless!"

Bates and Al sat in silence for a while. Finally, Bates leaning in toward Al and flickering his eyes around, making sure no one else could hear him, said, "This happened once before, I became separated. When I first joined the platoon and hadn't got the machine gun yet. LT would move me from squad to squad, you know, balancing out the sizes of the squads. Anyway, I was in Olsen's squad and was Tail End Charley. You know it's almost as dangerous as walking point. You have to stop at intervals and take the time to make sure no one is following you."

Bates paused, took a swig of water from his canteen, and continued, "A new guy had the spot ahead of me and he was supposed to not lose sight of me. We were in some very heavy cover and the trail came to a fork. I couldn't see any clear footprints but I could tell by the scuffed dirt, people had taken the left fork. As I hurried down the trail I came to a slightly muddy spot in the trail and I could clearly see out lines of shoe marks with tire tread marks in them, a sure sign of Ho Chi Minh sandals."

Bates took off his cover, wiped his brow, and softly said, "I quietly backed down the trail back to the fork and waited. I was pretty scared then too. In about five minutes I heard Olsen softly calling my name. Shit, was I ever relieved and never so happy to hear his voice. He came over and patted me on the shoulder. The new man was right behind him and had a swollen lip."

Al frowned and said, "Who was that guy anyway?"

Bates thought for a moment and finally said, "You know, I really don't remember his name. He wasn't with us very long. We did call him Speedy's brother. He was in Speedy's fire team. Speedy called him three fingers, because he was missing the trigger finger on his right hand. He wore a K-bar on his back over his right shoulder and a bush hat with the sides turned up, like a cowboy hat. He had thick glasses, thick black plastic rims and always, always a blank stare."

Al scratched his head and said, "I kind of remember him, but I can't think of what happened to him?"

Bates chuckled and said, "Well we were in the middle of a firefight with the NVA and Three Fingers jumped to his feet and started waving his arms and yelling for the enemy to shoot him. Speedy tackled him and laid on him to restrain him until the shooting stopped. He was medevaced and we never saw or heard from him again."

The company settled in for the night. The entire company was nervous; they weren't sent out to Antenna Valley because it was safe and quiet. Around two o'clock in the morning an enemy 82mm mortar could be heard pumping out rounds in the not too far distance. Shortly after, the sirens at LZ Ross could be heard sounding the incoming alarm.

After a dozen rounds had been dropped by the NVA, the Marines figured the enemy would be quickly packing up shop and running. Immediately, though, the sharp sounds of explosions erupted from the area the enemy tubes had been working. About fourteen more rumblings explosions rapidly followed.

Around the company's perimeter, a rolling echo of "counter battery fire" could be heard.

At the far end of LZ Ross, on a small knoll, was a radar unit. A modest bunker sat next to it. Inside the bunker Marines had tracked the incoming rounds and determined the location of the enemy mortars. The coordinates were swiftly relayed to the Marines 81mm mortar crew. They immediately adjusted their mortars to the proper calculations and began dropping 81's high explosive rounds on the enemy.

All was quiet after the last volley of friendly mortar fire.

The next morning LT was called to the company CP. The skipper met him at the edge of the CP, handing him a piece of paper and smiling said, "Want to take your platoon on a stroll and see how effective the 81's were last night?"

LT studied the paper showing the grid coordinates the 81's had targeted. He pulled his map from his pocket, opened it, and found the location on his map. "Sure. I guess you want a simple investigation, to see what we can find?"

"That's actually what battalion wants."

LT marked his map, folded it, and put it back into his pocket and casually said, "And are you going to remain here or are you going to move the company?"

The captain thought for a minute and finally said, "The company will stay here for now. Let's see how long you will be and what battalion may have to say once you report back."

LT hesitated and then said, "Since the company is staying here I think a squad with a gun should be enough and it will be faster than taking the entire platoon."

Captain McCarthy agreed and told him to take whatever he thought best.

He tasked 2nd squad, Bates' gun and himself to go out to investigate the site.

They cautiously moved to the location given by battalion. It was a grassy area surrounded by brush with a circular depression made by the mortar base plate. Scattered around the area were increment propellant charges and cardboard tubes with Chinese writing stenciled on them.

More importantly, though, the area was pock marked with craters the size of garbage can lids. Brown stains on the ground and torn open battle dressings revealed an excellent counter battery fire. There were no bodies. The NVA, if at all possible, always removed their dead. They did not want the American forces to know how effective they were.

At the far end of the position Bates saw an opening in the ground. Closer examination revealed a bunker covered by corrugated metal, with dirt piled on the steel.

Speedy hurried over to LT and said, "Let me have your pistol and I will climb into the bunker."

He looked at Speedy and asked, "You sure you want to climb in there?"

Speedy drew his one hundred and twenty-five pounds up and in a very dignified manner acclaimed, "I am a Mex-Tex Marine and I can do anything!"

LT jerked his head back, smiled, and said, "Yes, Lance Corporal Albert Speedy Gonzales, I do believe you can too." He then, with a serious expression, handed Speedy his 45 pistol and Marine flashlight and said, "Two things. First, use ear plugs. Second, shoot and ask questions later. I don't want you coming out deaf or dead… got it?"

Speedy grinned, grabbed the light and pistol, and immediately lowered himself on his stomach and inched his way into the bunker. His light revealed the bunker floor was covered with ammo belts for the RPD machine gun, the staple machine gun of the North Vietnamese.

Speedy exited the bunker, grabbed the ammo belts, and dropped them near the mortar base plate then glanced at LT said, "That's it. It sure looks like the gooks got a nasty surprise last night."

LT scanned the area, noticing the brown spots, bandages, depressions of the base plates in the ground along with the spent cartridges and said, "Yea, pay back is a bitch."

His reinforced squad returned to the company location. The report was made and then sent to battalion. The skipper then decided to move the company down the valley, to what he considered a better defendable position.

The company moved north about two and half clicks to a new hill. The captain assigned the platoons sections of the new perimeter. These positions did in fact provide superior and decisive defensive locations should an attack come from the north, west, and south, but not the east.

LT scrutinized the terrain from his location to the base of the mountain. The land was flat, mostly open for about three hundred meters, then quickly rose sharply into the Que Son Mountains. He once more looked up at the mountains and wondered how long it would take the morning sun to reach his section of the perimeter.

He walked back up the hill a few feet to a rock which resembled a large loaf of bread. It was about three feet high by eight feet long and four feet wide. He turned and sat down on the rock and began studying the terrain for the best possible avenues the enemy might use to attack the company's position.

The skipper, who had been walking around checking the perimeter, stopped and sat down next to him and said, "So, Geronimo, how do you like your panoramic view?"

LT chuckled said, "Well, the first few hundred meters are great, but the rest of it into the thick bushy mountain side is not so pretty. I did notice the other platoons have a much better panoramic view."

The skipper, smiling, said, "Yea, but the other two platoons don't have mortars or machine gun teams. Think your boys are up to defending this side of the perimeter?"

He laughed and said, "And you say that after what we did in the contest in Pagoda Valley… come on skipper, of all the people, you know we are more than ready."

Laughing, the skipper started walking away and over his shoulder yelled, "Get me your machine gun positions and mortar pre-planned fires in an hour."

LT got with Corporal Ray Agula and worked out the pre-planned fires and gun positions. He left Ray to get the mortars set up and reported to the captain. He then set out to position the guns so they could better support the perimeter.

Ed Cruz and Billy Baker were assigned a position on the left one-third of the platoon perimeter. They had a small crevasse to cover plus some bushy area.

LT found Larry Bates and Al Brown on the right side of the platoon and delegated them a large gap cut into the hillside leading straight into the perimeter of the platoon's area of responsibility.

After assigning Bates and Brown the place he wanted them to build their machine gun defensive position, he hurried down to Jersey's squad. He explained to Jersey he needed one of his men to help support the gun team and returned with Bob Wolf.

Lance Corporal Bob Wolf was from Texas, intelligent, friendly, quiet, steady, and as solid as a twenty-dollar gold piece. He had mastered the ability to locate his position on a map, along with enemy positions, and call in supporting arms.

LT took Bob up next to Bates' gun position and said, "Bob, I want you to put yourself right here and act as an observer to shoot any sniper that may try to knock out Larry's gun. If you can't get them with your rifle, call in a mortar fire mission, verbally, to Corporal Agula right up there." He pointed to Ray about twenty feet over and above the position.

Bates walked up to LT and Bob and said, "LT, you want to hear something stranger than fiction about Bob and me?"

LT, looking at Bates while he was talking, glanced over at Bob, who was shaking his head up and down. Turning back to Bates, he hesitated a moment, smiled, and said, "Sure," not knowing what Bates was about to tell him.

Bates drew a deep breath then said, "What I am about to tell you is true, and Bob and I can prove it. About a month ago you sat Bob next to the gun, like you are doing now, and we got to talking."

Bob, normally a very quiet person, jumped the conversation by saying, "I told Larry my father was in the Navy during World War II and was a POW in a Japanese prison."

Bates, agreeing, then said, "Well, I told Bob my father was in the big war, too, and also was a POW in a Jap prison. He was in Manchuria China, a place called the "Mugden Hotel."

Bob, becoming more emotional and excitable, raised his voice and quickly said, "My father and Larry's father were good friends at the prison."

LT, rather amazed at what he had heard, said, "So, you are telling me both of your fathers were in World War II, both prisoners at the same time in Manchuria, and they were good friends while POWs?"

Bates, grinning from ear to ear, said, "Yes! My dad made a cribbage board in the prison machine shop and our fathers played cards almost every night. And we have the letters our dads sent verifying all this."

LT thought for a moment then said, "I find this truly astonishing. I mean you two grew up halfway across the United States from each other, one not knowing the other. You both are the same service, same unit, standing side by side and fighting in Vietnam. You are paralleling your fathers' life stories… almost implausible. You're right Bates, truth is stranger than fiction."

He left Larry and Bob to check his lines, still thinking of what a fantastic story he had heard a moment ago. He walked a little way, stopped, and thought he must focus on his section of the company perimeter and check with the skipper and find out what was on the agenda for tomorrow.

The captain had a new mission for the platoon the next morning. The company was to cross over to the west side of the valley and sweep around Hill 309, past Thach Bich then east back toward Que Son Valley. 1st platoon would remain on the company's right side, across the valley during the operation.

CHAPTER 21
OUT NUMBERED

It was a bright, sunny, beautiful day. The temperature was not overly hot and the air was much drier. Early January the monsoon rains had dropped from around twenty-two inches of rain to about five a month. The terrain was open with knee-high grass, small bushes, and trees scattered here and there.

LT felt good about the sweep. He was proud his platoon was selected to work alone on the flank. He had his entire platoon with him. It was not an overly taxing route, hopefully allowing for a more relaxed atmosphere.

The platoon had been operating for about an hour or so and had not made any enemy contact and he began to think this was going to be a nice, uneventful operation.

The platoon was about two clicks from the rest of the company and was patrolling between Hill 309 and the Song Tranh River. There was a hill which was shaped like a pork chop; the side the platoon was passing by was steep. The top of the hill sloped down on the other side to a small stream, which paralleled a line of trees.

Abruptly, without any warning, LT stopped the platoon, looked up into the sky, and spotted an OV10 spotter plane. He yelled into the hand set, "SAY AGAIN, HOSTAGE JIM!"

Swiftly, he jerked his head in the direction of the hill top. His face became very serious and in a bellowing voice he yelled, "SPREAD OUT ON LINE. DROP YOUR PACKS. ON MY COMMAND DOUBLE TIME TO THE CREST OF THIS HILL."

In a matter of seconds, the platoon was on line and the signal to charge was given. About a hundred yards up the hill, LT glanced to his right and left he could see a perfect alignment as the platoon attacked up the hill.

About halfway up the hill, LT grabbed the radio hand set and suddenly stopped and screamed, "STOP, STOP! GET DOWN. DOWN ALL THE WAY!" He watched, from the middle of the line as each of his Marines on both side of him went down on their knees.

Then, speaking into the hand set, he said loudly, "Understand, I'm the mark!"

He then turned around and looked back over the valley. Coming toward him was an Air Force F105 jet. The jet was level with his eyes. He could see the white helmet and large black goggles over the pilot's face. The pilot looked like an alien bearing down on him and his platoon.

Without warning, flashes of what appeared to be large sparks sprang from the undersides of the two wings and belly of the plane. Quickly following the "sparks" was the roar of machine gun fire.

The troops began jumping up and down, screaming and yelling, thinking the pilot had mistaken them for the enemy.

Don swirled around and screamed, "STAY DOWN, STAY DOWN AND SHUT THE HELL UP!"

The plane suddenly shot straight up over the Marines. The roar of the plane was deafening and the afterburner blast from the jet engine shot a burst of extremely hot air down on them. LT felt a burning sensitization on the back of his neck. He grabbed the cause of the pain and realized it was from a brass cartridge from the twenty-millimeter machine gun the pilot had fired, trying to insure the Marines stayed down.

Many of the platoon members were now rolling around and throwing off the red hot brass cartridges raining from the sky.

The pilot was now in a barrel role heading back toward the platoon.

LT once more screamed to his men, "GET READY! AFTER THIS NEXT PASS WE ARE GOING TO TAKE THE HILL!"

Everyone knew they had to take the hill top. Going back down the hill without cover would be more suicidal than trying to fight through the enemy.

On the second pass, the pilot once more flew eye level with LT, and aligned his plane on him, the mark, the only standing figure.

LT's eyes swept from left to right. He could see some of his men making the religious sign across their chest, others were in the fetal position, no doubt asking God's forgiveness or to spare their lives. Some, however, were looking up the hill with anger and hate spewing from their faces.

He once more focused on the plane, as it was eye level again and tearing towards the platoon. He stood watching the plane rapidly closing ground on him. There was no sense hiding, there were no adequate cover from a high caliber machine gun bullets. He would rather be defiant if he was going to die, so he merely stared at the death machine ripping through the morning sky.

Suddenly LT jerked back in shock! From under the plane's belly and wings, three objects dropped. The middle one was in direct line with him. It now tumbled over and over, coming at a high rate of speed. It quickly rose over his head making a swish, swish sound. He immediately knew the tumbling effects and sound was from napalm bombs.

The three bombs hit the crest of the hill, almost at the same time, causing over a hundred-foot wall of burning sticky jelly to splash down the other side of the hill away from the platoon. The exploding napalm immediately sucked up the air around the platoon, causing them to gasp for air, momentarily halting their charge.

The Marines quickly recovered from the temporary loss of air and continued the charge to the crest of the hill. Live trees and bushes with green leaves could be seen burning. Many bodies of the enemy lay burning. A few of the soldiers were alive, running down the hill, on fire and screaming. One NVA was on fire from the waist down, and ran down the hill only to trip and become a rolling, screaming ball of fire.

LT could not believe his eyes. It was, to him, an almost apocalyptic destiny, not only of the hideous and almost paralyzing situation of human agony, but the number of the enemy which were on the run away from the crest of the hill, where the bombs had been dropped. There had to be at least a regiment of NVA's at the top of the hill in the beginning.

Between the fires, and bodies of the unfortunate enemy soldiers killed by the napalm scattered about, LT fought for mental and physical control of himself and the tactical situation.

Taking command of the situation, he hollered at Bates to put his machine gun on a flat space in front of him and support Jersey's squad, who was pushing the enemy down the hill toward the stream. He then yelled at Olsen to take Billy and Ed's machine gun and stop those fifty or so enemy running off to the left of the main group.

Grabbing Rathbone, he informed him to protect the platoon's left side and make sure no one came up from the back.

Bullets began flying past him. The enemy had now started to regroup and was showing signs of resistance. He was turning to holler at Bates when Lee yelled, "The captain is on the net. He wants to talk to you!"

LT swiftly surveyed the situation and cried out, "I'M TO BUSY TO TALK NOW!"

He glanced up in the sky and saw the F105 coming back, making a run across the front of Jersey's squad. He grabbed the hand set and told Jersey to hold up.

The pilot dropped two parachuting five-hundred-pound bombs. The bombs hit further down the valley between Jersey's men and the stream, shaking and rattling the ground, making it feel like an earthquake. Tall columns of black smoke and debris rose from the explosions.

The bombs took out more of the enemy. Those remaining were about three hundred yards from the tree line and as he was about to tell Jersey to hold his position, Lee interrupted him once more, yelling, "LIEUTENANT! The captain said he was *ordering you* to get on the phone!"

LT fumed; he was stressed and becoming frustrated with the captain and shouted, "I'M GOD DAMN BUSY! GO TO HELL!"

He quickly moved Bates and Brown to a new location. They were doing a great job lying down, plunging fires hitting the enemy, when they stopped and tried to set up defense.

Converging his attention on Jersey's squad, he suddenly jerked his head back in dismay. The enemy had spread out in a line and were about to enter the stream when, unexpectedly, a heavy volume of repeated small arms fire shot out from the tree line. The remaining NVA troops twisted and fell to their deaths.

Unknown to the Marines, a US Army Mike Force unit of Special Forces and ARVNs had sprung a perfect ambush. The Mike Force had been working a few miles back behind the enemy monitoring the developing tactical situation. They flew in their helos at tree top level and were able to land behind the tree line undetected and set up the ambush.

He swiftly ordered his troops move back to his location to regroup.

As the men were moving to the CP, he moved off by himself. He needed to do his own regrouping, sorting out and try to fully understand what had taken place. He scanned the area of small burning fires where bodies still smoldered; the pungent smell of roasted human flesh. He felt nauseous from the site and smell, which filled and lingered on the hill top. His stomach groaned. He swallowed hard, choking back the urge to vomit.

His eyes teared up and he looked up to the heaven and thanked God for saving his platoon. He also thanked Hostage Jim and the F105 pilot. His entire body quivered. He reached and grabbed the trunk of a tree next to him, steadying himself. He did not want to appear weak in front of his men.

After a few minutes of silence there was a sound gently creeping into his mind. He looked up; the sound, whop, whop, whop, was a CH-46 helicopter which was about to land. Someone in the platoon popped a green smoke, marking the LZ.

Lieutenant Colonel Folsom, the battalion commander, came charging off the helo with a smile a mile wide. He slapped the Marines on their backs as he passed by them on his way towards LT. He stopped briefly to talk to Joe and Jersey.

Captain McCarthy also got off the helo and tore straight towards LT. He never stopped to talk to anyone and did not have a smile, but rather was very tight-jawed. Reaching LT before Folsom, the skipper, with a now sinister smile and terse voice said, "You and I are going to have a little meeting when the CO leaves... UNDERSTAND?"

LT gulped a quick, "Yes sir!"

Colonel Folsom reached LT and grabbed his hand, shook it, expressed joyfully how happy and proud he was of the platoon. After a few minutes of congratulations, he said he wanted to personally thank each Marines in the platoon and bubbly hurried off.

Captain McCarthy quickly placed his fingers on both sides of LT's neck and squeezed hard. He felt like he had been grabbed by eagle's talons which were meeting in the middle of his neck.

"Now lieutenant, you were saying something about me going some place after I ORDERED YOU to talk to me on the radio, remember?"

LT stammered, "Yes sir, I kind of remember something about that… but there was an awful lot going on. Burning trees, bodies on fire, bombs, bullets flying around my head and troops to maneuver against an entire NVA regiment. Shit captain, my plate was pretty damn full!"

"Okay. What about the part when you told me to go to hell?"

Don, gasping for air and in a somewhat convincing and appalling voice said, "SIR. I would never tell the CO… captain… skipper to do such a thing. I did tell you I was damn busy."

"Yea, you still haven't answered the 'Go to hell' part."

Muscular convulsions caused him to squirm and twitch as the skipper's fingers dug deeper into his neck.

Going through mental gymnastics and somewhat desperate, he carefully and very distinctively said, "Sir, you had to be there to see the physical rather than the mental picture. See… when I said 'Go to hell,' I was looking at Lee. Not talking to you!"

The skipper squinted his eyes at him, curled his lips, and said, "You little cretin, you're lucky the battalion commander and I are in really good spirits. I'm going to let this slide this time but you had better not let it happen again… got it?"

LT gratefully acknowledged he understood, then stumbled back to the platoon CP.

Lee looked at the lieutenant and said, "Well, I guess you were Geronimo today, right?"

"Nope. Not only was I not Geronimo, I wasn't LIEUTENANT! I was a CRETIN!"

The helo lifted off, taking the senior officers off the hill, putting a damper on the festive atmosphere. No, "take the rest of the day off," or "steak and cold beer." In fact, the platoon, by direction of the skipper, was to patrol to the company's current location and join them.

LT, rubbing his neck, walked over to Lee and said, "Next time we get... no... *every time* we get in contact with the enemy, turn off the damn company radio!"

The company continued its patrolling around Hill 309, heading toward Que Son Valley. LT was happy to be walking, it helped him shed some of his built-up anxieties. His entire platoon could have been wiped out if it hadn't been for Hostage Jim and the Air Force F105 pilot. His body quivered when he thought of what happened earlier.

The company spent the next two days conducting sweeps towards LZ Baldy. The only "encounter" happened on the day mail was received by the platoon and handed out. Bates acquired several pieces of mail from home. A few from family members and two from girls he knew back in the states. By the time the supplies and mail were passed out, it was time to move out, so Bates shoved the letters into his helmet.

The Marines were taught to walk in the rice paddies and not on the dikes because the enemy loved putting bobby traps on to the dike paths. The platoon was crossing a paddy when Bates, being Bates, wandered off the route established by the point.

There was about four inches of water in the rice paddy and about half way across Bates fell forward and completely submerged himself in a bomb crater which was invisible under the shallow muddy water.

His gear, flak jacket, helmet, pack, machine gun, and his many letters pulled him right to the bottom. He had two choices; shed his gear and swim up or raise the barrel of his gun and hope someone would help him out of the watery grave.

He raised the barrel and Moe Sabanos grabbed the gun with his long arms and started pulling Bates from the crater. While Moe pulled Speedy, Louis Lujan acted as an anchor for Moe.

When they reached dry land, Speedy and Louis looked at Bates and began rolling on the ground in hysterics at Bates' soggy appearance.

Bates repeatedly cursed and flipped them the bird. The two only laughed harder, pointed at him and deliriously repeating, "*Rato ahogada.*"

Bates was lucky because the next day the skipper called LT over to his CP and told him he needed a mature, honest, and fair NCO for the company supply in the rear.

LT informed the captain he had the perfect individual, Lance Corporal Moe Sabanos. He had noticed with Moe's age that life in the bush was taking its toll on him physically. He also knew Moe would take care of 1st platoon so he recommended Moe and the skipper quickly took him for the rear company supply NCO.

CHAPTER 22
PROMISE NOT KEPT

Is it possible that because of 1st platoons run in with the NVA regiment, they were sent to LZ Baldy, while the rest of the company went to LZ Ross.

The platoon, in late afternoon, reached the gates of LZ Baldy. 1st platoon's men were fatigued to the point of almost collapsing, burning up from the heat, soaked from sweat, and permeating an invisible cloud of human stench.

As the platoon entered the gates of LZ Baldy, LT surveyed the area in front of him and could see they were going to pass through a series of offices. Offices containing the non-fighting pogues, which now were coming out standing along the street. It suddenly reminded him of when he was a child and watched the Saturday morning westerns. When gunfighters walked down the streets and the towns people would gather on the side of the streets whispering and pointing at the gunslingers.

LT raged in anger. His Marines were not a side show. Twirling around, facing his men, in a contemptuously manner and very stern voice, barked, "Listen up! Heads up, shoulders back! Eyes forward! We are the ragged, stinking, very proud… Horrible Hogs!"

In a single motion the platoon's heads jerked up, shoulders snapped back, and rigid stares faced the front. Any and all despair vanished from the platoon members. It was reconstituted, in each single platoon member, instantaneously, by a sweeping, almost prophetic, emotional euphoria of brotherhood.

Then, with great pride, the platoon passed by the open-mouthed, silent, wide-eyed, improbable gawkers.

A jeep came down the road and stopped in front of them, and the platoon came to a halt. A major stepped out of the jeep. He was six feet tall, thick, and barrel-chested, with jet black hair and equally dark, dense eyebrows. With a frown on his face he walked up to LT, carefully looked at him from head to toe then casually examined the platoon. Once finished he peered at LT as he was making his final inquiry into the group.

With a chuckle and then a big smile, the major said, "I'm Major Black and it's great to see a platoon of combat field Marines." Pausing while taking another quick glance of the platoon, he said, "Been out awhile?"

LT, shaking his head affirmative, grinned, and said, "You could say that sir. We are really looking forward to a shower, clean clothes, and hot food."

Once more scrutinizing the platoon and LT, he said, "I bet you are. However, I was sent down here by your regimental commander to show you where you, and your men, will be filling perimeter positions tonight."

A little stunned LT said, "No sir... I mean I don't think the major understands. We left our position this morning before day light. We were supposed to be helo-lifted in but wound up walking over twenty clicks to get here. We are supposed to get showers, clean clothes and hot meals... not stand perimeter watch."

With a very concerned look on his face, Major Black said, "I really don't know what to tell you. When I was leaving the command post Colonel Codispoti grabbed me, told me to find your platoon and show you where you are to stand watch tonight."

Major Black, after a short lull, continued, "Look, I'm on my way to the battery. I have duty over at 12th Marines. When I get there I'll get hold of the command and inform them of your platoon's situation. In the meantime, here is the positions I was told tell to fill." The major then pointed to six positions between the perimeter wire and road where they stood. "Right down there is a mess hall. I'm sure they can help you get some hot chow. I have to go but I'll talk to you later. Good luck!"

Reluctantly, the platoon filled the perimeter fighting locations shown by the major.

After getting the platoon set in, LT told Joe to stay with the platoon in case new word came down. Ballew and a couple other men went with him over to the mess hall to, hopefully, set up arrangements for hot chow.

They entered the mess hall's dining area and found it empty. He looked around in the dim light and finally called out, "Anybody here?" He waited a minute, then started to holler again, when suddenly an individual opened a back door and walked into the dining hall.

The person who walked in was short and heavy, with a pop-belly, and wore a dirty white t-shirt with no rank insignia. Startled, he said, "Who… who the hell are you people? This mess hall is closed today!"

LT unconsciously stomped his feet, crossed his arms over his chest, and said, "I'm Lieutenant Garrett, Platoon Commander, H 2/7. And you are…?"

"Sergeant Grims. I'm in charge of this mess hall, sir."

"Great! I have forty Marines that have not had a hot meal in over forty days. And I was told this mess hall would provide those meals."

Sergeant Grims' face turned white, his eyes darted from each of the platoon members then back to LT, and he hesitantly said, "Sir, I don't have the man power to prepare the meals. My people are on a cook out and I told you the mess hall is closed."

LT once more stomped his feet and yelled, "Cook out! What the hell is this cook out shit?"

Squirming, not sure what to say, Sergeant Grim in a fury said, "Yes sir! I guess a bunch of steaks, over at the main mess hall, were thawed out. My people were given the day off, a twenty-four-hour break, a cook out of steaks, beer and no perimeter duty!"

LT slowly stammered, "No… no perimeter duty." Pointing in the direction they had now came from, he asked, "Would your perimeter duty happen to be down the road about thirty-five yards?"

Sergeant Grims, gleaming, said, "Yes sir! How did you know… ooh shit!" His eyes darted from man to man and swiftly dashed to a back room yelling, "Wait… wait, I can help you. HANG ON!"

Ballew, Pizza, and Johnny "Crazy" Cox all started stomping their feet. Ballew screamed, "Shit! Those are maggots on our boots! They are everywhere!"

LT, almost listless, peered at the maggots and nonchalantly said, "Probably the only way to get rid of those maggots would be to burn this place."

Johnny Crazy Cox quickly looked at Pizza and winked in agreement.

LT, now feeling somewhat feeble, sat down on the edge of a dining table and steadied himself and mumbled, "I cannot believe this. This can't be happening. Are we that *expendable*?"

Sergeant Grims returned holding four loafs of packaged bread in his left hand, a long wooden spoon, half gallon jar of real Mayonnaise under his arm pit and a twenty-some-inch-long tube of Baloney in his right hand, and nervously said, "This sure beats C-rats… right?" He dropped them on to the table.

The four platoon members, utterly depressed, lethargically stared at the sergeant's collection of offerings in total apathy.

The mess hall doors were violently pushed open, causing the door to slam against the wall. A tall, slim, young lieutenant marched up to LT and in a loud voice said, "I'm Lieutenant Henry, Geoffrey Henry. Major Black sent me over here to inform you… I guess you already know what I was going to tell you from your dejected look."

Lieutenant Henry paused, glanced at the mess hall offerings on the table, and said, "I see the command has offered up a degree of cuisine."

Lieutenant Henry, after some prolongation, took a deep breath, exhaled, and in a deliberate manner, said, "Look the major is sorry he couldn't be here himself. There is a fire support mission going on right now and he can't leave the battery. He did, however, call regiment and, after learning what you, no doubt, have already learned, he tore into the command and offered to 'knock some sense into their dumb asses.'

"The major also sent over some food, which we think you will find more appetizing than… baloney. Come on, I have it out in the jeep."

The platoon members walked out to Lieutenant Henry's jeep. He opened a cardboard box and pulled out a plastic-wrapped package and said, "These are LRP's, Long Range Patrol meals, freeze-dried dehydrated field rations. We are testing them. They are very light to carry, no cans. Comes in several menus and are rather tasty. The only thing you have to do to get a great meal is add hot water… one canteen of hot water."

LT carefully leaned against the jeep, took a deep breath, slowly exhaled, and said, "Let me see if I have this right. DOD, Department of the Navy or the Marine Corps, sent an artillery unit Long Range Packaged meals to test. A unit which is *always* in a static position, *never* conducting long or *any* patrols."

Lieutenant Henry grimaced. "Yes."

LT threw his hands into the air and said, "Is there no sanity in this place?"

LT took the packaged meal from Lieutenant Henry, bounced it from hand to hand and said, "You know I believe this would have lighten our hundred-pound pack by twenty, maybe thirty pounds, and would have extended our days before needing resupply."

He gently tossed the meal he was holding to Ballew and said, "Well, Lieutenant Geoffrey Henry, if you would be so kind to deliver these meals to the platoon area I would greatly appreciate it. And if you would let Corporal Ballew ride with you, he can organize a working party to unload the meals."

Lieutenant Henry chuckled and said, "I have a better idea. Let your corporal and two troops take the jeep down to your platoon area, we can walk and talk back."

The two lieutenants, after reaching the platoon, sat for a couple more hours talking. They discussed mostly about where they were from and their lives before entering the Marine Corps. Geoffrey was from Georgia, graduated from the Citadel, majored in nuclear engineering, spoke English, German and could "get by" in Spanish. His great-great grandfather invented the Henry Rifle. All in all, LT found Geoffrey to be an extremely intelligent, friendly, good-humored person possessing a great personality.

Once Geoffrey left, LT immediately checked his platoon's positions, and found Joe and confirmed his 0300 watch. He took his pack and laid it on the slightly sloping ground. Spread out his rubber poncho, he lay down and covered his body with his poncho liner to keep the mosquitoes off him for the night. It had been a long day and he fell asleep instantaneously.

"LIEUTENANT!" LIEUTENANT!"

He flung his torso up to a sitting position, threw off the poncho liner, and stared at Joe. Joe, who was kneeling at the foot of where LT was sleeping, once more yelled, "Lieutenant!" He then pointed down the road.

LT swung his head toward where Joe was indicating. His eyes stopped and locked on to the mess hall. It was a giant red and orange ball of flames. The flames were leaping a hundred feet or more into the dark morning sky.

They ran down the road to the edge of the burning mess hall. No sooner had they arrived when a jeep pulled up with a captain in it. He jumped out and quickly asked, "Any idea how the fire started?"

At that moment someone in the background yelled out, "I THINK A ROCKET HIT THE BUILDING!"

The captain walked around the building trying to find some clue as to what happened. He finally walked back to where LT and Joe were standing and hesitantly said, "Well, it's not the first time an enemy mortar round has caused a building to burn up in the compound."

Others from the platoon started to gather at the edge of the fire. LT, looking around and noticing the number of his men there, said, "Okay, let's get back to our perimeter. The enemy might use this as a diversion to attack."

On the way back to the platoon area, a thought suddenly flash through his mind. He froze in place, turned around, and once more stared at the flames. He had a knot suddenly growing in his stomach. Had someone acted on his half-baked muttered comment, "This mess hall should be burned?"

The next morning the platoon was ordered out of LZ Baldy and joined the company. The company was tasked with providing a blocking fore for the ARVNs out by the Barrier Islands. From the Barrier Islands the unit was rumored to start a long and demanding operation in the Que Son Valley.

CHAPTER 23
QUE SON VALLEY

The land out around the Barrier Islands was strange. It consisted of very white, sandy soil, short, almost stunned-growth pine trees, flourishing cactus, and small gently rolling hills, none more than three to four feet in height, like small sand dunes. It was hot and humid. The local population was almost nonexistent.

The ARVN was conducting a large brigade and combined operations with the Marines. The idea was for the ARVN to span out across a large area of Que Son Valley and sweep toward the sea, driving the NVA/VC into the waiting Marines.

The Marines mission: destroy the NVA/VC forces as they were driven into their lines.

Higher command had developed the operation because the NVA/VC had become more brazen in the rice-growing Que Son Valley. The enemy was moving further and further out into the valley gathering rice by force and recruiting with their "Join or Die Program."

The company arrived early in the evening, hot and exhausted, and established a company line with 1st platoon in the middle, 2nd on the left, and 3rd on the right. The company CP was positioned directly behind 1st platoon.

In the morning, before sunlight, the Marines were stretched out across the barren landscape waiting for the ARVN to drive the enemy into their lines. By 1000 there was nothing, not a single soul in front of them.

As time continued to pass, the skipper became frustrated and anxious and began calling higher headquarters in hopes of trying to determine when the Marines might expect the enemy to appear.

At last, dust could be seen out in front of the Marines' line, about a mile away. No sooner had they spotted the dust, when they suddenly took heavy, large-caliber machine gun fire.

The captain, suspecting the incoming rounds were from the ARVN, through "tough language," convinced higher headquarters to issue a cease-fire.

The ARVN commander came up to the Marines lines with a big smile and joked about the situation. He told the captain his forces were conducting reconnaissance by fire, scattering the enemy rather than driving them toward the Marines lines.

The Marines from the company to higher headquarters found no humor in the situation and immediately canceled the operation. This left Hotel Company in the middle of a barren land and, with no mission.

Towards evening orders were finally received, sending the company to a large hill mass called Three Fingers Hill. Three Fingers Hill was a finger which extended off the Que Son Mountain Range, providing a partial landmark between Que Son Valley and Death Valley. Once on Three Fingers Hill they were to link up with Golf Company.

The captain called the officers and staff NCO's together and laid out the new orders and the company's new mission.

The captain told everyone to get their maps out, and after pausing for a minute, then said, "The company will be tactically air-lifted to an area about five clicks from Three Fingers Hill. We will move to Three Fingers, meet up with Gulf Company. From Three Fingers, sweep to the north along the sides of the Que Son Mountains, between the mountains and LZ Ross. Once the company reaches Happy Valley, which lays north of Que Son Valley, the company will to swing to the right, still following the fingers, which will lead us basically to the Rock Crusher, where we stop. We will get new orders at the Rock Crusher."

The officers and staff looked around at each other with questionable looks on their faces began to mumble among themselves.

The captain cleared his throat and said, "Our mission is twofold, and yes, I know it covers over thirty miles; however, we will not do it in a week, or so, but rather several weeks or more, in a slow methodical manner."

The skipper hesitated, eyed each officer, then continued, "The first part: Two platoons and the company headquarters will concentrate on locating stored enemy rice, gather it up, destroy their warehousing area and then send the rice back to regiment for redistribution to the Vietnamese people."

Once more the captain paused and said, "The second part: One platoon will work alone from the rest of the company at the base of the Que Son Mountains as they head north. They will also locate enemy rice storage areas, gather the rice and ship it back to the rear. Additionally, they will look for and mark the trails the enemy is using to come out of the mountains to get the rice or to haul the stolen rice back into the mountains."

"The location of the marked trails will be sent up to higher headquarters. Intelligence units will set up electronic monitoring devices seismic-triggered on these trails, hopefully allowing the artillery and/or air to eliminate this type of enemy activity."

"Okay, platoon commanders, here are your assignments. 2nd and 3rd, you're with me and the headquarters. 2nd on the right, 3rd on the left of headquarters. And by the way, 2nd platoon, Golf Company will tie up with you on your right side."

Looking directly at LT, the skipper said, "Geronimo, your platoon will work the base of the mountains." The skipper paused and said, "Now remember, we are going to be air-lifted out of here in the morning. Once we reach the landing site by Three Fingers, we will tactically march to the hill. 1st platoon will lead out, then 2nd and 3rd. I'll travel between 1st and 2nd platoons. Any questions?"

LT knew his platoon would be the one to work alone before it was announced. The platoon always worked alone and that was fine with him. He didn't mind working with the captain and the other platoon commanders, but he really liked working with his platoon.

As the rest of the staff talked among themselves and drifted towards their areas, the skipper walked over to where LT was sitting and said, "Well, were you surprised with your mission?"

He grinned and said, "No. I am very happy, as my platoon will be. We look forward to this challenge and I know we will be able to carry out the mission to its utmost."

"Good, an officer from G-4 will met us at Three Fingers and he will brief you on what they actually want on the marked trail issue."

"Yes sir."

The skipper paused and said, "I want your platoon to lead us too Three Fingers. I have a route drawn up, so copy it over to your map. We leave at sunrise."

LT went back to his area and called up Jersey to his platoon CP. "Jersey, I want you and your squad to lead the company out of this repulsive place." Handing Jersey his map, he said, "Here is the route the skipper has worked up. Copy the grids onto your map. We leave at sunrise. Any questions?"

Jersey took the map from him and carefully studied the route laid out on the map and finally said, "All right LT, and thanks for the opportunity to do something other than merely follow the Marine in front of me."

Jersey happily headed back to his squad and in a not so subtle manner could be heard throughout the company area saying, "Come here pukes! We have an important mission!" It sure reminded and sounded like his old squad leader Jersey.

Jersey was proud to lead the entire company. LT knew he and the squad were more than capable of completing the assignment and it provided another opportunity to demonstrate and display his squad.

The company was ready to move out before daylight the next morning. None of the Marines liked this place; it did not provide protection from enemy fire. No shade during the day and at night the sandy soil housed hundreds of scorpions and thousands of sand fleas.

The entire company was lifted out of the Barrier Island area to a landing site a few clicks from Three Fingers.

After an hour and a half on the route to Three fingers, Jersey saw movement ahead. The squad tactically moved forward close enough to see several men dressed as VC and three or so as NVA soldiers. Some approached the group from several directions and joined the group. Others remained while a few would join the group then leave.

Suddenly, the men saw the Marine squad; some of the men started running away and a couple of the NVA soldiers began shooting at the Marines.

The Marine squad laid down a very effective base of fire, killing those who remained at the gathering and most of those who tried to run away.

The gathering place turned out to be a local enemy post office. There were considerable letters and packages. One of the packages was from Russia and contained a metal mechanical part, which could not be identified.

Division was notified of the captured post office and materials. They immediately sent out a helo and a G-2 intelligence officer to pick up the mail and the precious metal mechanical part from Russia, which the intelligence officer seemed particularly interested in.

Corporal Rathbone's squad took over the point element for the company. Lance Corporal Patrick K. Rouse, known as PK to his platoon members, was designated as point man.

PK was from the state of Louisiana. His ability to function as a superb point man was because of his upbringing. He grew up hunting and had those quick eyes, noticing the slightest movement, off colors, patterns or materials that did not fit into the natural surroundings. He was also notably big in spirit and fight, and like all the other platoon members was inordinately capable, totally trustworthy, and reliable.

PK led the company through what was productive agriculture land. The population also dramatically increased, with a few farmers being seen working in their fields.

Early afternoon the trail came to a fork. The left fork headed southwest, toward Death Valley. The right fork turned to the northwest, in the direction of Three Fingers and the Que Son Mountains.

PK studied the tracks in the trail. Most of the human tracks were coming his way, too many for it to be farmers carrying out their daily duties. He also noticed a dead giveaway: the shoe or "flip-flop" tracks contained automobile tread marks. The VC/NVA were well known for using old tires to make flip-flop shoes.

Some forty minutes later the point squad came to a hill where the trail went around the side of the hill. From nowhere, eight NVA soldiers dressed in green uniforms and carrying AK-47s slung over their shoulders appeared.

The lead man went immediately in a martial arts stance, shouted at PK then advanced toward PK. PK, not knowing what really to make of the situation at first, then regained his thoughts and said, "Dumb shit!" and opened fire with his shotgun. He was muttering something about, "Grandpa always said, 'Don't take a knife to a gun fight.'"

The other enemy soldiers froze in place, watching the event unfold. Then, realizing their own circumstance, tried to flee into a nearby sugar cane field. Five failed to make the field but two slipped into the tall sugar cane.

Lance Corporal Johnny "Little John" Sims shot his M-79 grenade launcher, into the field where the two NVA entered. The sugar cane was maturing to the point where it was becoming dry and the round lit the sugar cane on fire, causing the field to burn.

LT quickly sent Corporal Rathbone and his squad to the back and right side of the field in order to catch any one trying to escape. Jersey and his squad covered the left side and the front. No one came out, nor was any yelling or screaming heard.

The skipper arrived shortly after the field finished burning. After a few minutes he decided not to wait while it cooled so they could hunt for the two bodies. He thought it was far more important to make this the company's objective.

Around noon the following day the company reached Three Fingers, about an hour behind Golf Company. The two company commanders selected a position on the hill for the two units to defend and tie in together. The rest of the day was used to dig fighting positions and setting up platoon and company command posts.

Late afternoon, Captain McCarthy called LT to his CP and, in very matter-of-fact manner, said, "Geronimo, each company is going to run a platoon night ambush off this hill tonight. I'm offering your platoon the option of taking it or not, because of your work guiding the company to this position."

LT looked at the skipper for a few moments, folded his arms on his chest and said, "And if we take on the ambush, what's in it for the men?"

The captain grinned and said, "I knew you were going to ask that question. And your right, your Marines deserve some consideration for what's happened in the last few days. So… as a reward, I'll pull your platoon off perimeter watch for the next two days and nights."

LT took a long deep breath and slowly released it. Knowing he would never get any better terms, he said, "Deal!"

Hotel Company was to conduct a platoon night ambush off the northwest side of the current company's positions, while Golf Company was to set up an ambush on the northeast side of the unit's position.

LT called his CP group and squad leaders together that evening and told them of the new mission, the night ambush, and the benefits in conducting the mission. They were very happy and felt the rest of the platoon would be equally thrilled.

At the platoon meeting LT decided to check his platoon for any items they might still need from supply. He glimpsed over to his side and saw Joe and Ballew talking. He said, "Hey, Joe, can you spare Ballew a few minutes and also take over command of the CP?"

Joe said, "Sure, going to do a last check of the platoon?"

LT nodded and then motioned for Ballew to join him. "Ballew, we have time to get a last request for supplies. I want you to go with me and make a final check. Not only with the squad leaders, but a random inquiry of the troops wouldn't hurt either."

The last stop of LT's inspection was Olsen's squad. He and Ballew walked through the area and talked to a couple of the squad members as they made their way to the squad leader, who was talking to Lance Corporal Lynn Stroop, the point man for the night ambush.

Lance Corporal Lynn Stroop was from Virginia. Lynn was small in stature and frame, standing only five feet four, and weighed about eighty pounds, carried close to a hundred pounds on his back and had as much spunk and fight as any two people. His voice was high pitched and the subject of some friendly kidding at times. However, his outstanding ability to walk point and meet or succeed every task earned him total respect of his platoon members.

LT, Ballew, and Olsen greeted each other. Ballew looked at Olsen and said, "You have any last-minute supply request? We have time to get it in tonight."

Olsen shrugged his shoulders and said, "Well… no. Wait, I do have a question. Why can't we get jungle boots for Lynn, instead of regular leather boots, which wear out in about three months?"

LT quickly looked at Lynn's boots, then turned to Ballew and said, "That's a good question, why can't we get some jungle boots for him?"

Ballew, noticing everyone was looking directly at him wanting an answer, said in a defensive manner, "Well… supply says they never have his size. Olsen, I asked you about two weeks ago if Lynn got new boots and you said he did, remember?"

"Sure I remember. I told you he got new boots, not new *jungle* boots!"

Ballew dropped his arms to his side, rolled his eyes, and looked up and started to say something when LT cut him off.

"What size boots do you wear, Lynn?"

Quietly Lynn said, "Five and a half, sir."

LT held up five fingers and said, "Five and a half?"

"Five and half regular, sir."

LT looked at Lynn and smiled and told him he would do his best to get him a pair of jungle boots. He thought, "Hell, I haven't worn a five-and-a-half shoe since third or fourth grade."

Walking into the CP, he said, "Lee, get me the first sergeant on the radio."

Lee quickly glanced up at LT, then turned his head toward Joe, who was sitting cross-legged about ten feet away.

Joe also looked at LT, then Lee and quickly lipped an unspoken, "Well!"

Lee grabbed the radio frequency knob and changed it to the administration setting and hurriedly called the rear. After several attempts to reach the rear they finally answered. Lee informed the rear 1st platoon commander wanted to talk to the first sergeant. There was about another ten-minute wait before the rear responded.

LT took the radio hand set, cleared his throat, and slowly and very carefully choosing his words said, "Hotel rear. We are in need of your support. Have a point man who needs jungle boots. Size five and half, regular. *Previous* request gone unfilled.

Recommending the first sergeant go to the battalion sergeant major and let him know. *Hopefully* the battalion sergeant major will inform the *new* battalion CO of situation. Could be a win-win for both *senior staff non-commissioned officers*. We have a resupply in *two* days. Over."

The radio was silent for several moments. LT looked at Lee then Joe. Both looked down at the ground. The entire platoon was aware of LT's run in with the first sergeant at stack arms. Suddenly, the silence was broken, the radio squawked out, "Hotel one, *understand*, rear out."

Once again the CP fell silent. The three looked at each other and LT finally said, breaking the silence, "Guess time will give us the results."

1st platoon moved off the hill before dark; ideally, they wanted to be within a hundred yards or so of their ambush site before dark. This would allow them to observe the site before dark, making sure the enemy didn't set up at the same place, and, equally important, making sure the enemy couldn't see where the exact ambush site was.

Lynn went up a slope on the trail before the ambush site and slowly lowered his body, crawling to the top of the incline, and peered down the trail. After a minute or so he slid down behind the rise and motioned for LT to come up.

He cautiously moved up to Lynn by a set of bushes off the trail and carefully scanned the trail ahead of him.

Instantly, he saw movement. He could make out through the dimming light figures what appeared to be human heads. He frantically searched for a site with greater advantage than his current one.

There, on the other side of the trail, was a group of bushes about three feet high on a knoll higher than his present position. The place offered great camouflage and a commanding view so he could more effectively scrutinize the situation.

With a great deal of discretion, he quickly moved to the new position. From here he could see over half of a torso; however, something was wrong. In the fading light the uniforms did not appear to be VC or NVA. He grabbed his binoculars and began scanning the area; all of a sudden, he saw a figure take off his hat. To LT's amazement the person's hair was *blonde*, not black.

He very slowly slid down the incline, stopped at the bottom, and momentarily sat there thinking. After a minute or, so he hurried back to the platoon and said, "Pass the word, 'possible friendlies.'"

He immediately got on the radio with the skipper and informed him of the situation. After a quick meeting between Hotel and Golf Company's commanders it was decided each of the platoons would shoot a green pop-up cluster into the air on the count of three.

LT held the pop-up cluster in his hand up toward what he hoped was Golf Company. When the person on the radio counted to three, he drove the cap of the pop-up into the palm of his hand, sending a green stream of light into the evening sky, which burst into a fountain of thousands of green particles. Instantly, another green pop-up exploded in the sky, right in front of his position.

His emotions went soaring within seconds he went from relieved, to fully outraged, and finally settling with exasperated. He thought, "What if we hadn't fully checked out the situation? What if I had called mortars on top of them? I could have been responsible for killing a lot of friendlies. CHRIST!"

In an instant he felt weary and the gigantic weight of responsibility was shoving him into the ground. With great deliberation, he reeled in his feelings and began to focusing on what to do next. He had, after all, promised the skipper he wouldn't lose control of his emotions again.

He called Golf Company's platoon commander to notify him he was on his way over to his position.

The two lieutenants met in-between their positions. LT could hardly believe his eyes; the Golf platoon leader looked like he was right out of high school. His uniform was clean and crisp, the camouflage pattern was sharp and his web gear was unused. He smelled brand new... like his equipment.

LT's annoyance grew dimmer and in an impassive manner said, "Lieutenant, do you know where you are on your map?"

The Golf platoon commander pulled out his map and with a noticeable amount of uncertainty pointed to a spot on his map and said, "Right here sir."

LT was surprised the lieutenant called him "sir," especially since both were second lieutenants, then said, "Well that's right, you should be there, but you are actually right about here." He pointed to the spot on the map where they were currently standing.

Looking closer at the Golf platoon commanders map LT said, "When you left for your ambush site, where did you go through your company's lines?"

Golf platoon leader placed his finger on the map and said, "Right here."

LT studied the map for a minute then said, "I think your mistake was following the ravine off the hill. It looks like your point man may have let the terrain dictate his direction and went northwest instead of northeast. Did you check your compass to insure he was going the right direction?"

The new lieutenant squirmed a little and in a low voice said, "No, I didn't."

Almost in a dogmatic manner LT said, "You are responsible for your point man's direction. You need to check on him at all times. You wound up almost in the center of my ambush site…it could have been very costly."

Lee, jogging up to the lieutenants, nearly out of breath, said, "The skipper wants the two platoons to return immediately to the company's perimeter through Hotels position."

Once back into the company areas, Golf Company commander quickly grabbed his new lieutenant and led him off, rather unhappy.

CHAPTER 24
BATTALION COMMANDER'S VISIT

The company remained on the hill for two more days. They had to wait an additional day on the hill because the skipper refused to take a resupply while on the march too Three Fingers and the resupply had to be rescheduled.

LT climbed up the hill behind his CP, high enough up so he could see his entire platoon's area and men. Below him he saw Lee come out of their make shift CP and start to scan the area, no doubt looking for him. He smiled cupped his hands over his mouth and loudly yelled, "LEE!"

Lee twirled around, then looked up, grinned, gave a thumbs up and returned back under the poncho liner top of the CP.

He leaned back on a rock, took out a cigar, started chewing on it, relaxed and soaked up the sun rays. He lazily began watching his Marines, some cleaning weapons, others writing letters but most enjoying the down time "bull shitting" with each other.

After watching the men for a while, he began to ponder why they were called the "Horrible Hogs." Marine units were often given nicknames, ie., Dying Delta 1/9, medevac Mike 3/26 and the Walking Dead 2/9.

Hotel was no exception and was often called by the unflattering title, Horrible Hogs.

Although the title probably started out as a derisive description, it had become a badge of pride for Hotel Marines.

He noticed every Marine in Hotel Company, not only his platoon but the entire company, had one thing in common: no two were dressed the same or carried exactly the same field gear.

Whether it was a symbol of self-expression or personal convenience, each had a certain nuance. A green t-shirt, without or with sleeves, an ARVN bush hat, a US Army flak vest, and so on. Another favorite was waist belts made from gas mask bag straps, NVA belts, facet darts, decorated bush hats, and frag pin rings finishing off the display.

Helmets brandished all sorts of graffiti. Hanging around necks were crosses, peace signs, bullets, church keys, and rings, to name the most common items.

This freedom of expression was tolerated because field Marines seldom received new gear and clothing. The Marines in the rear commands had and held the supplies, allowing for more control and tighter dress restrictions. However, the main reason for the Horrible Hog appearance was because of the poor resupply system and because the "good stuff" was siphoned off before it got to the field Marine.

Someone yelled, "RESUPPLY BIRD INBOUND!" This broke the solitude and thought pattern. He chuckled and thought, "How ironic." Here, I am bashing the supply system and in pops a resupply bird. However, the real question was, what did it bring?"

Arriving at the platoon CP at the same time as LT, Joe said, "Ballew and I have the working party to pick up our supplies, two men from each squad. We're going over now."

LT glanced at Ballew and said, "Do you have your supply list with you?"

Ballew grinned and from his chest pocket produced a much-worn, pocket-sized green notebook and said, "Yes sir. I have the Christmas list right here."

He smiled and said, "Well, you have a Merry Christmas."

Walking toward to the LZ, LT noticed there were four helos: three CH-46's, once again from the Purple Fox Squadron, and one Huey Gun Ship, the security bird. Two of the 46's had slings of supplies hanging from their bellies.

The third helo did not have a sling, which meant it was going to drop off passengers.

As he neared the LZ, he heard the skipper say, "Okay listen up. The battalion commander, Lieutenant Colonel. A. E. Folsom, is going to arrive here in a couple minutes. He also has the battalion S-3 and battalion sergeant major. Gunny Dixon, you take care of the sergeant major."

The captain paused, consciously looked at each officer, and said, "Since the S-3 is with the colonel I suspect he will be talking to me about allowing the commanding officer time to roam through your platoons. When he is in *your* platoon area stick with him. I want an officer with him at *all times*! Do you understand, lieutenants?"

They all gave a snappy, "Yes sir!"

The skipper turned to LT and said, "Geronimo, I think the G-2 will also be on the bird. If there is a representative from the G-2, he may stay with the S-3 and both brief me, or the G-2 may break from us and want to brief you directly. So, you need to be prepared to deal with both of them."

Lieutenant Colonel A. E. Folsom walked off the helicopter with a big smile to go with his tall, six-feet-three, slim, lanky frame. He exuberated authority and at the same time, radiated a warmth in his eyes and friendly manner.

Behind Colonel Folsom walked the battalion sergeant major, an older, stocky man with a grisly appearance. The sergeant major had a history as a person one does not want to trifle with; yet his eyes gleamed of youth and a willingness to extend a helping hand.

The battalion S-3 and the division G-4 walked off the helo side by side. The S-3 was not as tall and the CO, but taller than the sergeant major. He was a senior major a man of determination and accepted no "if's or ad's." The G-4 was a younger major who wore the cleanest, starched camouflage clothes the lieutenant had ever seen. His boots were spit-polished, his brass sparkling—definitely not a field Marine.

The last person off the helo was a US Army specialist with a German Shepherd.

Everyone assumed the solider and his dog would be going back on the helo once it left and dropped off down at the army support base below in Death Valley.

As predicted by the skipper, after proper introductions and a little small talk, the colonel immediately split from the group and headed straight for the troops with four lieutenants in tow.

Colonel Folsom proved to be very likable officer with an outgoing personality. The troops immediately took to him because he acted and sounded as if he was genuinely interested in each one of them and their welfare.

LT was watching the colonel as he made his way toward the platoon, when Joe walked up to him and asked, "LT, want me to wait until the colonel is gone before we hand out supplies?"

"Nope, I want everyone to continue doing whatever they are doing. If someone should be lucky enough to get a new pair of trousers in this resupply, they can change right then. I don't care if they are butt-naked in front of the colonel."

Joe smiled and said, "Yes sir, sounds good to me. I'll pass the word around."

LT started moving toward the end of his platoon perimeter to meet the colonel; however, as he walked by the supplies being piled up by Ballew and Joe, he could see separate stacks of C-rations, ammo—lots of ammo—some clothing, and possibly a small stack of "care packages." He hoped there was a package of Swisher Sweets cigars.

Moving on, he arrived in time to greet the colonel and started down the perimeter introducing the colonel to his men. Once the colonel had finished meeting the Marines of 1st platoon, he casually started walking toward the lieutenant's CP area where the supplies were being handed out and said, "How is the supply system working, Lieutenant Garrett?"

LT took a deep breath, exhaled and with a serious look said, "Well… colonel, would you like a stock answer expected from a junior to a senior officer, or would you rather have an answer from someone who lives with the system?"

Colonel Folsom turned toward the lieutenant with a straight face and said, "How about an honest answer."

LT's face became flushed and he smiled and said, "Great, that works for me. Let me give the colonel an answer using an overall grade system, like in school. I would give division an "A," regiment a "B," battalion within the perimeter a "C." Outside of the battalion perimeter, where the fighting takes place, a "D" or a "D-".

The colonel stared at the lieutenant for a moment then, chuckling, said, "You don't mince words, do you?"

LT lowered his head and kicked the dirt around with the toe of his boot and finally smiling up at the colonel said, "Guess not. I imagine the skipper can vouch for that too."

The colonel leaned his head back over his shoulders, laughed out load, put his hand on LT's back and said, between laughs, "Oh, I'll bet he can!"

The colonel and LT soon reached the platoon CP, where Joe and Ballew were handing out supplies. The colonel placed his hands on a pile of C-rat boxes and said, "Your platoon is the one who has had an order for a small size jungle boot for over four months, is that correct?"

LT somewhat surprised said, "Yes sir. Lance Corporal Stroop wears a five-and-a-half size boot, but the supply people say they can't get a boot that small."

Colonel Folsom smiled and told Joe to hand him the small green canvas bag by a pile of miscellaneous gear they hadn't finished sorting. The colonel opened the bag and pulled out a set of jungle boots, size five and a half, handed them to LT, and said, "You simply have to know where to shop. The ARVN supply is full of those boots."

LT, Joe and Ballew swapped glances smiling from ear to ear. He thanked the colonel as he tossed the boots to Ballew and indicated for him to get them to Stroop.

He stared at the colonel for a moment and in a very serious voice said, "Sir, may I relate to a true supply story I recently had with one of my men?"

The colonel gestured for the lieutenant to continue.

"Lance Corporal Bates came up to me the other day right after a resupply. The resupply did contain clothing. The clothes were used, no rips, holes had been sewn, and they had been laundered. In fact, they had been washed so many times the cameo colors had all but faded out. His question to me was, 'Why, do the pogues in the rear get new uniforms and we get their old ones?'"

The colonel walked over to where the clothes were being handed out and rummaged through them. He then walked over and picked up a case of C-rats, took the case over by LT, stood it on end, sat down on it, and motioned for the lieutenant to do the same.

LT sat down hurriedly, as if he had to justify his previous comments, and immediately said, "I tried to put a positive spin on what I told Lance Corporal Bates, by telling him that all of us enlisted and officers have the same dirty, torn clothes out here and none of us like it. However, the uniforms in the cargo net were better than what we were currently wearing." Pausing for a minute he continued by saying, "Bates asked me 'Why? Sir, do you have an answer for me as to why?'"

The colonel, sitting on the case of C-rats, placed his arms on his legs, clasped his hands together, and carefully said, "I don't know that I can add any more at this time than has already been discussed, and yes, you are right, those uniforms have been washed many, many times."

Crossing his arms over chest, the colonel then looked out over the country side and said, "I think I have something you can share, hopefully with a positive spin, with your platoon. Your platoon has, for the last few months, been rated as the number one Marine rifle platoon in the Vietnam."

LT leaned back and said, "Sir, how do you rate a platoon in combat? It's not like competing in drill competition or something like that."

The colonel laughed and said, "No, there is a formula. It's based on KIA's, MIA's, POW's, contacts, and the such. The point is, you should be very proud of your combat Marine rifle platoon."

LT sprung from his C-rat chair and said, "Sir, I am very proud of my men. They are outstanding young men and I am honored to be their platoon commander."

He paused, taking his own time, and said, "You know, Captain Frank McCarthy deserves a great deal of credit for our success too. We learn something from him on a daily basis. He can be rather hard at times and I can sure rile his Irish temper in a heartbeat."

Looking around to make sure no one was listening, he leaned in toward the colonel, chuckling, and said, "Sir, the captain is known as 'Fightin' Frank' in the company."

The colonel roared with laughter as he stood up and said, "I have really enjoyed talking to you lieutenant, and I have certainly learned a few things. However, I see the sergeant major, Major Evans, the G-4 and 'Fightin' Frank' are headed this way. We must be going. Good luck and continue the good work."

CHAPTER 25
LEADERSHIP AND PHYSICAL CHALLENGES

At day break the rest of the company scurried off the hill and headed into the Que Son Valley. LT was not happy, though; his platoon had moved very little and he did not want to spend any more time on the hill. It was now a prime target for the NVA. The company had been on the hill for several days and had given the enemy plenty of time to plan a rocket or mortar attack.

He shifted his hundred-some-pound pack on his back and took a deep breath. He turned and looked at the sun, which now cleared the distance horizon and began sending its hot rays down on the land. He started walking down the line of his men toward the front of the platoon column. The platoon had several clicks to travel today in order to make their objective.

The men turned toward him as he walked past them but said nothing. He knew what they all were thinking: "What the hell are you going to do?" He then glanced at his point man, Lance Corporal "PK" Rouse. PK gave the lieutenant a "Polish salute" and in a slow Louisiana Bayou voice said, "What do you want me to do?"

LT peered at PK, said nothing, then gazed past him to the reason the platoon was not moving off the hill and glared. He took a cigar out of his breast pocket, jammed it into his mouth, and mumbled under his breath, "Dammit."

He stomped over to the US Army Specialist Jeb Jebson and his German Shepherd, Boomer, who didn't get back on the helo and was assigned to 1st platoon. He said, "Specialist Jebson you and Boomer are going to have to move a lot faster. We don't have time for Boomer to smell each and every damn crap pile on the trail. PK is going to take over the lead. You can keep ahead, with or behind him, but you are not going to slow us down any more. Do you understand?"

Specialist Jebson scrutinized the lieutenant and said, "Lieutenant, I don't think you understand this program. Boomer and I are assigned to you to find booby traps for your platoon, therefore you will have to move at Boomer's pace."

LT did a rapid boil, then calmed himself in a few minutes, smiled, and in a very composed but firm voice said, "Your half right. You and Boomer are assigned to *my* command. *My* command is *not* assigned to you and your dog. Therefore you are not correct when you said 'we will have to move at Boomer's pace.' I am the CO and I will set the pace. Now, Specialist Jebson, do you understand?"

Specialist Jebson looked down at the ground and said, "Yes sir."

Turning to tell PK to come up, he was startled to fine PK standing next to him with a grin from ear to ear. "Well I guess you heard what I said, now get us off this damn hill ASAP!"

PK, without changing his expression in the slightest, said, "Yeees sir!"

The platoon was making good time, yet moving in a tactical manner. Lynn Stroop, with his new ARVN five-and-a-half boots, was swapping out with PK as point, therefore providing a break for both of them under the demanding responsibility.

They were both outstanding points but so much different in physical appearances.

PK was around six feet tall and had a husky build, probably weighting close to a hundred-seventy or seventy-five pounds back in the states, and was now about one hundred and thirty pounds. His voice was low key and deep in nature.

Lynn, on the other hand, weighed about eighty pounds and carried ninety pounds of gear on his back. His voice was high pitch, as though he had never quite completed puberty.

The platoon had been on the move for seven hours with only four breaks. LT noticed, after each stop, Specialist Jebson and Boomer fell back further and further. He glanced up at the sun and figured it was around two in the afternoon. He also thought the platoon was close to eighty percent of the way to his objective and decided now was not only a good time for a break, but that the terrain was highly defensible. He called a halt and immediately put the platoon in a defensive perimeter.

He walked through the platoon area checking on the perimeter and how the men were doing. He stopped at Lynn's position and said, "Lynn how are those new boots?"

Lynn jumped up and said, "They are great. No blisters and a heck of a lot cooler than those leather ones."

He smiled, then walked back toward the center of the platoon, took off his pack, dropped it and his cartridge belt on the ground, and said, "Lee, this is the CP. Call up the squad leaders, Joe and Doc Smith." He pulled off his sweat-soaked blouse from, what seemed like, his smoldering body.

He unbuttoned his blouse and waved both sides back and forth several times, allowing the built-up heat to escape from his body. He looked down at his green t-shirt; it was saturated to the point that it stuck to his body as if it were painted on him. He thought, "Not bad." Jackie, his fiancée, might really love his new sculpted look.

He sat down as the others began to arrive at the meeting place. He noticed their uniforms, once drenched in sweat like his, were now drying. As their clothing dried, large lines of white salt lines were forming around the waist, shoulders, and back.

He greeted each man, smiled, and said, "Okay, who knows where we are at on the map… coordinates-wise?"

No sooner had he finished speaking, when Corporal Rathbone fired off the coordinates.

"Who agrees and who doesn't agree?" They all agreed while managing a few playful slaps of their hands or maps on Rathbone's head and back.

"All right, settle down and listen up." He laid his map on the ground and said, "We will stay here long enough for eating and changing socks, since we have no more streams to cross before we get to our objective."

"Squad leaders and Docs, check for blisters. This has been a long, hot walk. Doc Weston, I talked to Lynn Stroop; he says his feet are fine. However, make sure you actually look at his feet."

As the meeting was breaking up, Lance Corporal Ed Cherry, Jersey's right hand man, came running up to the CP. Suddenly, from Ed's left and slightly behind him, Boomer tore out from under a bush and bit Ed in the left buttock.

Ed was knocked to the ground with the force of Boomer and screamed all the way to the ground. Specialist Jebson, who was lying down on the ground striped to the waist, jumped up, grabbed Boomer's nylon leash, and yelled for him to stop and return to him. Boomer immediately released Ed and obediently returned to Jebson. Jebson quickly tied Boomer to a shorter leash.

LT, Jersey, and Doc Weston ran to Ed. Doc told Ed to loosen his pants belt so he could pull his trousers down to check the wound. Ed, moaning, did so then laid on the ground cursing.

Doc Weston examined the wound and finally said, "Well Ed, you are going to be fine. You have four perfect small holes in your butt. There is no ripping or tearing. I'll clean the wound and you will be good."

Ed rolled part way over, looked up at the three standing over him, and said, "You going to medevac me?"

LT, Doc, and Jersey, with a flash of their eyes at Ed, said in unison, "HELL NO!"

Ed rolled back on to his stomach and began cursing until Doc poured iodine into the wound. Ed stopped cursing and instantaneously screamed like a girl, shattering the afternoon tranquility.

Without warning, Jersey leaped over to Specialist Jebson, unlocked his safety on his M16, and shoved the barrel up against Jebson's face and screamed, "I'M GOING TO KILL YOU AND YOUR DAMN DOG!"

LT leaped up, raced to Jersey and Jebson, where he wedged himself in between the two. With a calm but stern voice he said, "Jersey, look at me! You aren't going to kill him or his dog. Ed is going to be fine. Take Ed back to your squad and take charge of your men... they need you *here* not in a prison."

Jersey's eyes were blood red from anger. He slowly focused on LT and his eyes began to change back to their normal dark brown. He allowed LT to slowly push the barrel of the weapon away from Jebson's face. At his continues urging, Jersey finally walked back toward Ed a little ways then whirled around facing Jebson, and yelled, "YOUR ASS IS MINE, SHITHEAD!"

LT could see Jebson was trembling and visibly upset. He coaxed him to sit down before he fell to the ground.

After a few minutes, Jebson gained some composure and rubbed his hands through his hair, looked up at LT, and said, "That is one crazy son-of-a-bitch you have there, lieutenant."

LT glimpsed toward the direction where Jersey had gone then focused on Jebson and said, "Well, I don't know if that's true or not. I do know Jersey is nineteen, been here over a year and in that time has gone to hell and back several times. So… yes, maybe he is a little crazy. Then again we might be as crazy, or possibly even worse, when we have spent as much time as he has in this hell hole."

He sat down next to Jebson and waited a few minutes and finally said, "You and I have to have a very serious talk… are you up to it?"

Jebson put his hands on his knees took a deep breath and said, "Sure, a serious talk, about what?"

LT cleared his throat and, in an amicable manner, said, "You and Boomer are in a perilous situation. First, I can't guard you twenty-four/seven from the platoon members. Secondly, each passing hour you and Boomer fall further and further behind, rendering you both ineffective. The hard facts are the program is not working."

He waited a few moments while he hoped Jebson was comprehending what had been talking about. Then with great earnestness said, "Your face is flushed, Boomer is spent neither one of you can go another mile, This is our normal pace and every day activity. Do you think you and Boomer can do this for the next month or longer?"

Jebson slid his head down to his knees and softly said, "I can't go another mile and I'm not sure Boomer can go another half mile."

After a few minutes of silence LT put his hand on Jebson's back and said, "Okay. Let me offer this to you for consideration. Let's examine this, for what it is. First and foremost, this is a *test*. A test to see how credible this dog program is. Do you agree?"

Jebson gradually raised his head up from his legs, smiled, and said, "Yes... that's right."

"Fine. You and Boomer are out here testing the program. Granted it has not gone the way they envisioned, I'm sure. However, you have done what they asked. Now go back and report the facts. They now have data to refine the program or whatever they want to do."

Jebson nonchalantly walked over to where Boomer was lying and suddenly rushed back to LT and said, "Boomer is really sick!"

Less than an hour later, an army helo arrived at the platoon's position, and Boomer and Specialist Jebson were medevac to the rear.

The platoon, drenched in sweat, trudged on in silence for another hour and a half, trying to make up for the lost time due to the medevac. Finally, LT called for a break.

Rice paddies had become more numerous along with small, scattered villages. However, this resting place was a small knoll with several large rocks, coconut trees, and was well defensible, out of the watery paddies, and provided needed shade.

LT found two rocks, about three feet high and four to five in length beside a large coconut tree. The rocks formed a loose non-joined V, making it a perfect place for Lee and the radio. He pointed to the position and Lee immediately headed toward the place. He dropped his pack next to one of the rocks and started checking the machine gun placements and the rest of the platoon positions.

He checked 1st and 2nd squads, saving 3rd for last because he wanted to discretely inquire on Ed Cherry's wound and Jersey's mental condition.

As he walked into 3rd's area he saw Jersey, Ed, and Wolf sitting near a fighting position, talking. Jersey, Ed, and Wolf were kidding Pizza.

Pizza, Paul DiBenedetto, was from Boston and an avid Red Sox fan. His heavy Boston accent did in fact lend itself to much of his bothersome teasing.

Ed and Wolf were clearly ragging Pizza about his beloved Red Sox. Pizza was throwing his hands around saying, "Yea, yea, yea, whatever."

Ignoring Jersey, Pizza scanned the area, spotted a coconut in a tree, and said, "I'm going to get that coconut."

Pizza threw several long sticks he found at the coconut before it finally came crashing down to the ground. With great pride, he took the coconut over to the three. Jersey took it from his outstretched hand. The coconut was only the size of an average orange. Jersey very carefully studied the coconut and derisively said, "That ain't a coconut, it's a lousy Red Sox baseball."

Pizza stormed off throwing the small coconut a good thirty feet. Jersey, Ed, and Wolf rolled on the ground in hysterics.

LT smiled. Things appeared to be getting back to normal, if such a thing existed.

The platoon began to form somewhat of a routine each day moving from old to new positions up the valley. They now had been in the Que Son Valley several weeks. The work was hard, constantly moving and continuous daily contact with small enemy forces. The humidity was in the high sixty percentage, which felt more like a hundred. The temperatures ranged from ninety to over a hundred degrees. The mosquitoes were huge and appeared by the millions at night. Everyone in the platoon was getting about four to five hours of sleep in a twenty-four-hour period.

Each squad was either on day patrol, night ambush, or perimeter watch. The cycle never changed, never stopped, and the men were starting to really show the stress. They were now losing more weight, were dirtier and stunk to high heaven.

Captain McCarthy had sent over a new mission for the platoon. The platoon was to go on a full platoon sweep. The sweep ran along the base of the Que Son Mountains, north to Hill 110. Hill 110 was more of a finger jetting out of the mountains into the valley. From the hill, the platoon was to move out east, more into the rice growing areas.

LT felt good about the sweep. The day was bright and sunny, temperature in the high eighties, but very humid.

The platoon had been operating for about two hours, in and out of the jungle, with no enemy contact. He thought this was going to be a nice, uneventful patrol.

Suddenly, there was a loud *CRACK* and LT was immediately knocked back a few feet, then to the ground. Dazed, he tried to get up, only to be shoved back down by Jersey, who said, "STAY DOWN, LT, you've been hit."

He tried to make sense out of the hollering, small arms fire, then a blast from a machine gun. Joe ran over and started barking out orders and pointing towards a tree. LT felt strange. He heard the yelling and gunfire a few seconds ago, now he could not hear what Joe was saying and he was standing right over him.

Someone was unsnapping his flack jacket, then they lifted his head and placed something under it. This allowed him now to see where Joe had pointed and he saw a tree. The tree had shinny leaves and they seemed to be falling slowly off the tree, in slow motion, like a movie. He then saw a long stick fall from the tree, hitting branches and slowly bouncing off the limbs it hit. He thought the whole scene was very alien. He blinked his eyes, tried to better focus on what he thought he was seeing. As he glanced at the tree again, he saw a larger stick slowly slumbering down through the branches, only this "stick" bent and wrapped around a limb then slowly slide off the branch and dropped to the ground. It was a person.

He then felt someone repeatedly patting his cheek and he began to hear them as they said, "LT, LT, look at me. Focus on my voice. Can you hear me?"

Lethargically, he tried to converge all of his mental capacity on what was being said to him and happening around him. Bit by bit, he was now starting to put things in order and understanding what had happened.

Doc Weston said, "Can you understand me?" He shook his head yes. "Okay, that's great. You have been shot. Your flack jacket stopped the round from going into your chest, probably your heart. I think you have some broken ribs though. We need to get your flack jacket and gear off. Do you think you can stand up?"

After a few moments, he sluggishly attempted to stand. With help he was able to stand. He was a little wobbly but managed to get his equipment and shirt off. By now he had a large bruise on his chest, which was turning very black and blue.

Doc gently applied pressure to the bruised spot. LT gritted his teeth, wrenched, and tears welted up in his eyes.

Doc frowned and said, "We are going to have to medevac you, LT."

Gaining more composure, he said, "How many were there?"

Joe reluctantly said, "Well, we believe there were three of them. Two were guards, one was a sniper. You were his target. We got him and one of the guards. Think we may have wounded the other one."

Without showing any trepidation LT said, "Well I guess he won't collect any bounty."

Joe lowered his head and almost in a whisper said, "Are you going to be medevaced?"

LT took a real slow, cautious, deep breath and stared at Joe as he tested his lungs to see how hard it was to breath. He then looked around at some of the men standing close by. He could hear mumbles and low groans they did not want him to be medevaced. Joe was a nineteen-year-old sergeant, an outstanding one, but certainly did not want to take over the platoon.

Doc Weston, sizing up what was going on, said, "Look, I know you don't want to be medevac but I think you have at least two broken ribs. You won't be able to keep up with the platoon or even carry your pack."

LT walked away from the group to get a feel of what he might or might not be able to do. Then slowly hobbled back to the group and said, "Tell you what Doc. If I can't carry my pack I'll medevac myself. If I *can* carry it, I stay."

Jersey picked up LT's pack and dumped the contents out. He and Joe then helped him gingerly put on his flack jacket and pack. Jersey took LT's poncho liner and stuffed into the pack. "You okay, LT?"

He smiled and said, "Yes. Now add the star scope and binoculars."

That was enough; the weight pulling down on the flack jacket caused pressure on the ribs. He then picked up some of his C-rats and stuffed them into his cargo pockets in his trousers. He gingerly walked around and said, "I came over here to command a Marine rifle platoon, not hand out volleyballs in the rear. I have my platoon. There will be no medevac."

The platoon didn't move from one location as fast as they had previously, but they met all assignments and missions. After a few days the pain was less noticeable and he was able, to some degree, ignore the pain.

CHAPTER 26
THE MACHINE GUN MYSTERY SOLVED

The platoon moved to a position that would be their home for two days. Mail would be sent out, sometimes stored for weeks, until the platoon was in a location to accept it. LT thought it very strange the mail was always delivered in large bright red nylon bags, which made great targets for the enemy. He envisioned, as a child, those were actually the type of bag Santa Clause would use to deliver presents on Christmas.

A few hours before the mail was to be delivered, Lee informed LT he had a call from the rear. It was the first sergeant, who seldom, if ever, called platoon commanders in the field. These calls had happened before and Lee thought them somewhat odd.

LT took the call, said, "Yes and thanks," then hung up. He took a deep breath, exhaled, and said, "Lee, please get me Bates, Pizza, and Ray."

Lee soon returned with the three. LT mustered up a smile and said, "Gentlemen, we once more are going to conduct the Camouflage Test. Larry, you and Al take your gun over to that knoll." He pointed to the small hill five hundred meters from the CP's location.

"Pizza, you and your fire team provide security. Ray, work up preplanned protective mortar targets around the knoll. I want you off this hill by 1330 hours. Remember, no one is to see any of you from the helo. Any questions?"

LT stood by his CP and watched the "Camouflage Test" unit reach the knoll and began their task of hiding themselves and the gun.

Joe walked up to the lieutenant and asked, "You ever going to tell them why they are hiding the gun?"

Chuckling, he said, "Not for a long time anyway. Remember the old World War II saying, 'Loose lips sink ships'? Well, the fewer who know, the better off we are. Right now there are only five, including you and me, and one of them is back in the states. No, let's keep it among us for now."

As warned, the helo landed, bringing mail and the NIC agent. LT went down to the LZ and welcomed Agent Forest Walker.

"Agent Walker, what a surprise. Are you responsible for all this mail or merely making sure it reaches us safely?"

The agent grinned, nodded at LT, and said, "Sure, I wanted to make sure you and your men got their mail… nothing too good for the fighting man."

LT laughed and said, "Well, the part about 'nothing' has some truth to it. So tell me, what really brings you out to the bush and don't tell me you miss it from your Marine Corps days as a company commander."

In a pleasant, smiling manner, Agent Walker placed his large hand on LT's back and slowly started ambling toward the CP saying. "Let's go to your CP and chat."

Agent Walker's tall bulky frame made it uncomfortable for him to sit in the small CP, so the officer and agent sat outside, under the coconut trees' shade.

Lee handed Agent Walker a cup of coffee. Walker smiled at Lee and nodded in thanks.

After sipping, a few moments on the coffee, Agent Walker finally broke the silence by saying, "The last few times we talked, your machine gun was out on patrol and I couldn't check the serial numbers. So, what I would like to do today is to check its number. Is that possible?"

LT smiled at the agent and, in a very matter-of-fact manner, said, "Absolutely!" He turned to Joe, who was off to the side working with Ballew sorting the mail. "Joe, Agent Walker and I are going to go around the entire perimeter. Have everything uncovered so he can see nothing is being hid. Make sure the M-60 is uncovered. Remember, do not uncover it at its fighting hole. Move it up on the side of the hill and if Billy is working the mail, Ray can take care of the gun."

Joe froze, thought for a moment, then grinned and said, "Right away, sir!"

Agent Walker and the young lieutenant strolled around the platoon perimeter, talking in a cordial manner. LT was relieved when they approached the gun. Corporal Ray Agula was standing next to the gun, Billy could not be seen anywhere.

Satisfied with what he found, or didn't, find, Agent Walker left and LT breathed easier.

The "Camouflage Test" unit returned to the perimeter, with Bates loudly complaining. "LT, why are they conducting that test and for what purpose?"

LT shrugged his shoulders and said, "Don't know, Bates. They tell me what they want. Maybe it's a top secret project… you know, maybe some kind of heat seeker in the plane or metal locator, who knows." He winked at Joe and Ray and quickly walked away, not wanting to get into any more discussion with Bates on the matter.

The next day the platoon was on another platoon sweep. They headed in the direction of Happy Valley, close to the imaginary dividing line of the heavily-wooded ridge and rocks the size of pickups trucks which separated Que Son and Happy Valley. The point, PK, saw movement ahead, then found a tunnel entrance.

The tunnels were dug into a small hill, which covered about two acres. On the front of the hill was a flat wall or face of the hill, which measured about twenty feet long and eight feet tall. In the middle of this "face" was an entrance. About fifty feet from the entrance were two large boulders with about ten feet of open space between the two.

The lieutenant ringed the hill with his platoon. He placed Joe Tiger, with his M-14, Louis Lujan, and John "Hawk" Mihok, with their M-16's, by the boulders to guard the entrance of the tunnel.

After several attempts of dropping smoke and grenades in to the tunnels it became apparent it was not going to work.

LT scratched his head and pondered what to do next.

Larry Bates nonchalantly walked up to him and said, "You know, LT, those American-made CS grenades are aerosol based. The ARVN CN grenades are oil-based. The oil base will contaminate an area a lot longer than the aerosol ones. I'll bet the CN's will get those boys out of the tunnels real quick."

LT looked at Bates for a few seconds and said, "And I suppose you just happen to have some of those CN grenades?"

Bates, grinning, said, "Well… I may have happened to trade some… things to the ARVNs for a case of them."

Chuckling, he said, "And why aren't I surprised. Very well, get some of those grenades and toss them down these air holes and let's see what happens."

He then walked over the top of the hill to where Joe Tiger was guarding the entrance and told him to stand by, that the enemy should be coming out, hopefully, any minute.

Joe Tiger went into a kneeling position and aimed his rifle toward the tunnel entrance. Louis and John, still leaning on their weapons, stood on each side of Joe offering verbal support.

LT started to walk away to see if he could determine how Bates was doing with the grenades. Suddenly a VC charged from the cave, firing, and Joe, with his trusty M-14, shot the VC. This scenario was repeated four more times.

After fifteen minutes no one else came out of the tunnel entrance. C-4 blocks were dropped into the air vents and at the entrance of the tunnel. The explosions of the C-4 blocks sealed the entrance and collapsed most of the tunneling, causing the top of the hill to deflate.

LT finished his enemy contact report, handed it to Lee, and said, "Turn the company radio on and send this to the skipper."

The platoon had been out in the Que Son Valley over forty days without a break. Their clothes were dirty, becoming very ragged, and their bodies stunk because they had not had a bath since coming to the valley.

The C-ration meals were limited to a total of one dozen selections. The meals were mostly eaten cold because of security reasons or being on the move. The men averaged from four to five hours of sleep in a twenty-four-hour time period. Sleep was on the hard or wet ground. They were becoming more exhausted as each day passed. They ran day patrols, then day perimeter watch, followed by night ambushes. Most of the time day patrols included carrying tons of captured rice to an LZ to be flown back to the rear.

The high humidity and soaring temperatures combined with either rough rocky, bush-covered terrain or rice paddies filled with water made the movement and tasks of the heavy-laden Marines beyond burdensome. Their only saving grace was the fact that these young men were barely out of their teens and embodied with great endurance.

In spite of the Marines' perilous situation, the operation denying the NVA rice of Que Son Valley was extremely successful. The first thirty days or so of the operation the platoon had daily and nightly contact with the enemy. The last few days of contact was, however, about every other day and with much smaller groups of enemy carrying rice out of the valley. The platoon members also noticed where the ADSID's had been placed on the trails leading into the mountains; the firing of artillery on these sites had dropped from five to six a night to maybe one a night.

It had been raining several days, moral was low, troops were exhausted, and LT sat silently with his CP group when the radio broke the stillness with its squawking of an incoming call.

LT took the call and all that could be heard was, "Yes sir's," "No sir's," and "Are you sure," "Are you really sure," and finally, "You're absolutely sure?"

He hung up, then patted the hand set into his left hand several times before realizing Lee had been reaching for it numerous times. He quickly handed the hand set to Lee, saying, "Sorry."

Joe glanced around at the others then back to LT. After several moments of utter silence, he finally said, "LT, good news or bad?"

Wincing, LT said, "I fear both." Taking a deep breath then exhaling, he stated, "The skipper informed me regiment wants us to do one last thing and in return *promised* the platoon would then be flown into LZ Baldy for baths, new clothes, steak, and beer."

The four glimpsed at each other smiling, radiating total merriment, clapping their hands, and bouncing around the CP.

As Joe joyfully sat down, he immediately noticed LT was not involved in the festivities. He was solemnly staring at the ground. Joe held his hand up to stop the merry-making and said, "LT, what… what is the bad news?"

Bolting up from his seat, he hurriedly said, "Probably nothing." He paused, then with deliberation said, "However, I am not sure I want us to tell the troops about this plan right away. If we tell them and regiment doesn't carry through, I'm the bad leader. And it's not like that has never happened before, as we all know."

They all mumbled, groaned, and agreed it was very possible regiment might not come through. They did all agree though no one would tell the troops of the plan until the helos were actually coming into the landing site.

The next morning, before sunrise, the platoon moved out of their position to a designated area a few clicks west of the Rock Crusher. The platoon was to set up a

360 perimeter which would also serve as an LZ for a supply drop.

LT knew it was a clandestine operation or the unit would have taken supplies at the Rock Crusher. Why would the platoon establish an LZ so close to the crusher and take on supplies, especially since they were to go in right after finishing this "little last thing"?

By 0900 hours a 360-degree perimeter was established and the troops were told to expect "friendlies." Half an hour later, someone yelled, "Friendlies coming in!"

A lone figure emerged from the tree line at the base of the mountains. As he cautiously approached the lines, the Marines could see the person was wearing blue jeans and a green t-shirt, and had long, light brown hair which covered his ears. He also had a magazine pouch over his shoulder and carried a Swedish K sub-machine gun. He looked at no one, had no expression and no friendly gestures—simply a cold stare.

Five more men followed the first man out of the tree line. They were dressed in green uniforms, no insignia or unit patches, and carried M16s along with field gear. They never broke stride, went directly to the pile of supplies, picked them up and exited the perimeter.

LT could hear the troops whispering among themselves, "CIA." A few minutes after the secretive group left, he told Lee to check on the helos. Five minutes later Lee informed him the birds would be at least two or three hours late.

The platoon marched on the road to LZ Baldy. The helos never showed. The troops were exhausted and hot from the long walk and basically worn out. They needed a break.

As the platoon neared the gates of LZ Baldy, LT stepped out of the march formation, scanned the lines of his men, and felt proud of their accomplishments. Glancing up toward the gate, his heart suddenly stopped beating. There, at the gate entry, standing next to a US Army jeep and trailer, stood NIC Agent Forest Walker, an Army master sergeant, and a gunny. He had to think fast—Bates and Brown had momentarily passed him heading to the gate carrying *the* machine gun.

He tore toward the gate, passing up Bates and Brown. He could see Walker staring straight at him. LT waved at the agent, smiled, and over his shoulder yelled, "Gun up!"

Bouncing his pack, helmet, and equipment around made the jog awkward. When he reached Agent Walker, he stammered out, "Amazing, you're the one person I want to see." Pausing and taking in air he went on to say, "I think we found your missing machine gun."

Agent Walker, who had been smiling, watching him jog toward him, stop smiling and had a blank look about his face. The master sergeant quickly glanced at LT, then the agent, and back and forth, and finally asked, "Are... are you sure?"

Agent Walker crossed his arms over his chest, smiled, looked at the master sergeant, and said, "Oh, I bet he is sure... real sure."

Bates and Brown arrived at the group with the machine gun and bag of accessories.

LT, ignoring Agent Walker's comment, quickly, before Bates or Brown could say anything, told Bates to put the machine gun on the trailer and for both of them to go stand under a tree about fifty feet away.

Bates started to say something, but looked into LT's eyes, froze, and then gently grabbed Brown's arm and said, "Come on. Now!"

The master sergeant and gunny immediately started going over the machine gun. LT smiled at Agent Walker, who was now giving him an evil eye. The master sergeant broke the silence by announcing the gun was in fact the one stolen from the army. However, its condition was worn and dirty; he could not put it back into level "A Pack."

LT blurted out, "Worn a little, but not *dirty!*"

Agent Walker, with his arms still folded over his chest, stood straight up and, looking like a giant redwood tree, said, "And, lieutenant, you would know this because?"

LT again promptly dismissed the question from the agent, reached his hand out, and placed it on the master sergeant's shoulder and said, "Well, if you don't want it back. As a commissioned Marine Corps Officer, I have the authority to sign for the gun, transferring it from the Army to the Marine Corps... it's a win-win situation, master sergeant."

The master sergeant looked at the gunny then the agent. Agent Walker shook his head in agreement with the lieutenant and smiled.

Bates and Brown stood under the tree and watched every move. Brown, staring at Agent Walker, said, "Who is the big guy? Hell, he's half of a football team. And why is LT arguing and pointing his fingers all around?"

Bates glanced at Brown and said, "You ask a lot of questions. I don't know who the big guy is or the army SNCO's. LT is putting on one hell of a fight, for what, I don't know. Look, LT is signing something, he is smiling and looks real happy."

LT turned to Bates and Brown, then yelled, "GET OVER HERE AND GET YOUR GUN!"

Agent Walker watched as, Bates and Brown, gathered up the machine gun and scurried off to catch up with the rest of the platoon. The master sergeant and gunny crawled in their jeep and drove off, leaving LT and Agent Walker standing alone by the gate.

Walker broke the silence by saying, "Those two troops of yours didn't know the gun was stolen, did they?"

LT looked out over the road leading into the LZ and said, "No, and it wasn't stolen, it was appropriated."

Agent Walker roared with laughter. After a few minutes, when he had gained some composer, he said, "And tell me, my young lieutenant, can you explain to me the difference between stealing and appropriating?"

LT locked his jaws, swung his entire body toward the agent and, like a chained pit bull who had reached the end of his chain, stopped, glared at the agent, and in a tenacious manner yelled, "YES I CAN! Stealing is when you take something that doesn't belong to you and you use it for your personal use or gain. Appropriating is acquiring something in the system that you need and should have. This platoon has had a request for a machine gun for over eighteen months. The system isn't working. I didn't *appropriate* the machine gun for the Marine Corps, regiment, battalion, or company. The gun was *appropriated* for those young men. So they could have a better chance of fighting, winning, and a greater chance of living and surviving this hell hole."

Agent Walker stared at him, blinked his eyes, put his hand on the lieutenant's shoulder, and slowly said, "I'll take care of this. The gun has been found, signed for, and a great wrong has been corrected. Come, my young friend, I'm going to buy you a cold beer."

Instantly, to LT, it seemed one of his many "weighty responsibilities" had been lifted from his shoulders. He took a deep breath and, after a moment, slowly exhaled and stammered a genuine, "Thank you!"

Hotel Company's troops were given barracks to sleep in, semi-warm showers, and fifty-gallon barrels cut in half lengthwise, filled with charcoal and covered with metal grates, to cook steaks and hamburgers.

The wide-eyed troops grabbed up steaks, hamburgers, and baked potatoes, only to discover their stomachs had shrunk so much they could only eat portions of the food. They clutched their partially-eaten burgers in one hand and stared at the remaining steaks and potatoes on their plates, wondering how they could save the savory meal for another day.

The company spent two more days in the rear getting showers, clean clothes, and hot food. However, nothing better illustrated the importance of hot food more than the following example. The troops were so intent on getting hot chow that one day a sniper, in a ten-minute period, fired three rounds at them. Each time they would duck down, wait a few moments, then stand back up, never losing their place in the mess hall line. A Marine sniper silenced the annoyance.

LT's most-seasoned and heavily-relied-on squad leaders Jersey and Olsen both rotated back to the states. Lance Corporal Paul (Pizza) DiBenedetto now had 3rd squad and Corporal Gene Evans took over 2nd squad.

The company, at the crack of dawn, was trucked to the Rock Crusher, about three clicks southwest of LZ Ross.

CHAPTER 27
THE ROCK CRUSHER

All roads in Vietnam outside of the large cities were dirt. Therefore, the US Army developed the Rock Crusher, which provided all the rock used to surface the main roads used by the military in I Corps. Protecting the crusher was a major tactical concern for both the United States Forces and the South Vietnam government.

The crusher area consisted of a long, steep, narrow finger, much like a giant staircase standing alone and not leading any place. The finger overlooked the actual quarry and equipment used to mine the stone. This strange formation was formed by nature and the removal of the rock.

The finger was home to two rifle platoons, weapons, the CP group, and one squad from a third platoon. The two remaining squads, from a third platoon, were located at the bottom of the finger guarding half of a single culvert bridge. The other side of the single culvert was guarded by a small PF (Popular Force) unit. The culvert bridged a small stream on the road, vital in allowing trucks to enter the quarry.

Tactical doctrine called for an avenue, road, bridge, etc., to be guarded by a single unit and not split by two units. Why the culvert separated the two units was a mystery. It was assumed by most to give the PF's a feeling of responsibility and self-worth. To the Marines, it raised real concerns and doubts.

Hotel Company relieved Golf Company of the security responsibilities of the quarry and single culvert bridge. Captain McCarthy was immediately apprehensive about the road separating the units and tried to get battalion to change the situation. Battalion took the matter up with higher command and was told security responsibilities would not change.

1st platoon was given the responsibility to guard the single culvert using only one rifle squad and a machine gun. The area was not large enough for the entire platoon. LT begged the skipper to at least let him place two squads and himself in the defensive position. The request was denied.

LT had real concerns. Jersey, 3rd squad leader, had rotated back to the states before the company moved to the crusher, and Lance Corporal Paul (Pizza) DiBenedetto was appointed as the squad leader. Corporal Olsen, 2nd squad leader, had rotated only a few days behind Jersey, and Lance Corporal Gene Evans was chosen as Olsen's replacement. Corporal Rathbone was the only seasoned squad leader in the platoon.

He had personally selected each one of these men for their new, very important positions. He knew they all had the knowledge, capabilities, and leadership traits to execute their jobs at the highest level. It was a matter of "comfort" for him and the new squad leaders. He also knew time would provide the "comfort feeling" for all involved.

LT assigned Pizza's 3rd squad the mission of guarding the single culvert, along with Larry Bates' gun team. He was not happy having to assign anyone to the culvert but felt, since he had no choice, Pizza was the best selection of his new squad leaders. He got permission from the skipper to take most of his remaining platoon down to rebuild and improve the strength of their perimeter.

Both the Marines and PF's perimeters were like horseshoes, open at the facing ends. The PF perimeter, across the road, appeared to be more of a camping site, with hammocks strung up, some small bamboo huts, and a few fighting holes dug around the perimeter.

The skipper and LT questioned the PF's capabilities, willingness, and ability to communicate with the Marines. This was exacerbated even more when the officer in charge, and the only one who could speak limited English, rode off on his bicycle to an ARVN compound about a mile away each night.

The entire company knew the greatest risk of being hit by the enemy was the first night you moved into a new position. The Marines were uneasy, alert was high, and new pre-planned artillery and mortar fires had been put in place, especially supporting the single culvert.

Around two thirty in the morning, all hell broke loose. LZ Ross was struck by rockets and mortars, and the perimeter was breached by VC sappers. The Rock Crusher was bombarded by mortar and small arms fire. The valley's night sky was illuminated by flares, bursting rockets, tracer rounds, and exploding artillery rounds. The early morning silence was now a booming rhythm of roaring explosions.

The enemy mortars failed to land on the finger as the rounds landed in front or behind it because it was so narrow. The walls of the finger were steep and the enemy small arms fire flew up into the sky, only falling inertly back to earth far from the finger.

However, a major offensive attack was being wagered against the single culvert, especially on the PF's side. Satchel charges went off in the PF's compound. As RPG's flew in from the stream bed, the Marines could hear three to four enemy mortar tubes working and each must have had two loaders, as it was a steady "thunk, thunk, thunk."

An enemy attack on the Marines perimeter was met with stiff resistance and saved from being run over by the quick-thinking of the new squad leader, Pizza.

Pizza was a streetwise Italian kid from Worcester, Massachusetts who had been drafted into the Marine Corps after dropping out of college on a full gymnastic scholarship. Powerfully built, with a quick temper, he had been sent repeatedly to motivation platoon in boot camp, actually volunteering one time.

Pizza, seeing the direction of the attack, supervised a steady bombardment of grenades at the attacking enemy. Nearly every grenade was used in the initial attack. The VC had run into a literal wall of grenades and bullets. They simply no longer could sustain the attack and withdrew.

Scores of explosions and small arms fire finally ceased in the PF's position and it became quiet. Pizza then gave the order, "We're going over!"

The PF's position was a complete wreck; blood covered the ground and PF's bodies were scattered all over the site, many blown apart, others riddled with bullet holes. The only weapon left was an M16 destroyed by the explosions.

By morning light the Marines had regrouped and stood ready for another attack. However, they heard a strange sound. A small bell was going ring, ring, ring. Then they saw a light of a bicycle coming toward them. It was the ARVN officer riding a bicycle, leading a troop of South Vietnamese to the site.

The ARVN's combed the area around and in the PF's perimeter, and gathered up the bodies, and any ordnance left. The PF's lost; out of about twenty men, twelve were killed and seven badly wounded, and one was missing.

Bates was standing in the middle of the road, surveying the situation, when an ARVN officer approached him, dropped off a large green bag in front of him, smiled, and walked away. Bates, being the curious one, opened the bag and said, "Shit. This bag is full of unexploded ordnance." The sack contained eight RPG rockets, two satchel charges, and about a dozen homemade chi com grenades, each one made from tin cans with labels marked A1 Mackerel, product of Japan.

Bates looked for LT; he knew he had led the other two squads down from the Rock Crusher perimeter during the attack as reinforcements. Finally spotting the lieutenant, he hollered, "LT, come here, I have something to show you."

LT walked over to Bates and said, "What have you got?"

Bates, grinning, pointed to the bag and said, "Thought you might want to see this stuff."

He leaned over and opened the bag and shouted, "Damn it, Bates!" He stepped back quickly and, with a disgusted look on his face, further stated, "Get the engineers over here and get the hell away from this bag of ordnance."

The attack on the Single Culvert Bridge was probably a diversion, as LZ Ross had been attacked, too, and almost overrun the same night. Hitting the culvert and Rock Crusher had kept LZ Baldy from sending reinforcements to Ross, which had a heavy toll of Marines.

Later that day, Captain McCarthy pulled the squad from the culvert perimeter and declared it was indefensible and he would not place troops there anymore. The entire time the company remained at the Rock Crusher, the single culvert was not manned by Marines.

The next night, the Rock Crusher was attacked by enemy mortars. The skipper had a general fix on where the fire was coming from and told LT to form a squad and go out and find the exact place where the enemy was entrenched, firing their mortars.

LT quickly formed up 2nd squad, Lance Corporal Evans's unit, and headed out into the black night. He chose the high ground leading to the suspected site. The unit left the perimeter running through the night, dodging limbs and fallen logs in the dense jungle terrain. Finally, stopping, he turned around and, looking back to his squad, realized no one was behind him. He immediately froze making himself as small-as-possible target and listened intently.

After a few moments, he heard movement behind him and softly said, "Gene, I'm over here."

Much to LT's relief, the squad appeared from the deep shadows. Gene, much to his relief, said, "LT, you were moving too fast, we couldn't keep up in the darkness."

LT, without thinking, uttered, "Shit, I'm sorry, guys. I forgot to tell you, I can see in the dark."

The squad members glanced from one to the other and then, looking at LT, said softly in unison, "Ooh."

They went for another five hundred meters when LT suddenly stopped, pointed in the direction of a bright flash in the night, and said, "That's where the enemy is shooting their mortars from."

He checked his map, determined where the rounds were being fired from, and called the grid into the skipper. In a few moments, the area exploded into massive balls of fire. The artillery unit at LZ Baldly fired two batteries of guns and completely blew the area around the site away. The enemy mortars immediately ceased.

The unit returned to the Rock Crusher with many thanks of gratitude and a welcomed "well done."

The next morning the skipper announced the existing defensive obstacles were not adequate and the company was going to greatly improve the defense by adding new obstructions.

At the far end of the Rock Crusher hill was an area that at one time had been rice paddies. However, since the rock had been quarried from the place, it now was a swampy smelly mess. The skipper decided to place a string of razor wire across the swamp so a working party was selected by the company gunny.

Gunny Dixon thought it was only fair that each rifle platoon give him three troops apiece, for a total of nine men. This way the platoons shared in the nasty job. The lieutenants also agreed; it was better to share than stick one platoon with the task. Bates, Little John, and Speedy volunteered from 1st platoon, according to the platoon sergeant, Joe Loerzel.

The working party waded into the marshy water and pounded metal engineer stakes into the slimy ground. After driving the stakes into the ground, rolls of German tape razor wire were uncoiled and carefully attached to the downward-pointing hooks on the stakes. With the wire positioned in this method, a VC sapper could not slither under the wire to breach the new defenses.

Bates was holding a sledgehammer in his hands. He had just drove a stake into the boggy ground, and was watching Ski, a big red-headed Marine from 2nd platoon, kneeling over next to the stake in about eighteen inches of stagnant water. Ski had finished hooking a strand of wire to the pole when Bates saw a centipede, about eight inches long, running across the green, scum covered, water.

The centipede ran up and crawled onto the back of Ski, onto a patch of his bare skin between his trouser top and his green t-shirt. Horrified, Bates tried to knock the creature off Ski but the long, flattened arthropod drove his venomous fangs into Ski's back before Bates could knock it off.

The fangs, now buried into the skin, released toxins, causing Ski to leap into the air as if shot out of an ejection seat, screaming and swearing the whole time.

Bates yelled, "CORPSMAN!" Immediately, other Marines ran to Ski's aid. They carried him to dry ground and laid him on his stomach. By now, he already had a red welt the size of a half a grapefruit on the small of his back and it was growing larger by the seconds.

Fortunately for Ski, First Sergeant Knight had the company jeep at the crusher, because he had brought paper work out for the skipper to sign. Ski was swiftly loaded into the jeep and taken to LZ Baldy, about three clicks away for medical treatment.

First' Sergeant Knight also brought with him important news. Lieutenant Colonel Folsom was leaving as the battalion commander in the first week of April, only a few weeks away.

This information caused LT concern. He had joined the battalion about two weeks before Folsom had joined the unit. This meant he could be leaving the platoon soon and he did not want to do that. Maybe, just maybe, he could convince the new battalion commander he should stay a little longer with the platoon.

The next morning, as LT walked over to see the captain, he glanced over toward the single culvert and his heart sank as he saw three jeeps. Two were escorts with ring-mounted 50 caliber machine guns, and the middle jeep was carrying the battalion commander, Lieutenant Colonel Folsom, and the battalion sergeant major.

The jeeps pulled up to the company CP and stopped. The skipper and gunny both came tearing out of the CP, slid up next to the jeep, and enthusiastically greeted the CO and sergeant major. The gunny and sergeant major peeled off from the officers and began to talk. The colonel and captain started walking around the area, checking on the defensive projects.

The two commanders strolled through the area for a good hour. The colonel, it seemed, wanted to talk to every Marine in the company. As the two finished up their tour, they ended by the colonel's jeep, not far where LT was checking on some of his men.

He was watching his men, but at the same time, out of the corner of his eye, he could clearly see the captain and colonel. He saw the skipper turn and look right at him then turn and say something to the colonel. The colonel, in return, glanced toward him and then the two spoke again. The colonel turned and started walking, not to his jeep, but toward LT.

LT waited until the colonel was only a few feet away then quickly turned, with a pounding heart and a forced smile, saluted and said, "How is our fearless leader today, sir?"

The colonel chuckled and as he waved his hand from one side the other, said, "I'm doing fine, thank you. It seems where ever Hotel goes they make it better. Darn fine work here."

LT glimpsed around and said, "Thank you sir. Captain McCarthy's motto is 'make it better than you found it.' I believe it's a good one and I have adopted it myself."

Smiling, the colonel said, "That's a good one. Wished more people would buy into it." Then, with a serious look, he continued by saying, "You know I'll be leaving in the next few weeks. But before I go, I want to offer you a chance to come into the rear. I'll place you in any one of the shops you want to go to."

LT swallowed hard, looked down at the ground, and slowly raised his head up and looked the colonel in the eyes and said, "Colonel, *when* I go in, I would like to go to the S-3. But I really want to stay with the platoon as long as I can."

The colonel grimaced, said, "Why am I not surprised? Okay, you stay as long as I'm in charge. Can't promise anything longer than that, you understand? Or until you piss off 'Fightin' Frank' and he fires you."

LT grinned and said, "Well, I manage to piss the skipper off on a weekly basis, so I doubt that will change. However, I'll try not go overboard with it."

The colonel roared with laughter and headed to his jeep.

He was thrilled; he felt like jumping up and yelling at the top of his lungs. He swaggered off to see the skipper and find out what else might be going on.

"Hi skipper, did you find anything new going on?"

"Hey, Geronimo how did it go with the CO?"

Beaming, he said, "Really good. He told me I could keep the platoon while he was CO… well, as long as you don't fire me."

Smirking, the skipper said, "Well you know there is a pretty good chance of that happening, if you piss me off one more time."

LT ignored the skipper's last comment and said, "Any news as to what the company may be doing in the near future?"

The captain, with a good deal of thoughtfulness, said, "Sit down. I guess the CO wants us to finish the work we are doing here. Then we are going to Tu Cau Bridge. It appears the division will be moving all military units closer to Da Nang during Tet."

"How about you, skipper, do you know when you're leaving or where you will be going?"

The captain took a deep breath, released it, and slowly said, "I have been offered the S-3A job at battalion. I like Major Evans, but I'm not sure I want to go to any 3 shop… not right now anyway."

"By the way, last week when 1st Bn., 7th Marines got hit real bad, you asked me if I would check on a Lieutenant Paul Gibbs, one of your OCS classmates. Well, the colonel brought me the list of KIA's and WIA's." The skipper paused, then solemnly said, "Your friend is on the wounded list and was shipped back the states."

LT slid forward in his seat, leaned down, and placed his hands on his face and was quite for a while and finally stammered out, "Do you know how bad he was hurt?"

The skipper slowly said, "Well, since you gave me his name and I passed it on to the battalion commander, he went through the medical channels and found out that your friend was shot several times by an enemy machine gun in the leg. They don't think he is going to lose the leg but will be in the hospital for well over a year because he will have to have numerous operations."

LT slowly stood up and uttered a low, "Thank you and the colonel for getting me the information."

"Geronimo, I am sincerely sorry about your friend. He is alive; you know it could have been worse."

As he was shuffling out of the CP, he turned to the skipper and, through misty eyes, said, "I guess that depends on Paul."

The company finished its work on the new defenses and on the third day was helo lifted close to Tu Cau Bridge.

CHAPTER 28
TU CAU BRIDGE

Tu Cau Bridge was a wooden bridge which spanned a tidal river. When the tides were up, the water under the bridge was salty; tides low, the water was fresh and flowed out into the ocean. The area above the bridge resembled a dumbbell. The local farmers and merchants used the bridge extensively during the day; at night it was closed to all traffic.

The road the bridge was on ran west to Highway 1, about a quarter of a mile away. At the "T" conjunctions of Highway 1 and the Tu Cau Road was a garrison of ARVN's. They kept to themselves and seldom made contact with those guarding the bridge. To the south, a good mile and half away, was an old French Fort now occupied by an ARVN battalion. They were friendly, but, again, no relationships with those guarding the bridge.

The bridge was seventeen miles south of Da Nang. Apparently the military higher command did not want a repeat of previous years' military attacks during Tet, therefore the rifle companies were moved closer to Da Nang for the greater protection of the city and military installations.

Hotel Company was helo-lifted about a mile from the bridge, then they marched the rest of the way to the bridge. Why the company wasn't dropped off at the bridge remains a mystery, because there was a working LZ at the bridge. Some thought it was a display of American Forces, others thought it was to keep the Marines unhappy and thus make them even better fighters. The ideas were as many and varied as there were men in the company.

The new "home" of the 1st platoon was a moderate-size French bunker made of concrete built into the sides of the ground, which supported the end of the bridge. It was large enough for the entire platoon to get themselves and their gear in and out of the elements. It also allowed them to lay down their worldly belongings and not have to carry them on their backs all the time.

There was, much to LT's delight and satisfaction, a small cubbyhole which offered him a place to lie down on a rubber mattress and sleep in a dry place. More importantly, it provided a spot for the radios and operators out of the weather.

After spending over two months in Qua Son Valley, the men were exhausted, their clothes were ragged, they were dirty, and they smelled "to high hell." The Marines of Hotel Company were ecstatic when moved to Tu Cau Bridge. They all, to the man, were thinking and dreaming of warm showers and hot food.

Hot showers proved to be two general purpose tents placed end to end. The first one had three-quarter-inch pipes in four rows, which were suspended about seven feet above the wooden pallets placed on the floor of the tent, so those showering wouldn't get muddy feet. The other tent served as a dressing area. Hot food was another story. Once a week trucks would arrive with vats of food. At least it was not poisonous, and far better than C-rats.

The duty for the Marines of 1st platoon was light considering what they had been subjected to in the past: one day of patrols, followed by night ambushes and perimeter duty between the two. While it lightened the individual troop's burden, it brought new leadership challenges for the new squad leaders and LT himself. The platoon had the west end of the bridge to guard. They also had two sawhorses they manned during the day. The sawhorses were covered with concertina wire, used to hold up traffic until a number of people could be escorted across the bridge at one time. At night the sawhorse served as part of the bridge perimeter.

Additionally, the platoon was responsible for providing two guards who walked back and forth across the bridge checking the river on both sides for possible sappers trying to blow the bridge up from the river.

On 1st platoon's end of the bridge, at the bottom of the down-sloping bank from the bridge, was a small flag football field. On the other side of the river, adjacent to the football field, was the company three-hole latrine, also known as a "head."

The latrine was a wood-framed ten-by-eight-foot building with four-by-eight plywood front. Screen wire made up the remaining height of the front structure. The back and the end without the screen door were of solid plywood facing. The entry to the latrine was a regular screen door.

Each platoon stood "latrine duty" every third week, for a week. This duty required daily burning of the barrels, which held the human waste. The barrels were fifty-five-gallon barrels cut in half and placed under the hole where people sat to do their private business. The burning involved taking the barrel out of the building and mixing part gasoline and diesel fuel and lighting the waste, burning it up. Sweeping out the inside of the latrine was also a requirement, along with making sure plenty of toilet paper was available.

LT's platoon had finished their latrine duty a couple days ago. LT was crossing the bridge on his way to turn in his evening report to the captain when he heard, then saw, the rather loud and boisterous squad leader of 3rd platoon, 1st squad.

The squad leader was standing outside of the latrine and in an egotistical and blaring voice screamed, "I declare this shitter clean and I shall be the first to use it… undisturbed!"

The squad leader hollered at one of his men to stand guard on the screen door and instructed the young guard to let no one enter while he was using it or it would be the troop's ass. The bullying squad leader then grabbed a *Playboy* magazine from the young Marine and slipped it under his arm. He then calmly took a cigar out of his breast pocket, and lit it. The self-centered squad leader looked around and boldly entered the clean latrine, yelling at the young Marine to "post" himself.

LT sat down on the bridge rail, crossed his arms over his chest, and mumbled to himself, "What an ass!" He thought about going down to the head and messing with the squad leader but decided he had more important things to do than screw with the jerk.

As he started, once again, to make his way to the skipper's bunker, he glanced at the squad leader through the screen wire front, he was totally startled by what happened in a flash. The squad leader had taken a couple long drags on the cigar, looked around for a place to deposit his ashes, and decided to drop them in the empty hole next to him… which he did.

Out of the half drum, which contained diesel fuel and gasoline, a single flame roared all the way to the top of the head. This, in return, caused the squad leader to jump up screaming at the top of his lungs and tear toward the screen door. His action also prompted the fumes from the hole he was sitting on to clash with the flames. Another column of flames shot up and finally the third hole erupted into a fountain of fire.

The squad leader hit the screen door with such a commanding force that he tore the screen door from the frame, knocking it and the young guard to the ground. The now shrieking squad leader, with his pants down to his ankles, stepped on the screen door and the young guard, then he tripped, sending him flying through the air, with a blue streak of flames from his buttocks rapidly following. He then unceremoniously went crashing and landing on his back loudly, squealing, "My ass is on fire… HELP… HELP!"

Unfortunately for the squad leader, his obnoxious, "look-at-me" attitude in fact gained him many observers, who saw the whole caper. Many of those now were lying on the ground face down and slapping the earth. Others were flattened on their backs and holding their stomachs, all in uncontrollable laughter.

LT, trying to maintain some kind of dignity, held onto the railing post of the bridge while trying to cover his face with his other hand to conceal his laughter.

Captain McCarthy and Gunny Dixon charged out of the command bunker toward the burning latrine with pistols held high. The skipper quickly yelled at a group of Marines and, pointing to the head, told them to put the fire out.

However, several other Marines had already pulled the burning barrels from the building and were in the process of dousing the flames.

The skipper swiftly turned his attention to LT and walked over to him and asked, "What the hell happened, anyway?"

LT, trying to stand up, still laughing, pointed toward the latrine down the road, and, in a choking and stammering voice said, "That dumb shit…

cigar… flames… human rocket…" Then, laughing uncontrollably, he sat down awkwardly on the side of the road.

The captain looked at LT then at Gunny Dixon, who in return gave him a hunched shoulder response. The skipper, then frowning at the gunny, said, "Well, go down there and see if you can find out what the hell is going on."

The gunny quickly ran down the embankment toward the latrine and a bunch of Marines standing around pointing and laughing.

The captain carefully watched the gunny trying to pick up any information he could better understand the situation. After all, the lieutenant, in his present condition, was of no value. He once more stared at the lieutenant and slowly shook his head from side to side. He then noticed the gunny trotting back to him.

Gunny Dixon, chuckling, ran up and sat down next to LT and said, "Well skipper, our loudmouth squad leader "got his up and comings." He accidentally burned the hair off his ass." The gunny then slapped LT on his back and they both roared in laughter. They leaned against each other for mutual support, so neither would roll down the slope.

The captain scowled and said, "Jesus Christ," throwing his arms up in the air and stomped back to his bunker.

LT spent the next morning "unofficially" inspecting and talking to his troops. Every time he had an opportunity to talk to his men, he did. He learned a great deal about his Marines and it also allowed him to keep a close pulse of the platoon's morale. As he checked the platoon's area for cleanness, he saw Corporal Ballew handing out mail. Mail was always a big event for everyone, if they got mail or not. The men stood bouncing around in excitement hoping for mail from back home.

Mail was such a big thing for the Marine infantry man. When in the bush, packages were not normally sent out to them. So many of these packages that they were now receiving may have been in the company mailroom for days, weeks, or even a month or so. Now in a static place, they were sent the packages.

The reason packages were held in the rear was because the men would get things like electric razors, radios, small cooking burners—all useless to the infantry man because there was no electric power in the bush. The military bases were normally the only place which had electricity. Every time an item did make it to the Marine in the bush it would eventually be thrown away because the lack of electricity or the item's weight proved to add more weight than he was willing to carry day after day.

Lance Corporal Robert Kumlien, "The Swede," got a large package from his folks in Wisconsin. The Swede didn't talk a lot, was strong as an ox, and was liked by all of the platoon members. The lieutenant didn't know for sure if Robert was of Swedish decent or not; however, he never objected to the name, so LT assumed he was Swedish.

The Swede, with one hand, ripped opened the package. Several of his squad members hovered over him, ready to lend a hand if he needed help in getting the "goodies" out of the box. He immediately pulled out a brand new football and tossed it in the air. Five of his buddies jumped and dove over one another in order to capture the ball. He then handed out several novelty toys. Robert handed Bates a plastic mouth of teeth that chattered when held in the palm of the hand. The rest of the packages contained cooked goods from home… "the mother lode!"

The other thing the young Marines really enjoyed about being at Tu Cau Bridge was the fact there was a "pogey bait truck" which came by every week. The truck came down from division offering candy, gum, sodas, magazines, and countless types of snacks, all for sale to the Marines. This truck was by far the best thing the bush Marines had come across so far. The men could see the truck coming a half a mile away and once they spotted it, the cry went out, "POGEY BAIT TRUCK, POGEY BAIT TRUCK!" Once it stopped, the troops, in what could only be described as an "orderly stampede," would swarm the vehicle.

The Marines on duty would yell out their pogey bait orders to their buddies who were already charging the truck. Their excitement was only second, LT assumed, to when they were children and raced to the Christmas tree on Christmas morning. As orders were filled, young men would exit the side of the vehicle with their helmets filled, or even overflowing, with goodies, and would then be met by a barrage of cat calls, which were endless and at times very colorful.

It was the end of the second week at Tu Cau Bridge for the platoon and a good smooth routine had been established for the unit and LT. Since things were running mirror-like, Lance Corporal John "the Hawk" Mihok asked LT if he could go visit his friend stationed with 1st Tank Battalion in Da Nang.

John Mihok was an excellent Marine who could always be counted on and was reliable, extremely intelligent, and trustworthy. He was in 2nd squad and they didn't have any patrols for a few days, so LT decided he would let John go, if it was all right with his squad leader Corporal Gene Evans.

Evans was more than happy to let John go because almost everyone in the squad had given John a list of items they wanted from the Da Nang Exchange.

Bright and early the next morning, John gathered his gear, ran down to the main road, and hitched a ride with an army truck convoy going to Da Nang. LT told John to be back before dark the next day and knew he would make it back on time.

Later in the morning, at the sawhorse barrier, a burst of small arms fire erupted from a crowd of about thirty civilians. Bates and Billy Baker, who had bought ice cream cups from the pogey bait truck, grabbed their weapons and ran to the scene.

Upon arriving, they found an elderly Vietnamese man lying in the middle of the road, who had been shot several times. The man was still in the seated position, hands on the bike's handle bars as if he was still driving, only his bike was tipped over, lying flat on the ground. They saw a couple of suspects running with five or six other Marines chasing them.

LT was over by the skipper's bunker talking to Gunny Dixon when the gun fire broke out. He and the gunny ran over to the barriers and found Bates and Billy standing over the dead civilian casually eating ice cream. The lieutenant and gunny glanced at each of the two Marines then each other and shook their heads in disbelief.

The group of Marines who had been chasing the suspected assassins came down the road and stopped to tell the lieutenant and gunny what had happened. They reported they had chased the individuals into the French Fort. The ARVN's refused to let them in and shut the fort gate. They also reported the fleeing men were wearing the South Vietnamese 51st Quang Da patches, the same as those stationed in the fort.

The ARVN's immediately put out word the man killed was a village chief and killed by men dressed as ARVN's.

As it turned out the chief, Dang Ditch, was assassinated not by the VC, but the South Vietnamese because he was a VC supporter, which explained why the Marines were not allowed to pursue the assassins into the fort.

The next day, 1st platoon received a new member. Lance Corporal Richly "Bunky" Taylor was from Maryland and had played football at the university. Bunky was a slim but muscular built individual, an easy-going friendly Marine, and had an accent which sounded more like he was from deep Georgia rather than Maryland. He was assigned to second squad, which seemed a perfect fit for both him and the squad.

That afternoon the platoon lined up to get haircuts. The barber was a Vietnamese contract barber and the haircuts cost each Marine forty Military Payments Certificates.

Haircuts were a fact of life in the Corps, in peace or war; Marines accepted this as part of the game. However, LT did slip the barber an extra five dollars worth of MPC to ensure Joe and Evans got a little more than their request for "just a light trim."

As 1st platoon had finished getting haircuts, LT crossed over the bridge to report to the skipper and noticed a US Navy patrol boat come from under the bridge, towing a small sampan about the size of a canoe. They tied it up to the small dock and left. He figured they were tired of towing it and dropped it off, leaving it on the doorsteps of the Marines to deal with.

As he turned toward the skipper's area, he noticed Bates coming across the bridge. Bates and the rest of the weapons squad were the first to get haircuts and left early to fire their machine guns. Wondering about the rest of the squad, he asked Bates about them.

Bates, grinning from ear to ear, said, "Oh, we got back a while ago. I was over at the skipper's bunker. You know, LT, I'm kind of scared of the captain. He sure is intimidating, but he was nice to me."

With some concern in his voice, LT said, "And why did the skipper want to see you?"

Boastfully, Bates said, "Well, he told me he had been in the Marine Corps since 1957 and he hadn't heard a better five round machine gun burst. I thanked him and got out of there as quick as I could."

He chuckled and congratulated Bates on his excellent shooting and then continued on his way over to make his report.

That evening John "the Hawk" Mihok returned from his visit to tank battalion as promised. He told the men he had not one but two hot showers and three glasses of *cold milk*. He also acquired a brand new pair of jungle utilities and, along with them, new under garments, which was unbelievable to the other troops. He slid down his new jungle utilities slightly to show his buddies the new undershorts when accused of lying about it.

John also brought back several of the items on the squad's list. However, the biggest trophy he obtained on his adventure was a blow-up rubber pillow given to him by his buddy at tanks. The pillow was bright red on one side and white with red stripes on the other. It measured sixteen by ten inches when inflated. To John it was pure luxury; it kept his head out of the dirt, rocks, puddles, and mud. All were very envious of John.

LT was up early the next day checking post. He started towards the sawhorse barrier at the end of the bridge where some of the local farmers were gathered waiting to cross the bridge, when suddenly a loud explosion broke the morning silence. The explosion came from the old French Fort up the road on Highway 1.

He quickly looked around and saw Bates coming off guard duty with his rifle. He told Bates to come with him. In addition, he grabbed up two Marines from 3rd platoon who were coming off guard duty at the sawhorse barrier. They all four jogged up to the fort. When they arrived they found total chaos. People were running around screaming, and motor bikes and little farm trucks were driving off into the field next to the road, trying to get past the mess in the middle of the road.

In front of the fort doors lay five ARVN's, all dead; their bodies were ripped up and limbs were torn from their torsos. Bright red blood splattered the gate doors and was now slowly running down the large wooden doors.

It was obvious some type of bomb had been set off in front of the fort and had killed several ARVN's standing duty.

In the middle of the road, two ARVN's were holding down a young Vietnamese girl. She appeared around sixteen or seventeen years old. She was in sitting position and the two soldiers where holding her up by her arms and a third was beating her over the head with a six-foot bamboo pole. Her head was partially split open, blood was gushing from her head and her eyes were open with a blank stare.

A second young female was lying spread eagle in the road and was being held down by an ARVN, while another soldier kicked the girl repeatedly in the crotch, cussed her and spit on her several times. Each time the solider kicked her, a screeching scream echoed off the giant fort doors out across the rice fields. Her pants were soaked and after each kick blood gushed from her body.

LT grabbed the soldier by the arm, who was beating the girl, and yelled for him to stop. He then hollered at the man kicking the female lying on the ground to stop. Both soldiers paused and focused their attention on a Vietnamese major standing between the two girls, watching the beatings and making no attempt to halt the egregious acts.

The major glared at LT, his jaws tightened; he said nothing as his gaze rapidly became a sharp, piercing, hot, penetrating stare. After a few moments, the major slowly began sliding his hand down to his holster on his hip. Suddenly, his eyes darted for a millisecond, down the road past the lieutenant. He then cautiously lifted his hand from his holster.

The two officers were locked in a "No Win Situation" and they both knew it. The ARVN soldiers, as well as the Marines, were frozen in place. LT could feel the sweat running down his legs or at least he hoped it was sweat. Onlookers said nothing. They all stared at the two officers. It was deadly quiet.

The major, still fixed on the lieutenant's eyes, stood as erect as he could and in a very rigid voice barked out a command to his men. Apparently, they did not move as fast as he desired, so he screamed out the same order much louder. The soldiers jumped to life, immediately dragging the two women through the partially-opened fort doors, and dropped them both between the doors inside of the fort.

The major, in a very belligerent manner, marched behind the men dragging the women, and stationed himself over the two women. He then turned, looked directly at the lieutenant, smiled, drew his pistol, and shot both women in the head. Now smirking at the lieutenant, he slowly placed his pistol back in its holster and the two large, bloody, wooden gate doors slammed shut.

The lieutenant took a deep breath, closed his eyes and in a low, solemn voice said, "You son of a bitch…you bastard!" LT's rage was almost uncontrollable. His hate was instant and deep. He swore he could shoot the major himself.

After a few moments of slow burning, he slowly turned to where Bates was standing and now understood why the major had withdrawn to the walls of the fort. Standing next to Bates were at least twenty US Army Special Forces soldiers, fully armed.

LT allowed a smile at the senior staff NCO in charge of the unit and said, "Thanks."

The staff NCO grinned and said, "Anytime lieutenant." He then told his men to get back into the trucks.

LT told his men to let the traffic through and head back to the bridge. On the way back to the bridge, Bates said, "LT, I think the major wanted to kill you. He looked like he was really pissed."

LT chuckled and said, "You think?" He then became a little solemn and went on to say, "I want to thank you men for going with me, and I apologize to you all for getting you involved." The three Marines looked around at each other with puzzled expressions on their faces. Noticing their confusion, he went on to say, "I don't blame the major for getting so upset with me. Hell, if someone killed five of my men I would want to kill them too. The major is Vietnamese, as are the two girls and it's their country. However, the combination of raw brutally and a total lack of chivalry really got to me."

CHAPTER 29
MORE CHALLENGES

LT was restless; he kept thinking about the encounter with the ARVN major earlier that day and couldn't sleep. He never woke Joe or Ballew for their watches. Instead, he stood them; there was no sense waking them when he couldn't sleep anyway.

He walked on the bridge, watching the guards, every ten to fifteen minutes, throw small chunks of C-4 explosives over the side of the bridge and explode in the water below. This kept sappers from swimming up the river and blowing up the bridge.

By mid-morning he was feeling the lack of sleep and must have been showing it because Joe highly recommended he get some sleep. He decided Joe's suggestion was pretty good and went to his billeting area and crashed on his poncho liner, with the promise from Joe that he would let him sleep no longer than two hours, and that he would immediately wake him if anything happened.

An hour into his sleep, something happened. Joe and squad leader Gene Evans woke him up. Joe waited a few moments to make sure he was fully awake and then reluctantly told him Lance Corporal Joe Tiger had lost his rifle.

Lance Corporal Joseph Prentice Tiger, a Native American from Oklahoma, was a graduate of the Marine Corps Sniper School. He was never placed with a sniper unit but rather sent to 1st platoon. He was unquestionably the best shot in the platoon. He was an easy going, quiet individual who was more than willing to do his part. All the platoon members liked him and considered him an invaluable member, not only for his marksmanship abilities, but also his personality and work ethics.

Tiger had asked him several times for a transfer to a sniper unit, but each request was denied. LT, through Corporal Mount at the battalion armory, got Joe an M14 rifle. The M14 was more in line with the old M1 and could be used as a long-range weapon, unlike the M16 used by everyone else in the platoon. The M14 made Joe happier, and no doubt helped him feel somewhat special and an important member of the platoon.

LT was lying on his back, and snapped up to a sitting position with a puzzled look, and said, "Lost? Care to elaborate?"

Joe cleared his throat and, somewhat wavering in his speech, carefully stated, "Well, Tiger was on duty, walking back and forth on the bridge, watching for snipers. He laid his rifle against the bridge rail to tie his boot lace. Unfortunately, about then, a six-by truck started across the bridge, which created a bouncing sensation, causing the rifle to slide off the rail, hit the floor of the bridge, then launched off into the river."

LT got up, splashed water on his face from his canteen, dried, and, looking at Joe, said, "Guess I had better go see the skipper. Wish me luck."

He walked to the captain's bunker. The skipper was half lying on his cot with his back against the bunker wall, reading messages. He peered over the top of the papers and said, "What's up, Geronimo?"

He was somewhat relieved, because when the skipper called him "Geronimo," he knew he was in good grace. However, if he had called him "lieutenant"… not so good.

LT slowly sat down where the captain had indicated for him to sit and hesitatingly said, "Is there any chance of getting a diver down here today or tomorrow, sir?"

The captain stared at the lieutenant, then, as he laid his messages on the end of the cot, sat all the way up and said, "Diver. As in one who dives into water?"

Smiling, he said, "Exactly skipper!" He then went on and explained what had happened on the bridge.

Frowning the captain said, "What kind of Marine is Tiger, lieutenant?"

"Outstanding, sir."

The captain rolled his eyes and said, "Are all of your Marines outstanding? Wait, don't answer that question, it is a rhetorical question." The skipper, smiling and shaking his head from side to side, yelled, "Communications! Get me the battalion operations on the radio."

Two days later, two Navy divers arrived, and LT showed them where the rifle fell from the bridge. They dove into the water when the tide was low. The water was calm but murky. In about five minutes one of the divers surfaced with the M14 in his hand. LT motioned for him to take the rifle to Tiger, who stood on the river bank.

Tiger immediately took the weapon to the lieutenant, who was on the bridge. LT removed the magazine, carefully inspected the outside of the rifle then opened the chamber and inspected it to make sure there was nothing in the barrel. He turned to Tiger and asked for dry ammo. Joe quickly produced a single round from his bandoleer.

He placed the round in the chamber and scanned the riverbank and saw an old Coca-a-Cola can. He took aim, hollered "fire in the hole," shot, hitting the can and popping it into the air. Among the many on-lookers there was a low but firm moaning of approval, probably for both hitting the target and the rifle actually functioning.

He handed Tiger the weapon and said, "Clean it up and let me know when you're through. I want to see it before you put it back together."

Tiger quickly took the weapon and headed to his sleeping area at the end of the bridge.

Joe Loerzel walked up to him and asked, "LT, what are you going to do to Tiger?"

He looked at Joe and said, "I don't know yet. But I do know I want to handle it, not the skipper, and keep it unofficial."

Joe, nodding his head, said, "Good...good. I hope it works out that way."

LT walked over to the skipper's bunker and had a short meeting with him. He left the meeting happy. The skipper agreed to let him handle the matter.

He immediately went to the billeting area, found Tiger, sat down next to him on the edge of the blanket, and began inspecting what he had cleaned so far. Then he told him to watch closely as he methodically broke the rifle down even further, until there was nothing left to separate.

Tiger sat wide-eyed, staring at the parts, wondering how he was ever going to be able to put the rifle back together.

Noticing the look on Tiger's face, he chuckled and told him to watch. Between the two of them they assembled and disassembled the M14 five times, and finally he said, "Great job. Now you know how to put it together, take it apart, and are able to really clean it."

Joe was standing outside of the billeting area watching and listening to what transpired and as LT exited, he said, "Okay, what next?"

He took Joe by the arm and pulled him a few feet from the bunker and said, "Give Tiger, on top of his regular duty, additional guard duty for five days and make it during the day so the rest of the platoon can see him."

Joe grinned and said, "Sounds good. I'm sure glad we get to handle it at the platoon level."

The lieutenant would not have normally taken as much time with Tiger, or any of his Marines, but would have had Joe or the squad leaders handle the matter. However, in this case, he was the only one in the platoon who could totally disassemble and assemble the M14.

Security was always a top priority and the skipper became concerned about the elephant grass growing inside the perimeter long the banks of the river that separated the unit. He therefore charged the company gunny, Gunny Dixon, to organize a working party of eight Marines from each platoon to cut and burn the grass.

Some of the Marines would cut the grass with their E-tools, then someone else would pour diesel fuel on the grass. The diesel fuel was allowed to soak in the grass, then regular gasoline was poured, thus the gasoline, a very combustible liquid, would immediately combust into flames and burn the green grass.

Joe "volunteered" Al Brown, Louis Lujan, Ed Cruz, John Cox, Lynn Stoop, Mark Serrano, Bob Kumlien, and Richly Taylor. The new guy would always be selected for working parties.

Bob Kumlien's job was to pour two GI cans, five gallons each, of diesel fuel on the grass, which he did. He then was to throw a coffee can of gas onto the diesel fuel, which he also did. Finally, he was to light a cardboard shelf of a C-ration case on fire and toss it onto the mixture.

Normally it would take a few minutes for the diesel to catch on fire, resulting in a slower flame building up across the area of soaked fuel. This time, however, it suddenly exploded into a giant fire ball. Bob was knocked back to the ground with flames leaping up from the front of his body. Several members of the working party jumped on him and quickly put out the fire, but not before it had caused him second- and third-degree burns.

LT, from the far side of the compound, saw the flash of fire and by the time he reached the site, Gunny Dixon had things under control, and was calling for a medevac.

LT looked at the gunny and said, "What happened?"

Gunny Dixon glanced at him and said, "I don't know. I watched Kumlien do this at least two or three times before with no problems. I frankly don't know what happened."

He then walked over to the two cans Kumlien had used to splash fuel on the grass. He picked up the first can, smelled it, and moved on to the second one. He sniffed it, jerked his head back, and cried out, "This is gasoline, no wonder the place burst into a fire ball."

It became apparent that whoever had filled the cans of fuel didn't know or didn't care that cans painted red held gasoline, while diesel was put into cans marked with black paint—the color Bob had spread over what he thought was diesel, not gasoline.

Lance Corporal Bob Kumlien was medevac and sent to the states for his medical recovery, never to return to the platoon.

It was late one night and LT finally completed his rounds and was getting ready to turn in when a loud explosion rocked the area. He tore from his bunker and ran to the middle of the bridge. The guard on duty told him one of the other guards saw a sampan coming up the river and threw a stick of C-4 into the boat and blew it up. He swiftly surveyed the area; the end of the sampan was barely out of the water and was sinking out of site. He also noticed the other guards were not acting nervous but rather clam and grinning. Not the expressions seen when encountering the enemy.

The captain, the other platoon commanders, and the gunny all came rushing onto the bridge a short time later. The skipper immediately started barking out orders and asking questions. After fifteen minutes or so, the captain determined that all was clear and the guards had spoiled an attempt by the enemy to destroy the bridge. He quickly notified battalion of the attempt.

Joe had joined LT on the bridge and as they started to leave they met Bates, who was on duty, and he asked Bates where was the sampan that was tied up at the little dock for several days.

Bates' eyes flicked from him to Joe and then back several times and he finally stammered out, "Sampan… tied up… it's not there." He then paused for a moment, sweat started to pour off his forehead, and said, "I'll find out for you sir," and raced off the bridge.

Joe looked at him and said, "Shit, you don't think that was the enemy boat?"

He shook his head and said, "Yes. Attack, my ass. I suspect we may have some bored troops. Joe, if it is true, find out who. I am sure you can find something for them to do."

The following day Joe had five volunteers who worked several days cleaning the camp, filling new sandbags, and rebuilding fighting positions. Over all, according to Joe, they seemed eager to spruce up the area.

Not long after the sampan incident, LT was standing at the end of the bridge, looking down, watching some of his troops playing flag football, when he looked over and saw the skipper coming across the bridge his way with a big smile on his face.

The captain walked up to him, causally patted him on his back, and said, "Hey Geronimo, how is it going over here with my 1st platoon."

LT stared at the skipper and thought, "He seldom, if ever, comes over here; he usually sends for me; he is smiling and I am Geronimo today." He whimsically said, "I can tell by your charismatic charm you want something. What do you want, skipper?"

Captain McCarthy chuckled and said, "Well, since you asked, my friend, General Wheeler is coming down here around 1400 hours to visit me and I would like for you to put together a team to escort him around. You know, like the team you put together over in Pagoda Valley at the monk's temple when we got the well water… nothing fancy."

LT sighed and said skeptically, "In other words, you want me to get five of my Marines in the same identical, clean uniforms, shined boots, and brass, parade ready, is that right, skipper?"

The skipper, wavering a bit, said, "Yea… the gunny has some boot polish and Brasso. You know, you don't have to make it sound like I'm asking you to win the damn war by yourself."

LT closed his eyes, counted to ten, and opened his eyes, only to find the skipper right in front of him, staring at him. He took a deep breath, exhaled, and then said, "When and where?"

The skipper broke out in a big smile and said, "Our little LZ at 1330 hours."

"1330 hours! You said he was coming at 1400. Damn it, skipper, I'll have them there before he lands."

The skipper frowned and snapped, "You damn well make sure they are there before he lands." Then he stomped off mumbling something about ungrateful lieutenants.

He found Joe, informed him of the skipper's request and told him Lance Corporal Ed Cherry was to be in charge of the detail.

Ed Cherry was his "go-to Marine." Ed was very intelligent, hard-working, and always eager to help. He had many capabilities—not only operating a movie projector, as he did at Stack Arms—he also could type. He helped type up promotion warrants once when the platoon was in the rear for a couple days.

As per LT's instructions, the guard detail kept out of site until the general's helo was well inbound. The skipper, in the meantime, paced and grumbled along the side of the LZ.

The general's visit was very successful and he commented on how sharp the guard detail looked, which caused the skipper to beam with joy. In fact, the skipper was so pleased he personally thanked each member of the team and actually smiled at the LT.

CHAPTER 30
THE KNOWN AND UNKNOWN

The next morning, at the CO's meeting, the skipper openly thanked LT for doing a great job providing the guard detail, indicating all was good between the two.

Tet was in full swing; the local villages were draped in colorful banners. Flags were flown from rooftops, poles, trees, anything which would hold them. Fireworks were set off at night, filling the night sky with explosive illuminations.

Both the South and North seemed to have taken time off from the war to celebrate. However, the Marine night patrols were still sent out.

Corporal Evans was assigned such a patrol, going out toward an old French fort or the Vu Ca Bases, located about a mile and a half south of the bridge.

The fort was occupied by an ARVN unit. The fort itself was triangular with high towers at each point and sturdy bunkers. Some thirty feet away from the wall, the white sand around the fort was raked daily, which enabled the guards to see sappers at night.

Unknown to LT, Corporal Evans, along with the rest of the squad, decided to skip the unpopular roving patrol assignment and headed directly to Vu Cau Base. It was twilight when they reached the base and the Vietnamese were pleased to have the visitors.

The ARVN's gave the Marines a large sand-bagged bunker to stash their gear and it was roomy enough for all of them to sleep in too. The squad members took turns standing radio watch, dutifully falsely reporting in in a timely manner at each check point.

Once settled in, the squad was invited over to a large GP tent which served as the fort's club. Inside the tent were electric lights, a large card table, and a small bar. The squad members started off with bottles of Tiger Piss, a Vietnamese beer with a Tiger's head on the oval label. The Marines drank every bottle the ARVN's had.

The South Vietnamese played a fast card game with both cards, and money, briskly changing hands. However, the Marines focused on the gallon jugs of a type of rice wine. The clear gallon jugs had about an inch of sediment on the bottom, which was also drank by the squad members.

An ARVN lieutenant passed out small packets of Lane cookies and said he had a big surprise. Leaving, he returned to the tent with two bottles of Southern Comfort whiskey. Smiles greeted this act of friendship. Generous amounts were poured into the Marines' canteen cups and it quickly disappeared.

After partying most of the night, the squad members stumbled into the bunker and slept until the radio watch woke them and then they headed back to the bridge.

When they entered the bridge perimeter, LT was waiting for them and, after a close look at them, said, "Looks like it was a rough night."

Gene Evans glanced toward him and said, through a pounding headache, said, "You don't know the half of it."

LT crossed his arms and slowly said, "Oh, I'm sure that's true."

A few days later, LT was leaving a company commanders' meeting and started to cross the bridge when he began taking in the sites. He glanced down toward the latrine and chuckled, thinking of the "Great Latrine Fire." He looked across the river and could see his men playing football with the ball Bob Kumlien had received in his care package from home.

For some reason, he was feeling fidgety and uneasy. He watched his men play for several minutes then noticed something odd. Two or three men would exit the living area and go down, joining those standing around watching the game. Then two or three different men would immediately walk back up to the living area. Once they reached the entry to the living area, they stopped to talk to a Vietnamese man, then entered.

The Vietnamese man was about twenty or twenty-two, wore white pants and shirt, along with sunglasses. When he turned, talking briefly with the Marines, LT caught the bling of jewelry around his neck and the men handing something to him.

LT leaped from the rock, thundered across the bridge in what could be described as an "erupting volcano." Guards on bridge duty quickly cleared a path for the lieutenant. Upon seeing the lieutenant approaching, the Vietnamese man first smiled, then noticed the charging pace, doubled up fist and very contentious scowl, and fled to his motor bike like a kicked dog with his tail between his legs.

In a rage, the lieutenant tore open the poncho liner door to the living quarters. To his shock, lying in front of him were two young Vietnamese girls, and they both were completely naked! Not expecting to see the two very attractive nude females, he merely stared. He thought, "Damn, they could easily grace the cover of *Playboy*."

Under his current mental state, he did not notice the explosion of young Marines shoving, pushing, and tripping as they grabbed clothes, escaping through the back entry of the room.

The two girls sat up in their makeshift beds and questionably glanced at each other, then the closest one to LT asked, "You want Susie?"

He swallowed hard and in a weak voice said, "Uh... no." He turned his head away from the girls, cleared his throat, gained some composure, and, in his best stern voice he could muster up, said, "You two get dressed and get out of here. Do it now, do you understand?"

The two young women nodded and promptly gathered up their clothes lying neatly folded on the floor.

LT backed out of the doorway and turned toward his troops, who were now milling around on the football field down the embankment. They were in small groups watching him and as he looked at each of the groups, they immediately lowered their heads and shuffled their feet.

Not wanting to look at his men anymore, he turned his head away and then saw the Vietnamese pimp sitting on a new white motorbike. "Slick Willy" was sitting on the bike talking to a couple Vietnamese boys, no doubt, in the lieutenant's mind, telling them how wonderful it was to be a pimp. LT moved fast and quiet as a large cat after prey toward the unsuspecting whore monger.

He was enraged, hatred like venom was bubbling from his pores; he loathed any and everything in his sight. His brain was exploding with disgust and scorn for the war, killings, deplorable living conditions, lack of supplies, even the damn insects which bit, chewed, stung, and sucked life from the men. But what really pissed off the lieutenant was the feeling of *betrayal* from his troops.

Reaching the Vietnamese pimp, LT grabbed the front of Slick Willy's white shirt and, with a handful of cloth, held on with a death grip. The other hand held his Grey Colt 45 pistol, now resting under the nose of the horrified pimp. His oriental "slant eyes" were now as round as plates and almost as large. He immediately began to sweat profusely.

LT, in a gnarly voice, said, "Asshole, you understand English?" The perspiration was so heavy now it fell off in large droplets from his head as he nodded yes.

"Good. Because I want you to clearly understand what I am about to tell you." LT slowly slid the pistol across the pimp's face while pressing it against his skin, then stopped, shoved it, with some force, into the ear of the extremely scared man. "I'm going to kill you. I'm going to shove this gun up your butt and empty the magazine into your ass, if I ever see you again!"

The frightened man squirmed and pleading for his life in a whining voice said, "Please, promise, no come back…please no kill me…PLEASE!"

LT, pleased with his ability to clearly communicate with the Vietnamese pimp, formed a sinister smile and said, "Your girls are here, get them on your bike and get the hell out of here before I change my mind."

The pimp lunged over the edge of the bike and grabbed up a small flat board lying on the ground. He placed the board across the seat and sat down on it, leaving about a foot sticking out on both sides. The two girls sprang up, sitting on the ends of the board at the same time, allowing the bike to be in perfect balance.

The pimp fired up the motor bike and peeled the back tire, throwing stones from the road as he rapidly took off. He tore down the road, blasting his bike horn, warning everyone to get out of his way. In his hast, he fish-tailed the bike a couple of times when changing gears, but managed to maintain control.

LT watched as the trio fled down the road until they turned north on Highway 1. He then slipped his pistol back in his holster, took a deep breath, exhaled, and turned around. Two Marines from 3rd platoon on sawhorse barricade duty gawked at him. In a decisive manner, he walked over to the two and said, "If that jerk ever comes back, I want to be notified. I made him a promise and I want to keep it. That's part of your standing orders, be sure to pass it on to your reliefs. Do you understand?"

Both sentries mumbled, "Yes sir."

As he walked away from the barricade, the taller guard turned to his buddy and said, "Now that is one crazy lieutenant." The other Marine nodded and said, "Yea, and if I was that pimp, I wouldn't stop going north until I hit Hanoi."

Still fuming, the lieutenant walked around the barricade on to the bridge. The troops down below playing football all froze to watch the lieutenant as he stomped across the bridge. He did not once look their way, but he could hear a voice saying angrily, "I told you sons-of-bitches he would find out and now we all are going to pay!" He then heard many other voices agreeing and shouting at what sounded like a couple trying to defend themselves. He needed some time alone away from his platoon.

He walked past the company CP, turned right, and went down to the LZ. The tower at the edge of the LZ was manned by 2nd platoon. The guard in the tower nodded at the lieutenant, then went about his duties, scanning the area for possible attacks. LT walked to the far side of the landing zone, next to the river. He found a large rock right off the LZ, in between it and the river. He sat down and tried to make sense of what had happened.

He tried hard to be a good leader. He carried his own load, walked the same rice paddies, jungle, heat, fought mosquitoes, slept on the same hard and/or wet ground. He had no privileges.

Good leadership required trust, without it you had nothing. Was the trust between him and his men broken? Could it be repaired over time? How long, if possible, would it take? All questions haunted the platoon commander.

He realized his troops were young, vibrant, and virile, had vigor, and, at the height of their courting years, were being cheated of this experience because of this duty to country. His men were not vicious or prone to cruelty. True, the nature of their responsibility to their country, to destroy the enemy, was a vicious dichotomy shared by all military personal.

After much time and many "mental debates," he came to the conclusion it was his fault. Joe, Ballew, and the three squad leaders were in Da Nang with Gunny Dixon getting supplies. He was "on duty," responsible for the supervision and welfare of his men… in his mind, he failed.

LT leaned back and stretched; the stress had caused his muscles to tighten up. He then heard a scuffle of a boot on the metal grading of the LZ. He turned and saw Doc Wolf, the company senior corpsman, approaching.

Doc Wolf hesitated, then said, "You all right, lieutenant? I noticed over an hour ago you were sitting here."

LT, turning away from Doc, toward the river, mumbled, "'I don't know' is the best answer I can give you."

Doc stepped closer to the lieutenant, squatted down on one knee, and with concern said, "I can see something is bothering you, want to talk about it?" Doc then quickly stated, "You know I have confidentiality authority and won't share this discussion with anyone, unless it's about an epidemic."

The lieutenant cracked a smile and said, "So tell me Doc, do they ordain you once you finish corpsman school?"

Doc thought for a moment and finally said, "No, but you may be on to something. I think religion and medicine overlap and both have confidentiality powers. God knows, I have heard a few repentance's over the years."

LT chuckled then his facial features changed to concern and he said, "This is a rather tedious and complex situation for me."

Doc studied him for a few minutes, then suggested, "I don't know about tedious, but complex can be broken down into workable parts. Does this by chance have anything to do with medicine?"

LT kicked a small stone in front of him with his foot and haltingly said, "It could be… you and Doc Smith might want to keep an eye on 1st platoon when it comes to, uh, social diseases."

Doc Wolf stood up, put his hands in his trouser pockets, and walked in a large circle, ending up next to the lieutenant, sat down beside him, and, in an analytical manner, slowly said, "So, your platoon had the two mama-san hookers. You're the 'crazy' lieutenant who threatened, no promised, to kill the Vietnamese pimp. And your entire platoon is scared to death you're going to hand them their asses, after you rip them from their bodies. Nice going, lieutenant!"

LT didn't flinch, nor did he indicate in any way whether it was true or not. He simply stared at the river and finally announced, "They weren't mama-sans, they were two young, stunning girls, believe me. And I may have shown a local person a close up view of the working end of my pistol. The platoon members can think what they want."

Doc Wolf slapped his hands on his knees and busted out laughing. He laughed so long and hard he eventually pulled a handkerchief from his pocket and wiped his eyes. Then said, "So, why are you so down in the dumps? Seriously, I don't understand what the problem is… care telling me?"

LT got up, walked over to a bush and broke a small limb off, and stripped it of its leaves. He strolled back to the boulder and sat back down next to Doc Wolf. He slowly drew some lines in the dirt then said, "It's a matter of trust and respect. I respect my men for what they do and under very serious conditions. I will go to hell with them because I trust them to do the best possible job and have my back, like I do theirs."

Questioning, Doc Wolf said, "So, what has changed? Your troops respect you and, believe me, they trust you. I think you're confusing respect and trust with what happened today. They are totally two different things. What happened today was out of some young horny males giving into the calling of nature, nothing more or less, and besides, I understand you got a real good view of the girls and you said they were attractive, right?"

Grimacing, LT said, "Oh, they were beyond attractive."

Wolf inquired, "I take it you have not talked to Captain McCarthy, are you going to?"

He hesitated, looked around, and in a low voice said, "No. I don't think I'm ready to admit defeat on this matter or ask him for his help. I need more time to think about it. However, Doc, you have really been a big help, and thanks. Thanks, a lot."

Doc smiled at him and said, "Any time." He then quietly walked off toward the company CP, leaving the lieutenant to ponder his options.

He was exhausted from examining and reexamining his plight as he headed back to the platoon area. As he started across the bridge, he saw Bates with a couple of ARVN's in the middle of the bridge, apparently kidding around.

Honing in on the situation much closer, he saw the ARVN's giggling and laughing as they playfully ran a few feet, stopped, waited for Bates to catch up with them and then repeat the same thing again.

LT kept walking and, as he caught up with the group, he could see Bates had the plastic chattering teeth in his hand. The ARVN's thought the teeth were very funny but were somewhat leery of the toy.

As the lieutenant passed up Bates, he quickly turned toward the side of the bridge and swiftly looked down, like he'd suddenly seen something of importance. LT passed Bates and, without looking back, said, "Bates, damn it, quit screwing with the locals."

The next morning the lieutenant attended the skipper's morning briefing, where he received several knowing glances from his peers. He quickly slipped out after the meeting was over; he did not want to get into any discussions about the war or where they might be going next. He sure didn't want to explain about the hookers, or what punishment might be appropriate by the CO or even by him, if allowed to pass punishment.

As he crossed over the bridge back to his platoon area, he heard some yelling coming from the football field. Rich Taylor and Gene Evans were wrestling, pushing, and slamming one another down on the ground.

He briskly marched toward the two fighting men as he unwrapped a cigar and jammed it into his scowling mouth. As he started down the embankment someone yelled, "Hey, lieutenant, do you want to play some football?"

The two combative Marines momentarily froze in place, then jumped up, brushed the dirt off each other, smiled, shook hands, and walked back on the playing field as if nothing ever happened.

The next couple days the lieutenant's relationship with the platoon members improved dramatically. On the third day, the captain announced the company was to be helo-lifted to LZ Ryder, the artillery fire support base in the Que Son Mountains.

CHAPTER 31
LZ RYDER

Once airborne, the flight for 1st platoon to LZ Ryder took about forty minutes. It was uneventful and very much appreciated. This was one of the few times the unit got to fly rather than walk. LT watched as the flat rice paddy ground quickly passed beneath him. The level ground gave away to terrain climbing into the sky. The vegetation grew thicker and turned into denser jungle the higher the helo soared.

The map had not lied to the lieutenant, the sides of Ryder were very steep. The helo circled the landing zone twice, then ever-so-gently landed in the middle of the steel matting, which served as the actual landing pad. The Marines, without thinking, immediately exited the helo in combat formation.

As he departed the helo, he saw an older Marine standing off to one side of the landing pad and assumed it was the commanding officer of Fox Company, the unit Hotel Company was replacing on the mountain. He approached him and introduced himself.

The Marine captain, looking over LT's shoulder, said, "Where is Captain McCarthy?"

"Sir, he sent me ahead as the Bravo Command. He is coming in on the last wave with the Alpha Command. He wants me to make liaison with you and assign positions for the company."

The Marine captain chuckled and said, "Well, the positions, the platoons, weapons and headquarters are pretty much carved, literally, in stone, due to the limited amount of space on the mountain top." The captain finished showing LT the positions and explained the ground rules… there were always "ground rules."

After four waves of helos, Hotel Company was complete in its move to LZ

Ryder. LT showed the other platoon commanders their area of responsibilities, not without a good deal of harassment from them, though, and the skipper, his new CP.

Completing his assignment as the liaison officer for the company, he asked the skipper, "Sir, the platoon commanders are settled in their areas and all troops are accounted for. Do you have anything else?"

Captain McCarthy smirked and said, "No Geronimo, but I do have a couple questions. Do they have showers for the troops?"

"No, sir."

The skipper frowned and said, "Do they have a *damn* mess hall for the troops?"

"No, sir."

The skipper, scowling, barked, "LIEUTENANT, DO THEY HAVE ANYTHING ON THIS DAMN MOUNTAIN FOR US?"

Don took a deep breath and slowly said, "Sir, an occasional movie and the responsibilities of colors every other week, sir."

"Shit, lieutenant! Boy, you are full of glad tidings aren't you. Can you tell me who the *HELL* is in charge of this… *hill*?"

LT, in a serious voice, said, "Sir, I'm the messenger, not the rule maker! The officer in charge is a major. His last name is… Major. First name is Sir. Hell sir, I have forgotten his name, only remember his rank."

Captain McCarthy slowly rubbed his hands together as he calmed down and then, in an apologetic voice, said, "You're right, you are the messenger, not the one who makes the rules." He paused a moment, then smiling, said, "Hey, Geronimo, you did an excellent job managing the company's exchange of places and assigning the platoons their positions. Thank you. Now go back and take charge of your platoon."

As he headed back to his platoon area, he knew the captain was disappointed, as he was, and the rest of the company. The entire company was openly looking for a break and a chance to get a hot shower, eat hot food, buy pogey bait, and flat relax for a few days in some type of comfort.

LT entered his platoon CP. It consisted of wooden artillery ammo boxes filled with dirt and stacked about five feet high. The entire CP measured about eight feet wide and ten feet long, with wooden slats across the top, covered by a tarp, which made up the roof to keep the rain and sun out.

Lee, as usual, had worked his magic. LT's gear was already stored away and the small crude room looked somewhat inviting. Along the wall was an old iron cot; in the dim light, a thin, dirty mattress could be seen lying on the rusty bed springs.

Lee jumped up, hitting his head on the slats on the ceiling. Rubbing his head, he asked, "LT, is it okay to put the radio in here? There is not a lot of room in Sergeant Loerzel and Ballew's bunker."

"Sure. Now you can show me their bunker, yours, and Doc's."

The company had been on the mountain about five hours now, and sectors of the perimeter had been assigned and watches designated, and everyone was settled in and starting to relax.

LT sat on the side of his bunker, giving him a commanding view of his entire platoon area. As he sat there he began to realize he was really and truly tired. The Rock Crusher and Tu Cau Bridge never really allowed for any rest, showers, or hot food. He unbuckled his cartridge belt—it no longer mattered if he buckled it or not, it hung loosely around his waist, due to his weight loss, and was held up by the suspender straps. He had four canteens, a holster with a 45 pistol, K-bar knife, entrenching tool, first aid pack, and two ammunition pouches.

He slowly scanned the perimeter and noticed the troops were also appearing to relax. His attention was directed toward Rathbone, 1st squad leader, because he stood up and took off his camouflaged blouse and green t-shirt. He then walked over to a group and started talking.

Not fully conscious of what he was watching, LT realized something was nagging at his brain, something was different, odd, about the group. He studied them closer. They were sitting in a circle, cleaning weapons, joking and laughing, all had their shirts off enjoying the afternoon sunlight. Suddenly, like a strike from a lighting bolt from the heavens, his mind divulged the reason they all seemed peculiar: They all were slim, no, skinny, certainly gaunt.

LT was sitting straight up, staring towards the group, when Doc Smith walked up beside him and said, "What are you so intently looking at, LT?"

Doc's voice broke his silence and thought pattern. He blinked his eyes, turned to Doc, and asked, "Doc, you think that group, Lynn, Joe, Bob and Louis, appears skinny or maybe even emaciated?"

Doc sat down and gently laid his chin on his folded hands and remained silent for few minutes then said, "Have you looked at yourself lately? Of course you haven't. My point is: Do you think you look any different than your troops?"

LT jerked his head back and stammered, "Well, I have lost a few pounds, maybe ten or fifteen, but nothing like the troops."

Doc grinned and said, "What did you weigh when you first came over here to Nam?"

"When I left Quantico, I weighed one hundred and fifty-five pounds, pure muscle. I may have put on a couple pounds because of mom's cooking."

Doc chuckled and said, "Okay, let's say you weighed one fifty-five. What do you think you weigh now?"

"About one hundred forty, or forty-five."

Doc laughed and said, "LT, you weigh very close to one hundred thirty or thirty-five pounds... really. Remember when I went back to the rear last week to get some medicine for Speedy?"

"Sure, what about it?"

"Well some of the corpsman I hadn't seen for a while were kidding me about how much weight I had lost. It turned out I had lost over thirty pounds. I now weigh one hundred and twenty pounds."

LT sat silent for a while and finally said, "I need to find a set of scales, and by the way, how is Speedy doing?"

Doc sighed and said, "Speedy is the reason I came over here and sat down by you. I need to talk to you about him. He is not really making any progress. The treatment is not effective out here in the bush or in the swampy water at the Crusher. We need to send him to the rear for a few weeks, and he is not going unless you order him."

LT smiled and said, "I know, they all are like that. Can't leave the platoon."

Doc chuckled and, in a sarcastic manner, uttered, "Yea, wonder where they get that attitude?"

LT grinned, glancing at Doc, and said, "Yep, Marines are stubborn and corpsman are a pain in the ass." He paused, started getting a serious expression on his face, and, in almost a whisper, said, "I really hate to give him up for that period of time, but I guess this is the best time to do it. Okay, I'll talk to him. Make the arrangements."

Doc excused himself to go check on other Marines in the platoon.

LT sat there for a few more minutes daydreaming and wondering about his folks, his fiancée, and his friends back home. He then snapped out of his melancholic mood and focused on where Speedy had been sitting with his buddies in a circle. Sure enough, he was still there.

He ambled over to the group and casually spoke to each of them. After inquiring after Speedy's jungle rot, he asked to see his hands and feet. He frowned a few times, voiced concern, then emphatically said, "Speedy, I'm going to send you in to the rear so that you can get your jungle rot cleared up."

Speedy put up a defiant, but respectful case, as to why he shouldn't go into the rear and leave the platoon. However, he reluctantly gave in when LT told him it was an order, not a request.

Speedy was happy, he had delivered a worthy performance in front of his fellow Marines as to why he couldn't leave the platoon, but had to succumb to the LT's orders.

LT was happy; he had skillfully provided Speedy the avenue to receive treatment without losing face with his buddies. It was a win-win situation… it was Marine leadership at its best (in his mind, anyway.)

As the days slowly dragged by, LT became more bored at the passing time. The company was charged with running a squad-size day patrol off the only finger, leading to the top of the mountain. There were nine squads in the company, so a squad commitment was every ten days, leaving each squad plenty of free time.

Today, Corporal Rathbone took the resupply helo back to LZ Ross in order to rotate back to the states. All the squad leaders were now LT's appointments and he knew they would perform and be as skillfully as his old leaders. Lance Corporal Gil Galispi was his newest appointment, taking over 1st squad, Rathbone's old squad.

LT was coming back from pestering the CO about when the company might get off the mountain. He had, in fact, bothered the skipper so much he was now being addressed as lieutenant, rather than Geronimo.

He glanced over to the side of the hill and saw Bates sitting there with his elbows resting on his knees and his hands dropped down in front of his legs, holding a piece of paper. Bates looked very distraught.

Concerned, he walked over to Bates, and cautiously said, "Bates, are you all right?"

Bates slowly raised his head and stammered, "LT, I don't understand what is going on." Raising the paper in his hand then looking at it, he said, "I got this letter from an old friend of mine who was over here last year and really got burned bad by napalm. They had to drop a napalm bomb because the unit was about to be overrun by the enemy. Anyway, he's been in the hospital for over a year."

LT, passionately said, "And what is it you don't understand?"

"Well, my friend wanted to go home for Christmas. The doctors kept telling him no, but he kept after them until they finally said he could go. He got a new uniform, squared himself away, except his face, especially his jaw—it was still pretty much screwed up."

Bates took a deep breath, sighed, looked at the letter one more time, and said, "He says when he got to the airport a very well-dressed couple, maybe in their thirties or early forties, came up to him and asked what happened to his face. He told them and the woman said in a very harsh manner, 'Serves you right for going over there and fighting'!"

Misty-eyed, Bates stared at LT and said, "I don't understand why any one would say that to a young man who was sent to war by their country. THAT'S WRONG!"

LT agreed, but had no wise or comforting answers.

That afternoon, strolling through the company area near his platoon position, he suddenly heard three loud bangs from a 45 caliber pistol. He ran to where the sounds came from and found several Marines constraining Doc Smith.

Amidst the confusion, LT saw Joe holding what appeared to be Doc's pistol, and Joe hurriedly stated, "It seems Doc was in his bunker taking a siesta. When he woke up, a rat was on his chest. He grabbed his pistol and started firing away at it."

LT looked at Doc, who was staring back at him, and excitedly said, "LT, I can't stand those filthy creatures, they drive me insane; I had to shoot them!"

He calmly stepped over to where Doc was being restrained, motioned for the Marines holding him to let him go, and gently patted him on the back, and said, "I understand, let's see what we can do to get rid of those nasty varmints."

Looking into the bunker, he could see, through the dim light, several places where the rats had chewed holes into the wooden ammo boxes. He thought for a moment, then turned to Joe, and motioned for him to join him.

"Joe, I want the entire platoon, with the exceptions of those on perimeter duty, to tear down, inspect, and rebuild this bunker right now. Here is how I want you to do it: Take a few men, take down each box, one at a time, open the box to see if there is a rat or rats' nest in it. If the box has a rat in it, it will run away. I want everyone who isn't checking the boxes to be circled around the bunker with their E-tool in their hands. When the rat or rats run out from the boxes, those men with E-tools are to club the rats to death. Ensure each box is filled with dirt. I did notice several boxes where rats have chewed holes in them."

Joe frowned and said, "How will we stop the dirt from coming out of the boxes with holes in them?"

LT grimaced, folded his arms across his chest, and thought for moment, then smiling, said, "Back home, right before harvest, farmers inspect their grain bins. Holes in the bins would be patched by taking the metal lids from cans to cover the holes. We can do the same thing. Take our C-rat can tops and put them over the holes; pushing dirt against the holes will hold the lid in place."

Joe giggled and said, "Damn, this might prove to be fun for the men. I wonder who will be more agile and faster, the rats or our Marines?"

The incident proved to be a roaring success. The Marines found the diversion a great break from the mundane life, and seeing the entire operation from start to finish, Doc was satisfied. His bunker was rat-free and he slept well that night.

The next morning the skipper informed LT he would have to give up Lance Corporal John the Hawk Mihok. Golf Company has lost several people and each of the other companies were tasked with providing men to the company in order to bring up the company's combat strength.

LT frowned, then in a few moments a smile crossed his face and he calmly said, "I let The Hawk visit his buddy at 1st Tanks when we were at Tu Cau Bridge. He brought several things back with him. The most prized item was a rubber blowup red and white stripped pillow. He was the envy of the entire platoon because he slept on a pillow, keeping his head off the hard ground or mud."

He now chuckled and said, "As luck would have it, one night we got hit and Hawk was sleeping next to his hole with his pillow. Bullets were flying right above his head, so close he claimed he could feel the wind as they passed over him. He couldn't find the plug on his pillow to let the air out. He knew if he stayed elevated by the pillow, he was going to catch a round in the head. So he pulled out his K-bar and punctured the pillow."

LT chuckled and said, "Skipper, I think he actually cried when he threw the pillow away." He sighed and said, "Golf Company is getting a very smart and outstanding Marine."

The skipper laughed and said, "Oh hell, I knew that—after all, he is from 1st platoon."

A few days later, water became an issue. Clean drinking water on top of LZ Ryder could be a problem, especially during stormy weather. All the water was helicoptered in with five-hundred-gallon containers called water buffaloes. Water buffaloes were five-hundred-gallon steel water tanks mounted on a single axial trailer frame, allowing them to be trucked or flown into a position.

Each unit on the LZ had their own equipment, including the water buffaloes. On the side of each buffalo were stenciled embarkation letters and numbers, clearly showing who owned the equipment. Each unit was responsible for ordering water pick-ups and delivery through the air wing.

When assets are tight to start with and when someone fails to order their water, sprinkle in a good dose of male Marine testosterone, and the situation can turn quickly to a game of "King of the Hill."

Several members of 2nd squad, 1st platoon walked over to their battalion water buffalo, only to discover a Corporal from the artillery was guarding the buffalo, allowing only Marines from the artillery battery to get water.

Louis Lujan, after a futile discussion with the corporal, sent Lynn Stroop to get Sergeant Loerzel.

Sergeant Loerzel ordered the corporal off the buffalo and allowed the men to get water. In the meantime, the corporal standing guard duty sent one of his men to get his gunny. The gunny, out ranking Loerzel, ordered him and his men away from the water tank. Sergeant Loerzel sent for LT.

LT arrived and was briefed on the situation. In the meantime, the gunny sent for his first lieutenant. The artillery lieutenant was briefed and now both lieutenants were, possibly, locked in a no-win situation. While in a drastic huddle to come up with a "saving face" answer, magically a helo popped out of the clouds and delivered a water buffalo to the artillery side of the mountain. The two officers shook hands and headed back to their own areas very happy.

The next morning Captain McCarthy went to LZ Ross for the change of command ceremony. Lieutenant Colonel Vicente A. Albers, the new battalion commander, replaced Lieutenant Colonel A.E. Folsom.

Questions were still swirling: Was the skipper being replaced? After all, he was close to six months in the bush. Where would the company be going? Too many unanswered questions.

The day after Captain McCarthy returned from the change of command, about mid morning, Lee chased LT down and informed him the skipper wanted to see him, no hurry, when he had some extra time. LT knew the captain well enough to know it was a "baited" invite. The skipper had some news he would be eager to hear.

Acting very casual, he strolled into the company CP and offhandedly asked the skipper, "What's up, sir?"

"Hey Geronimo, I'm glad you found the time to drop by. Anything going on over in your area?"

LT knew the skipper wasn't upset with him, after all, he called him Geronimo, but he also knew the captain was disappointed he had not shown up earlier.

He cleared his throat and humbly said, "Gee, skipper I came over as soon as Lee informed me you wanted to see me. Is there something urgent going on?"

The captain wrinkled his face, waved him off, and indifferently said, "Nah… I was wondering if you were ready to get off this mountain."

LT slowly slid down and sat on an ammo box chair and hesitantly said, "Well, you know I have become real fond of this high level air; it's cooler, low humidity, no damn mosquitoes, does have big and vicious rats though. I don't have to carry around a hundred-pound pack, five-pound helmet, slug through mud, water, or talcum powder dust. And…"

The skipper cut him off by yelling, "I KNEW IT! You want off this damn rock pile as much as I do!"

"Hell yes! I'm bored to tears. When do we leave?"

The skipper moved across from him, sat down on the other ammo box chair, leaned forward, and in a hushed voice said, "I had a long meeting with the battalion commander, Lieutenant Colonel Albers and the S-3. I'm not for sure what all is involved, but I do know we are going to participate in the big operations on the horizon."

CHAPTER 32
NEW CHALLENGES

A few days later the Marines of Hotel Company cheered when the helos landed to lift them off LZ Ryder to LZ Ross. The men really needed a break, some time to unwind, eat real hot food, and possibly have a cold soda and hopefully a cold beer.

The men were ecstatic. They were billeted in their old hooch's and had racks with mattress, hot showers, hot food at the mess hall, and ice-cold sodas and beer. They were also given some new, mostly used, but clean uniforms; after all, they were in the rear and needed to look respectful. Life for them was truly great.

However, not great for LT. His chief corpsman, HM3 Tom Smith, received orders for the battalion medical station at LZ Ross. Tom had come to Vietnam about a month before him. He and the entire platoon would miss Tom, not only for his outstanding medical services but because he was their Marine corpsman and very trusting friend, who wore the Marine uniform, his choice.

Paradise found was on its third day when the skipper informed LT they were going to have a meeting with the new Battalion Commander, Lieutenant Colonel Albers, in the morning.

LT spent most of the rest of the day getting ready for the meeting. He did get a good, not new, but very crisp camouflaged uniform and new boots. He spit-shined the boots and polished his brass. He made it to the barber shop before it closed. He felt "squared away" and got a good five hours sleep, an hour more than normal. His new squad leaders were proving to be as reliable as his old ones. He was ready for the meeting but was concerned about what it was about. The skipper said he didn't have a clue.

He walked over to the skipper's hooch to meet him before the meeting with the battalion commander. As he approached the building the skipper came out smiling and said, "Geronimo, you look like a real Marine."

LT snickered and said, "Well sir, for an old, grouchy company commander you look pretty spiffy."

The skipper, obviously enjoying the battering of words said, "Yea, well, I'm the happiest person around most of the time; it's damn second lieutenants, smart ass ones, that make me grumpy."

The two officers reported to the battalion commander and LT couldn't believe his eyes. The CO had a wooden oak desk, state side type, the American and South Vietnamese flags, along with the regimental and battalion colors, all on flag poles behind him. A two-by-four piece of stained plywood held what appeared to be a brand new AK47 rifle fastened to the board. When really focused in on the brass plaque on the board, he could read the inscription, "Presented to LT. DR. Garrett by 1st Plt., H Co., 2/7." His chest swelled with pride.

The colonel told the two officers to have a seat. Once seated the CO looked at Captain McCarthy and then LT and said, "Captain McCarthy, your company was selected by me to lead the battalion in two night operations. Those operations will be back-to-back, maybe a week or two apart. Both operations will include other Marines and friendly forces. Skipper, you indicated 1st platoon would be your choice for the lead platoon, I agree, therefore we need to meet with S-3 and select the route we are to take. Gentlemen, let's go over to the S-3 office and nail down the track."

For three hours the colonel, major, captain, and the lieutenant worked the final routes the battalion would take to reach their objectives in the upcoming operations. LT went back to his quarters exhausted, he had never been involved in such high-level operations before, but felt useful and had contributed key information in making the final decision as to what route would be taken.

Over the next two days, elements of the battalion where helicoptered and trucked to LZ Baldy. On the third night, after sunset, 2nd Battalion 7th Marines marched out of the LZ led by 1st platoon, Hotel Company, heading for a finger fourteen clicks away in the Que Son Mountains, which separated Pagoda Valley from Arizona Territory.

The 5th Marines, an ARVN regiment, and a Korean regiment were conducting joint operations coming from the north, northwest and northeast, driving the enemy south toward the Que Son Mountains, where 2nd Battalion, 7th Marines would act as a blocking force and eliminate any enemy forces trying to escape into the mountains.

The battalion left LZ Baldy at night, and headed due west for about four clicks across open rice fields until they ran into the old French railroad berm. There was not a single railroad tie or track left on the berm, the NVA/VC had long ago taken them into the mountains to build fortifications.

This was the same berm the platoon had crossed back in November when they acted as a driving force into Pagoda Valley. LT and his men knew the area extremely well and was very comfortable leading the battalion in the dark. There are no artificial lights in rural Vietnam, so the nights were very dark. The only light was from the stars or moon. The half-moon provided ample light for the platoon to maneuver.

Once on the berm, the battalion headed northwest for another four to five clicks. They passed an army personnel carrier, which long ago had hit a powerful mine and was standing straight up on its rear door. It now resembled a large metal grave marker.

The battalion had been traveling for over five hours and about half way up the railroad berm when the colonel called a halt so the men could take a break. The idea was to make it to the foot of the mountains by day break. They were on schedule and the troops were in need of a rest period.

While the battalion rested, LT sent a squad ahead to recon the area. They had been gone for ten minutes when all of sudden the night silence was quickly broken by the firing of M16's and AK47's. In less than a minute, total silence again.

LT held on to the radio hand set waiting for the squad leader, Gene Evans, to report in to him. He figured he had a few minutes before either the skipper or the colonel would be calling him, wanting a report. Gene's call came in first. LT got the information and swiftly made his way back to update the colonel.

He immediately found the skipper and colonel, both standing side by side. Though it was dark he sensed Colonel Albers was calm and collective. Captain McCarthy, on the other hand, was mashing his teeth and jittery. He got close to the two officers and softly said, "I sent a squad ahead to check things out. They saw movement and opened up with fire. They killed two NVA and two VC. They also captured a NVA M49 machine gun.

Apparently the group was moving the gun out of the mountains up to one of the units the 5th Marines are after. There were no other enemy, only the four KIA's."

Through the darkness he could see the colonel smiling and he said, "Great. Good job. Tell me, are we going to make it to the base of the finger by daylight?"

"Yes sir. At our current speed Echo and Fox Companies will be in their blocking positions before daylight. My platoon will have the top of the finger secured right at sunrise. I think everyone will be in place in an hour after sunrise except the mortars. Those heavy base plates and 81 tubes will take a while to get up the steep slope."

Colonel laid his hand on LT's shoulder and said, "If we make your timetable it well be outstanding. Be ready to move in fifteen minutes."

As LT turned and started to leave the skipper reached out and grabbed his arm and nervously said, "Geronimo, you sure we are going to make it on time?"

He stopped, looked at the captain, and carefully said, "Yes sir. Look skipper, I know the responsibility of getting this battalion to its objective rest on your shoulders and you are in a position where you have little influence or say. Please believe me, 1st platoon is not going to let the company or the battalion down. Sir, try to relax and trust us."

The skipper sighed, then smiled and said, "You're right. 1st platoon hasn't ever let the company down and I know you won't this time. Go get 'em."

The remainder of the night movement was uneventful and by midmorning the battalion was fully in place.

Colonel Albers had managed to move to the very front of the battalion and stood near the top of the finger and thanked every man in the battalion as they reached him.

From the finger, at night, it was like sitting in a stadium overlooking Arizona and Dodge City territories. It looked like thousands of AK47 blue tracer rounds streaked across the land and green M16 tracer rounds swiftly answering back.

The second night proved to be the most dazzling display of color and sound. A C-130 airplane dubbed Puff the Magic Dragon flew over the valleys releasing thunders of "BURPS" while lighting up the sky and ground. The burp sound was caused when the plane fired thousands of rounds in a second, which covered an area about the size of a football field, with the bullets impacting every six inches apart. It was a deadly flying machine.

The third day the entire battalion was helo-lifted back to LZ Ross to prepare for another joint operation in a week.

This operation would be the battalion and a regiment of Korean Marines. The battalion would be helo-lifted, at night, into an area between Antenna and Pagoda Valleys and would push through the narrow passage containing the giant boulders, where Jersey had set up the night ambush and the skipper chewed him out for not springing it.

Once through the pass the battalion would start fanning out across the valley, pushing the enemy out toward the old railroad berm where the Korean Forces were waiting.

The Marines were thrilled they were being helo-lifted and not walking into the valley. The night lift was quick and flawless. However, when 1st platoon reached the other end of the passage connecting the two valleys, the unit was stopped and LT called to the front.

The point man found a booby trap consisting of a grenade, placed in a bush, next to the trail. LT crawled up the bush and with his red lens flashlight he could see the booby trap had been partially tripped. The grenade was cradled among three small limbs, the only thing keeping the spoon of the grenade from popping off. It was a tedious situation. He couldn't leave the booby trap, it wasn't an option. If he set it off, the sound might alert the enemy.

He hurried back to the colonel and explained the situation to him. After a moment the colonel asked, "I'm curious, how would you handle this matter?"

LT swallowed hard, cleared his throat, and slowly said, "Well sir, I think there are three possible courses of action. The first one, leaving it there, is actually not an option. Secondly, we could—I would, because I'm not ordering one of my men to try and get it—I could try to get it out of the bush but that's really risky and what are you going to do with it then? Third, blow it in place with a small amount of C4. Yes, the sound might alert the enemy, yet I have spent a month in this valley and every few nights you would hear small explosions at night. Probably booby traps set off by wild animals. Therefore, my choice would be to blow it in place."

The colonel smiled and said, "Good thinking, you made the right choice. Go do it."

By day break the battalion reached the crest of what the platoon referred to as Mount Baldy. Looking out over the railroad berm, the Koreans could be seen fighting the NVA unit 2/7 had forced out of the valley. The battle lasted less than an hour and the NVA lost another regiment.

The last three weeks seemed too fast and furious for LT. However, now his world was falling apart. Captain McCarthy was replaced by First Lieutenant Abanto. He was a good officer, but lacked combat experience and knowledge of the bush.

LT was becoming concerned about how much time he had left with the platoon. Colonel Albers, on more than one occasion, brought up the discussion of him going to the S-3 shop. But he could always come up with a good argument why he should stay a little longer.

The company was now at the Rock Crusher, hopefully out of site and out of mind, were his thoughts.

It was a bright sunny day and LT was happy when the company commander informed him the company would be leaving the crusher in a couple days for Antenna or Que Son Valleys. He was on his way to the platoon area to let them know when he suddenly heard the sound of a jeep coming over the single culvert. He jerked his head around and saw Colonel Albers's jeep. The colonel was in the front seat and someone else was riding in the back seat.

The jeep pulled up to LT and his heart sank. In the back seat was Second Lieutenant Jim W. McClurg, a classmate of his. His stomach felt queasy: he knew Jim was there for one reason and no other—to take over his platoon.

Colonel Albers stepped out of the jeep and in a stern voice said, "Lieutenant Garrett you are relived of your platoon. Lieutenant McClurg is taking over for you. I don't want any more arguments, get your gear and get in the jeep."

LT was shocked. Jim walked up to him put his hand on his shoulder with a degree of sympathy and said, "Don, I know you don't want to give up the platoon. You have a tight, well-disciplined fighting unit and I'm honored to be getting the platoon."

Misty-eyed, LT thanked Jim and then turned to Colonel Albers and said, "Sir, thank you for letting me command the platoon for a little longer. And I thank you for selecting Jim to take over for me. He would be my first choice to take the platoon."

LT got his gear and tossed it in the back seat. His mind was racing out of control with the many events which occurred over the last six months. He suddenly felt numb, his legs weak, and his eyes grew misty. He was devastated.

The ride back to LZ Ross was very quiet, not a word was spoken. The jeep rolled up to the officers' quarters. LT jumped out, grabbed his gear, started to thank the colonel for the ride, when suddenly the colonel got out too and told the driver he would walk back to his office.

Lieutenant Colonel Albers walked over and sat down on the steps leading into the quarters and motioned for LT to have a seat next to him. In a deliberate manner, the colonel said, "I know you are not real happy with me, but listen to what I have to say. I have watched you close for several weeks and I have seen a lot of very good things. In fact, I know that with your abilities, leadership, and loyalty you are going to be a great help to the battalion. I can count on you and you can count on me."

The colonel stood up, walked a few feet away, turned and looked around then at LT, and said, "I need a 'go-to officer.' Normally it would be a captain, but, I don't have that luxury, especially since Captain McCarthy left the battalion. You're going to work in the S-3 shop. You will be getting, let's say, projects from me and they will be your priority. I promise you, it well be fun, exciting, enlightening, and the time will fly by, trust me."

LT did trust Colonel Albers. He found being the "go-to officer" was everything the colonel promised. After two months in the rear, he was promoted to first lieutenant and took over a company when commanders were killed or medevaced, but only for a few days until a replacement was found. He worked with special forces on secret missions, and traveled throughout Vietnam and out of country. The colonel had kept his word and the time flew.

One thing Don really missed, he was now Lieutenant Garrett, sir, or, on some occasions, by senior officers, Don. No more LT.

The passing time was not as promising for the companies in the battalion. Hotel, along with the other companies, had lost commanders and 1st platoon was no exception.

Lieutenant James W. McClurg, Don's replacement and classmate, was killed one month after taking over the platoon. The next platoon commander, Lieutenant Warren Gather, another classmate, was medevaced from heat exhaustion. The third one, Lieutenant Conners, was wounded and medevaced. The fourth platoon commander, also a classmate, Lieutenant R. W. Poore, was doing a great job.

One night in the COC (Command, Operational, and Center) bunker, it was slow and Don was on duty from midnight to 0600 Colonel Albers, who also couldn't sleep, entered the COC and called Don over for a chat. He leaned forward in his chair and looked directly into Don's eyes and said, "You are my most experienced combat officer at the company level and you have been a first lieutenant for two months." He paused, took a deep breath, and slowly said, "I'm not getting senior, or experienced officers because this battalion will be rotating in a couple months. It's not right, but that is the fact of life."

Don shifted in his chair, ran his hand through his hair, and carefully stated, "I understand you're not getting senior, or experienced officers, but I also think your company level officers are not utilizing their supporting arms as much as they should be. Supporting arms is a key element to success on the battlefield."

Colonel Albers agreed. However, though neither officer at this time knew, Don would get a chance to prove his point in a couple days. He would take charge of the company under severe conditions.

Hotel Company was located in a small valley in the Que Son Mountains. Maybe a depression would better describe the area. The land was flat, about the size of two football fields side by side. On three sides were the mountains' steep sides, which had no trees, but rather knee-high grass and scattered scrub brush. On the fourth side, paralleling the plot of ground, flowed the Song Tu Bon River. Across the river the ground was also flat for about fifty yards, then immediately rose abruptly. The mountain side and flat ground had trees covering them. The trees actually grew right up the edge of the river.

The Marines were located on the far west side of the tract, in a drainage ditch about seven to eight feet deep and ten feet across the top. The ditch drained water from the mountain sides and the flat ground laying out in front of them. The trench ran straight towards the Song Tu Bon River, except fifty feet before it dumped into the river it made a sharp turn east and ran another hundred feet before tapering off into the water. This created an L-shaped berm, providing protection from the VC across the river in the trees.

To the far side, across the open field, or east of the Marines, was an entrenched NVA battalion. The NVA had machine guns, RPG's, and rockets. On the enemy's side was also a narrow pass which paralleled the river as it flowed down the mountain, approximately four miles into the vast valley of rice paddies below.

The company was in a desperate situation; they had no way out. They had an NVA battalion three times their size in front, and on their left side, a VC unit firing small arms at them. Their company commander had been wounded and medevaced earlier. They now had seven dead Marines they couldn't medevac, because the NVA now had the landing zone covered by fire.

Since there was no landing zone, it meant Don and Lieutenant Ted D. Jones, the AO (Aerial Observer), would have to jump from a helo into the Song Tu Bon River.

The helo flew, barely above the water, to a place between the Marines and VC, then came to an almost stop and the two officers bailed out, plunging into the river with flak jackets, helmets, and packs on.

The VC shot small arms at the helo, and the NVA shot machine gun fire and fired a rocket at the bird. The rocket missed. Out of the corner of his eye, Don saw the rocket exploded harmlessly, as it hit the mountain side above the VC. Other than for a couple bullets holes in its side, the helicopter escaped the attack and made it back to base.

Don splashed into the cold, clear, fast-moving water, sinking to the bottom. It took him a few seconds to get his feet under himself so he could push off the rocky floor of the stream and get air. When he broke the water surface he immediately began looking for the Marines. They were waving and yelling for the two officers to come to them.

The VC were now shooting at him and Ted, since the helo had left the two as the only targets. As the two fought through the water, heading for the berm, they could hear *spat, spat*. Ted, being six foot six in height, stood more out of the water and hollered at Don, asking, "What's making that *spat* sound?"

Don looked up to the Ted and yelled, "THOSE ARE BULLETS IMPACTING THE WATER. THE VC BEHIND YOU ARE SHOOTING AT US!"

Ted glanced over his shoulder, saw a muzzle flash from a VC's rifle, and screamed, "SHIT!" His long legs pushed him out of the water, and he tore up the bank and did a swan dive disappearing over the berm.

Don thought, "CRAP! Now I'm the only target the bastards have. Sure enough, the *splats* dramatically increased around him. He tried harder and harder to go faster, finally reaching the top of the bank, when two large arms from each side of him grabbed him and flung him over the berm.

He lay on the slope of the bank gasping for air. When he regained his composure he thanked the two big Marines for pulling him over the berm. He looked around, seeing if he could recognize anyone from the platoon. He then saw Mark Serrano coming toward him with a gunny.

Mark, grinning, said, "Hi, LT. You taking over the company?"

He stood up, took his pack off, dropped it to the ground, and said, "Yes, at least until I can get the company back in one piece. You still in 1st platoon?"

Mark lowered his head and mumbled, "No, LT. I'm the last of the platoon members in the company. Everyone else is gone, rotated, medevaced, or killed. I'm the company radioman and this is Gunny Smith, the company gunny."

Don could not stop grinning, he was called LT once more.

Don shook hands with the gunny and after some small talk, he asked if Staff Sergeant O'Tool was still with the company as the FO (Forward Observer) for artillery. The gunny assured him the staff sergeant was still with the company.

Don looked at his watch and said, "Okay, it's 1400 hours. I will have a company commanders' meeting at 1430, right here. Gunny, would you get Staff Sergeant O'Tool and the AO that came in with me. Mark, call the platoon commanders and inform them of the meeting." Suddenly, it felt strange to him, standing there calling for a company commanders meeting. He was in charge, he was being relied on to get the company out of its current mess.

Mark finished calling the platoon commanders and walked over to Don and said, "I guess you know about Lieutenant McClurg and Billy Baker?"

Don winced, took a deep breath, and quietly said, "Yes. Lieutenant McClurg was a great person and I was really happy he took over the platoon." He paused, swallowed, and softly said, "I simply never thought about him being killed."

He smiled and said, "You know I'll never forget Billy Baker's Texas accent hollering, 'THIS IS THE REAL DEAL!' I mean he said that about everything, what a character."

"Mark, I know several people were medevaced when Lieutenant Conners was wounded, do you know who they were?"

Mark glanced at him and thoughtfully said, "Sure, LT. Larry Bates, your machine gunner, Lee Graff, your radio operator, Louis Lujan, Bob Wolf, Rich Taylor, and you know Doc Smith was medevaced while in the rear at the battalion medical station. You know some Purple Heart awards were handed out."

Don nodded an agreement, then with a serious face, said, "I was back in the S-3 shop when Tom got hit. The NVA dropped a mortar round right through the hooch the corpsmen were sleeping in. Almost all of them were seriously hurt. The colonel had me heading up a reactionary force; by the time I got over to the medical station Tom had already been medevaced."

He then focused on the current problem: How to get the company out of this grave situation. He had a daring plan. Would the company support it? He would know very quickly; the meeting was about to start.

He started off the meeting by saying, "Gentlemen, the Marine Corps teaches us to improvise, adapt, and overcome. And that is what we are going to do. However, to make my plan work I need everyone to be on board. Here is our situation."

He paused and looked at each one of the people at the meeting, making sure he had their undivided attention. "We have enemy in front of us, enemy to our left. We cannot move from this ditch without losing a great deal of men; we are trapped here. And, if we don't do something by morning the enemy will have surrounded us, making us nothing more than sitting ducks."

He again waited a few moments to make sure what he had said soaked in, then he calmly said, "My plan is simple. We destroy the VC by air power, namely napalm. We dislodge the NVA with artillery, charge across the open area, and destroy them."

The group as a whole began glimpsing at each other and mumbling under their breath. Don produced his best smile, held his hands up in front of him, and in a reassuring manner said, "Listen, I have never asked a Marine under my command to do anything I wouldn't do; therefore, I will lead the charge across the open space. I'm not worried. There won't be any enemy left, because we are going to blow the hell out of the place."

Quickly turning to the AO, Lieutenant Jones, he said, "I want at least three napalm bombs dropped on the VC position across the river. The bombs will kill them by blowing, burning and/or suffocating them to death. We must inform the troops that when the napalm is dropped it will suck up the air and the troops must take a deep breath before the bombs explode. Believe me, I know, 1st platoon has been in that situation before."

"Sergeant O'Tool, I want you to call in a heavy artillery barrage, walking it from the side of the mountain down to the NVA's current position. As soon as the last round explodes, we charge across."

There was dead silence, no one moved, they merely stared at him. Ted finally said, "Well, it's not a bad plan and could work, except we are dangerously close, too close, they won't drop the bombs."

Sergeant O'Tool, hesitantly said, "Sir, I have to say the same thing, we are to close, they won't shoot the mission… not this close to the target."

Don smiled, then chuckled, laid out his map, and said, "So, if I move the company, let's say, to here," he pointed to a location on the map, "the company will be far enough away for the supporting arms to be deployed?"

The AO and FO both agreed.

Don roared, "GREAT! I'll move the company on paper. In other words, we are going to stay right here. Yes, we will feel the heat from the napalm and, yes, we will have shrapnel flying over our heads, rocks and debris falling on us. However, the heat from the bombs and shrapnel won't compare to what awaits us, if we do nothing."

This time the silence was broken by a unified group of, "Hell yes, it will work!"

Don was ecstatic. He had IMPROVISED, ADAPTED and OVERCOME!

"Gentlemen, I want the assault across the flat ground executed at dusk. We will attack in an upside down V. The four machine guns, two on each side of the assaulting force, will shoot as we attack. Bombs on the VC, then the arty on the NVA. AO and FO need tight coordination between you two. We attack right after the last artillery round explodes. On my signal, the machine guns open up, then we charge across the field. Any questions?"

Every man in the company was briefed and re-briefed, especially the machine gunners. Ten minutes before dusk napalm bombs were dropped and as predicted the heat was felt and the fire sucked up oxygen, causing difficulty in breathing for the Marines, but all were safe.

The artillery barrage was deafening; rounds ripped through the sky, sounding like the loud tearing of paper. Once the rounds hit the ground and exploded, the vibration lifted the men two to three inches off the ground. Shrapnel whizzed over their heads, and rocks the size of grapefruits came crashing down like hail, along with lots of other debris.

Don led the charge. The machine guns laid down beautiful suppressing fires, the company mortars saturated the enemy area, and the formation held its form. Only green tracers could be seen, no enemy blue.

The NVA had three machine gun bunkers before the artillery attack, now none were left, only holes in the ground. Trenches and fortification were blown apart; twisted rifles, beat up helmets, human body limbs, and burning tree splinters were strewed over the area.

The only resistance from the enemy came when the Marines started through the narrow pass. The small area only allowed a platoon at a time to push the NVA through the pass.

The lead platoon was given all the company's grenades and laws, and the fighting was done from tree to tree and rock to rock, most of the time under a hundred feet separating the two military forces.

By day break the NVA were forced out the pass and into the flat rice-growing land. The US Air Calvary swept from the early dawn light and quickly finishing off the remaining enemy forces.

The battalion conducted two more operations before rotating back to the states, Operation Imperial Lake and the last-named Marine operation in Vietnam, Pickens Forest.

The 5th Marines moved into LZ Ross and completed the turn over of command from 7th to 5th Marines. Colonel Albers would go to Da Nang in the morning to complete his transfer back to the states. Don would go to the Da Nang pier and board the navy vessel taking the battalion's colors and equipment back to Camp Pendleton, California.

That evening the seasoned combat colonel and the young battled-tested lieutenant sat in the colonel's office for an hour or so, quietly sipping Southern Comfort bourbon and reminiscing about their time in Nam.

After a while Colonel Albers fixed his eyes on Don and solemnly said, "I have really enjoyed your company, but I must go to my quarters and finish packing for tomorrow. However, before I go I want… must to tell you two things."

The colonel gently set his half-filled glass of bourbon on the desk and slowly sat straight up in his chair and said, "You and your men's gallant and very successful combat efforts on Hill F105, as you call it, against the North Vietnamese forces of over three hundred plus enemy has been written up giving the South Vietnamese the credit. It's a higher up political decision to supposedly build confidence in their forces and show the American public the war is going good."

Don stared at the colonel, not knowing if he should respond to the statement or not. He lowered his eyes to the floor and in a low voice finally said, "Well colonel I don't believe we expected anything. We felt like we were doing what Marines do." He then looked up at the colonel and, with a slight grin and bold voice, said, "Hell colonel, what matters is they lost and we won."

Colonel Albers smiled, stood up, walked over to were Don was sitting, and in a very serious manner said, "The last thing I want to say to you is I really appreciate what you have done for me and the battalion. There is an old saying about a true leader. I can't recall who said it, maybe too much bourbon, anyway it says, 'No man is a true leader until his position is ratified in the minds and hearts of his men.' I believe you achieved this with your platoon. I know you have in my eyes."

The colonel reached out and patted Don on the shoulder, turned and slowly walked to the door. As he reached the doorway he paused a moment, as if he were scanning the camp for the last time, and then, without turning toward Don, said, "Tell me, Lieutenant Garrett, what do you consider you greatest accomplishment here in Viet Nam?"

Don quickly stood up and with great earnestness and in a sharp clear voice said, "Sir, my greatest achievement, thank God… I never lost a Marine."

CHAPTER 33
HOMEWARD BOUND

Colonel Albers rotated back to the states a couple days before Don, leaving the task of embarking the battalion colors and gear aboard a US Navy ship to Don. The vessel would take the command group back to Camp Pendleton, California.

Upon arrival at the ship, Don checked in with the duty on the pier. The duty promptly motioned to a Marine sergeant leaning against a staff vehicle. The sergeant introduced himself as the commanding general's driver and informed Don he was going to the airport and not sailing back on the ship. The general decided the lieutenant would be way past his rotation date by the time the ship reached California.

The driver whisked Don to the airport where the freedom bird was waiting.

In reaching the top of the steps and entering the small entry compartment of the plane he could not see much because his eyes were still adjusting to the dim light but he felt a woman's soft but firm hand grasped his arm and gently but quickly moved him to the center of the small entry section. She closed and locked the outer passenger door and in an urgent manner said, "Please take your seat lieutenant. We need to get airborne immediately!"

A commanding and very stern voice, right in front of him, said, "Lieutenant, sit down right here so we can get this damn freedom bird in the air!"

Don's, eyes cleared up some, glancing down at where the voice came from and saw the individual pointing to the seat next to him. He realized it was a Marine colonel pointing and immediately sat down.

The plane darted down the tarmac and quickly jumped on the end of the landing strip. And with a greater roar and speed, equal only to that of a dragster streaking down a race track, the plane jetted down the runway and soared into the sky. Don grasped the arms of his seat and squeezed them so tight the colonel on his right side said, "Relax, lieutenant. If your seat were alive you would have strangled it to death."

Loosening his grip on the arm rest he looked up at the colonel and said, "Yes, sir. I haven't been concerned about dying this much since my platoon took on an NVA regiment."

The colonel chuckled and said, "An NVA regiment is a lot of soldiers."

"Yes sir, a little over three hundred. However, we did have a lot of help from Hostage Jim, the AO, who got an air force, I think a F105 plane, to drop some pretty good napalm and five-hundred-pound bombs on the NVA."

The colonel, who had his elbow resting on his armrest, pushed himself back up against the other side of his chair and said in a low but firm voice said, "Did you say, Hostage Jim?"

"Yes sir, Hostage Jim, I won't forget that name as long as I live."

The colonel paused a moment, glanced at the lieutenant, and said, "Lieutenant, did you ever meet Hostage Jim or know his real name?"

"No sir. Do you know who Hostage Jim is?"

The colonel grinned and said, "Yes, Hostage Jim is Major Jim Jahn… that's Jahn with an "A" not an "O." He is a great pilot, good man, you would like him."

"Sir, I don't even know him, but believe me, when my entire platoon and I say we like him, we mean it! He, and the US Air Force pilot, probably saved every one of our lives."

"Congratulations. I remember hearing about it. 7th Marines, right?"

"Yes sir."

"Well, your home bound now so enjoy it."

"Home." Don hadn't thought much about home because he had been so busy. As he began to think about it he slowly began sliding down into his chair and relaxing. The plane was very quiet now, with the exception of the steady hum of the jet engines, and the cabin temperature was cool. He was tired, no, he was beyond tired; he was physically and mentally exhausted. He quickly fell asleep, in a deep, sound, and for the first in, a long time, a safe satisfying sleep.

Three days were spent on Okinawa getting his gear and tons of new paperwork. Then he boarded another plane and headed for Los Angles.

Don looked out of the plane's window and could see Los Angles, well at least the smog over the city. After a few minutes the passengers felt the thump as the plane touched down and a loud cheer went up from the military personnel returning to their beloved country, which they all had put their lives on the line for.

The civilians hurried off the plane and straight through customs, while the military people, although eager to get home, hung back and never crowded or pushed their way to the front of the lines, seemingly happy to be this close to getting to their much-prized destination.

Don was in no hurry either; he had a couple hours before his flight to Oklahoma City. He mingled with the Marines and listened to what they were going to do when they got home… rest, eat "Mom's" great cooking, and mostly hang out with the family and girlfriends too, of course.

The talk of girlfriends and fiancées sent a sharp, almost overpowering pain of panic through his entire body. He knew if Jackie was at the airport in Oklahoma City all was good; if she wasn't, it was over.

As instructed, he laid his val pack on the table in front of him and unzipped it, then handed his orders and paperwork over, which had been handed out on the plane to be completed out and given to the custom officers.

The agent opened the val pack and slowly slid his hands into the several unzipped compartments of the pack. He asked Don several questions and looked directly into his eyes each time he answered a question. The custom agent then took the paperwork to a stand, stamped it, walked back to him, and handed him the paperwork. In a very mechanical type response said, "You can go."

Don took the paperwork, quickly glanced at the boarding pass which he had been holding, and asked, "Pardon me. Do you know which way gate 32 is?" The agent looking straight forward with a solemn expression said nothing. He once more said, in a little louder voice, "Could you tell me which way to gate 32?"

The agent, now with a sly smile on his face, turned, and as he walked away his demeanor immediately changed to contentious as he said, "If you can read, there's signs outside pointing to the gates."

Don blankly stared at the agent as he walked away and in a low skeptical voice said, "What… what the hell?"

Another agent, a woman about forty years old, walked up and, glaring at the agent who had walked away, said, "Sorry, it's been a long day." She then turned to the him and said, "You want to know which way to gate 32?"

Don slowly nodded and kept staring at the agent, who was now entering a door and out of the large customs room.

The woman agent half-heartily smiled at him and in a soft almost frail voice said, "It's to your right as you go out of those doors." She pointed to the exit of the customs offices. She then lowered her eyes toward the floor and walked back the way she had come from.

He sluggishly picked up his pack and walked toward the exit doors, glancing back several times in total disbelief. As he pushed through the double customs doors into the air terminal he suddenly heard the shrieking and deafening screams of "BABY KILLERS," "WAR MONGERS," "SHIT FOR BRAINS," and "DIE AND GO TO HELL," to name a few of the lewd and disrespectful calls from the crowed. The hecklers were lined up on both sides of the double doors, screaming at the top of their lungs.

Don immediately gained his senses and, as he was taught, tore from the kill zone of an ambush—only this ambush was from his fellow Americans, not the NVA. As he cleared the area, he suddenly felt wet blobs on his neck and hands and in utter disgust realized the wetness was human spit.

In an eruption of pure rage ran through the lieutenant's entire body as he turned toward the group and swiftly started building an attack plan in his mind. The group taunted him even more and began throwing things at him, yelling even more obscenities and egging him on to come and try to "kick their asses."

Their brave leader was a tall, long haired, bearded, loud mouth holding an oak walking stick in his right hand, slapping it repeatedly from hand to hand. Others standing beside and behind the leader also had various types of "stick clubs."

Don glared at the group but his military training hastened his understanding of the situation and knew he was facing a lost cause. He rapidly scanned the area to see if he could find support in the terminal. There were no military personnel to be seen and the civilians scurried into magazine shops or turned and promptly went the other way. There was no help; he faced the situation alone.

As he stepped backed and regained some resemblance of control, he reached into his back trouser pocket, pulled out a handkerchief, and methodically wiped the saliva from his neck and hands. Once more he peered around to see if he could find some, any kind, of support. Suddenly, an individual began to approach him. He smiled; it was a policeman.

The policeman walked up to Don, looked him up and down, smiled, and said, "Can I help you, lieutenant?"

Don turned and pointed toward the group who had now positioned themselves on both sides of the customs doors, apparently to ambush another unsuspecting military person, and he said, "See the tall, dirty, shaggy looking guy with the walking stick in his hands? I want him arrested for assault and battery. He spit on me and threatened me with the stick in his hands."

The officer turned and watched the group for a few seconds, began very slowly rocking back and forth on his heels, then placed his hand on his chin, rubbed it a couple times then said, "Well lieutenant, that's a big order. I can't see they are doing anything wrong and I never saw them spit on you, or, heard them threatening you. Looks like to me those boys are merely expressing their constitutional rights. And you know it's my job to protect their rights also."

Don's jaw dropped open and, almost dumb founded, stammered, "Constitutional rights, are… are you shitting me? I told you what he did!"

The cop smiled and said, "Well, I didn't see it and I have seen them fellers around here for several days and they haven't started anything." The cop looked Don up and down and said, "I'm thinking maybe a tough Marine like you may have started a situation where he came out on the short end and wants to use me to get back at them." He then lifted his arm towards the lieutenant's lapel and said, "Here, let me straighten that out."

Don slapped his hand back from him and said, "You asshole, don't touch this uniform, you rotten bastard!"

The cop frowned and, in a threatening manner, said, "Let me tell you this, you dumb-ass Marine, I am going over to the coffee shop to grab a cup of coffee and when I get back I had better not see your ass or I will arrest you for disturbing the peace. You got it?"

Don glared at the officer and said as he walked away, "Shove it up yours, you shit head!"

He was furious. He kept asking himself the same questions over and over, "What the hell is going on? Why all the hostility?" He looked back once more at the cop, only to see him raise his hand and wave to the "ambush group" as he made his way to the coffee shop.

He thought, "Is this the way people are treated after serving their country?" He tried to make sense of the situation but couldn't. The military made no mention of being careful or to get ready for ridicule or mobs once one returned to the states. The military papers made no mention of this type of "homecoming." He finally thought, "Maybe it is merely in California where this type of crap is going on." He hoped anyway.

He, haltingly, walked down the terminal towards his gate. He could not help being on guard as he passed people, not knowing if someone else or a group was going to strike out at him. He noticed a restroom up ahead and decided to wash up some. Maybe cold water on his face might help.

He entered the restroom and quickly glanced around. Not seeing anyone he set his pack down then took off his cover. He washed his hands for a long time then gently splashed cold water on his face several times, being very careful each time not to get water on his shirt.

Growing tired of trying to answer his repeated questions, he slowly put on his tie, jacket, and cover then stood in front of the wall mirror and checked his uniform to make sure it was perfect. He then leaned over and picked up his pack.

As he turned to walk out of the restroom he heard the gentle step of shoes on to the floor. He immediately turned and saw two shoes and pant legs in a stall in the restroom.

When he first walked into the restroom, he had checked and saw no feet; apparently whoever was in the stall had put their feet up so they could not be detected. The shoes were absolutely military and so shinny they had to belonged to a Marine.

He relaxed a little and stared at the stall. Almost immediately a face appeared around the corner of the stall door and in a hurried voice said, "Lieutenant, you were on the plane with me!" A Marine lance corporal stepped out from the stall and then said, "Sir, what the hell is going on around here? Were you spit upon and called names when you went from customs to the main terminal?"

Don gathered himself, cleared his throat, and in his best command voice he could muster up said, "Yes, I was on the plane and landed with you and yes I also was spit on and screamed at."

He then glanced back to the stall and said, "How come you were hiding in the stall?"

The lance corporal quickly looked at the stall then the lieutenant and in a very determined voice said, "I wasn't hiding in the stall. I was simply making myself not so conspicuous and trying to figure out what is going on."

Don smiled and said, "Well that sounds about right. Are you catching a flight out of here?"

"Yes sir, in about twenty minutes, gate 36."

"I'll tell you what, why don't I walk with you to your gate; mine is right next to yours and leaves a few minutes after your flight."

The lance corporal smiled from ear to ear and eagerly said, "Thanks, lieutenant, that's great!"

The two young Vietnam veterans walked down the long corridor to the lance corporal's gate and found two chairs away from the rest of those waiting to board the plane and sat down.

The lance corporal became a little melancholy, stared out the large glass window for a while, and finally said, "Lieutenant, do you know what is going on?"

Don slowly shifted his body in his chair, ran his hand through his hair, and in a thoughtful manner said, "No, but maybe if I tell you what I do know, maybe we can make some sense out of this crap. I do know all my life I have been told the majority rules in this country. Well, that's not true. The minority actually rules in this country. Let me ask you a question. When you were in high school did you start the day off with a prayer or the flag salute?"

The lance corporal sat up in his seat, looked down at floor, and thought for a few minutes then finally said, "Well around my freshman year we stopped doing the prayer, then in my senior year we stopped saluting the flag."

"Yep, the prayer was stopped by an atheist woman who didn't want her children exposed to Christian teaching in public schools. She sued the government and won… no more prayers in public schools. Would you not say a single person rates as a minority? Therefore, the minority had the prayer thrown out of the entire United States public school system.

"The saluting of the flag was thrown out because two families sued the government because they felt by having their children salute the flag the government was forcing its doctrine on their kids." Don paused, gesturing toward the group who had ambushed them, and said, "Now that bunch of shitheads over there, who spit on us, called us vile names and accused us of sordid deeds, I'll bet, represent the minority of how people really think in this country… I really hope so anyway."

The lance corporal gently slid back into his chair and after a few minutes slowly frowned then said, "Okay, I understand about the prayer and flag issues, but why are those jerks harassing us? We didn't start the war. Heck, most of us are draftees and can't even vote. We did what the government asks us to do, exactly like our fathers and grandfathers. When they came back from their wars they were treated like heroes. Why are we being treated like criminals?"

Don slumped down in his chair, raised his hand up to his head, and slowly began massaging his scalp. After a few moments he turned to the lance corporal and said, "Damn! You sure can ask some tough questions." Now, becoming somewhat frustrated, said, "Look! I don't have all the answers you are looking for but let's, once again, evaluate what we have here."

He gradually sat up straight in his chair, placed his hands together, rubbed for a few seconds, and finally said, "What is your father doing right now?"

The lance corporal turned toward the lieutenant and in a questionable expression on his face stammered, "Well, this is Friday, late morning back home, so he's at work and so is my mother."

"So both of your parents are working?"

"Yes, but what about it?"

"Those bunch of thugs over there are in their early to late twenties and we can assume they are not working because the cop said they have been here for several days. Your father, my father, and all the rest of the fathers are more than likely working today. So let's call them the 'Silent Majority' and the loud mouth thugs, let's call them the 'Loud Minority.'"

"You see, Lance Corporal, the 'Silent Majority' are busy with life, working, supporting their families. They have far more important matters to deal with in their eyes than a bunch of dirt bags. Quite honestly, people in general don't want to get involved in matters of unrest or possible violence."

"Now on the other hand, the 'Loud Minority' are trying to make headlines and justify their own cowardliness and sniveling by attacking the very people they don't have the guts or fortitude to be. Now they aren't stupid, they are smart, they have superior numbers, ambushing those who least expect it and in the large media cities, and of course the media is more than willing to run pictures of them and their stories of woe. I bet any amount of money this is not happening in our hometowns, and, speaking of hometowns, your plane is starting to board."

Don's wait and flight to Oklahoma City was uneventful, he was happy for that small favor. The late November weather in Oklahoma City was very wet, cold, and dark. It now was almost seven in the evening. He had waited until he landed to call his parents because he didn't want them driving the hour and a half drive until he knew he was actually at the airport.

His plane was the last one for the night and the airport terminal, in a very short amount of time, became an empty and lonely place. He stood at the double glass doors entrance of the terminal where the only light on was a small low watt bulb above his head. It had started to rain, at first a slow but steady rain, and now it was heavier and the wind had picked up a little and was gently blowing the rain against the glass doors.

He gazed, almost in a stupor, at the raindrops as they gently slid down the glass doors. His trance was broken suddenly by the sound of footsteps coming toward him. He quickly turned and tensed up as he squinted to see who was approaching him in the dim light.

"Are you waiting for a taxi or someone to pick you up, mister?"

Now the individual came into full view and Don could see by the man's dress and the keys dangling from his uniform that he was a custodian. He relaxed somewhat, cleared his voice, and said, "I'm waiting for my parents and my fiancée to pick me up. They should be here any minute." Then, realizing he was the only person in the terminal that didn't work there, he said, "I'm sorry, do you need to lock up?"

"No it's okay. No need for you to wait in the rain. So, you are a Marine coming back from Vietnam? My nephew was a Marine and came back from Nam a few months ago. He sure has had a rough time of it lately."

They both turned in unison as the front glass doors flung open and a man and woman scurried through, briefly stopping, quickly looking at Don, then at the black man in his blue custodian attire, and headed toward the main terminal.

"Mom, Dad! Where are you going?"

The man froze in his tracks, jerked around, and stared into the eyes of Don. He slowly looked from his head to his toes, then back to his eyes, and stammered, "Son?"

"Yes, who do you think I am?"

His father, stumbling with his words, said, "Well… it's the light, I couldn't really see your face." They both stepped forward and embraced.

After hugging his mother for some time, he said, "Well, we need to get out of here, this gentleman needs to lock up for the night." The three once more thanked the custodian and walked to the car outside of the glass doors.

As he placed his val pack in the back, next to where he would sit, and said, "So Jackie didn't make it?"

His mother uttered something about her having an afternoon class that she couldn't miss. The Vietnam veteran made a faint smile and, feeling totally dejected, crawled into the back seat, because he knew her last class on Friday was at ten a.m.

The Vietnam veteran sat in the back seat of the car. After a few miles of driving, the talking faded to silence, due mostly to the awkwardness in the initial meeting and the fact that his fiancée had not come to meet him. The veteran knew he had changed; hell, war does that to a person.

He then remembered getting a letter from his best friend Larry Wright, also a Vietnam veteran Marine lieutenant, who had recently returned to the states, and in the letter he said that while his mother was looking at him one day she said, "My son went to Vietnam and *you* came back!"

In the cold darkness, the young Vietnam veteran, felt rejected, alone, and in gut-wrenching pain, silently watched the rain from the heavens flow like a river of tears down the vehicle's windows.